*For Werner —
Wonderful friend and
personal supporter in this
+ other projects
Best, Fred*

Disastrous High-Tech Decision Making
From Disasters to Safety

Frederick F. Lighthall
Professor Emeritus
The University of Chicago

D1211950

Kilburn Sackett Press

© 2015 Frederick F. Lighthall

All Rights Reserved.

No part of this publication may be reproduced, stored in a retrieval system, or transmitted, in any form or by any means, electronic, mechanical, photocopying, recording, or otherwise, without the written permission of the author.

Cover photo on left: Deepwater Horizon oil drilling disaster—United States Coast Guard

Cover photo on right: Challenger shuttle disaster—NASA

Kilburn Sackett Press

In Association with Dog Ear Publishing
4011 Vincennes Road
Indianapolis, IN 46268

ISBN: 978-1-4575-3297-9

1. Psychology—organization decision making. 2. Sociology—leadership and intergroup conflict. 3. Safety—time-critical, high-tech situation assessment.

Library of Congress Control Number: has been applied for

This book is printed on acid-free paper.

Printed in the United States of America

www.High-TechDangers.com

For
Maureen Sylvia Lighthall
My cushion, rock, and compass

And

In honor of

Nikolaus Copernicus 1473-1543
Tycho Brahe 1546-1601
Johannes Kepler 1571-1630
Galileo Galilei 1564-1642
Pioneers of Systematic, Empirical Investigation

Contents

Preface

The space shuttle program is now history. Tokens of that era, four of the shuttles' winged orbiters, can be viewed in museums.[1] They remind us of technological achievement and of new frontiers imagined and explored. Behind the achievements, however, were two technical and human failures, the *Challenger* and *Columbia* shuttle disasters. Because those whose deliberations caused these two disasters survived, unlike many other high-tech disasters, a rich record is uniquely available in their testimony that traces how decision-making participants interpreted events and how they reacted. Decision participants' own testimony, including their commentary on their own and each other's actions, offered a rare opportunity to examine closely participants' perceptions, presumptions, and prior commitments. The official investigation of the *Challenger* disaster provided in its *Report*[2] both complete assessment of the physical cause of the accident and extraordinarily open availability of information about its human causes, but the Commission's own examination of the human causes fell far short of probing how and why the participants thought, felt, and acted the way they did. Probing the how and the why remained an open task.

The immediate *physical* cause of the *Challenger* disaster was identified by the investigating Commission accurately.[3] Most academic analysts of the accident, however, misidentified the technological dynamics that caused the disaster. Those are reported in a remote appendix of volume II of the Presidential Commission *Report*, in dense engineering language.[4] Engineers gave pronounced warnings about that actual danger hours before *Challenger's* fatal launch. The recently arrived cold weather, they warned, could well cause critical protective devices (O-rings) to fail. Managers at the time, and virtually all analyses of the accident since that time, focused not on temperature dynamics but on O-ring erosion, whose threat had actually been proven negligible, and on other distracting pressures.

The complex *human* causes of missing or denying the *real* danger of cold temperatures, therefore, have entirely escaped attention—the engineers' and managers' conflicting interpretations of data, the development of key individuals' mental models, the shaping forces of organizational culture and of leadership style, individual managers' fears and situations, interorganizational complexity, sensitivities to production schedule and market, and even the form of argument that the engineers and managers fell into.[5] Those are among the human causes that produced the wrong diagnosis of the shuttle's actual situation on that cold morning of launch. Those causes are explored in this book.

A perspective not before applied to this type of accident, macroergonomics, brings to light new dimensions of causality in such disasters. Ergonomics is the study of *persons*, using their available mental and manual *tools* and working from their *past experience*, who are attempting to accomplish a *task* in a particular social and physical *environment*. Macroergonomics is ergonomics applied to complex organizations, where "persons" translates to individuals, groups, and roles operating at different levels of authority and organization, and where "task" translates to organizational (or inter-organizational) function and mission. Delving into the causes of this disaster with this more differentiated and grounded framing than earlier analyses have employed has yielded two new dimensions of disastrous decision processes.

First illuminated is the unfolding sequence of a social psychological process in which deliberations of the decision participants (engineers and managers), traced from the first suggestion of a possible problem to the disastrous decision, proceed in the form of an evidence-based argument. This micro-history of a decision shows how sequence matters. It also pinpoints places where errors of various kinds were made.

The second new dimension of disastrous decision making revealed is a cluster of four previously unnoticed dangers that imperil the decision process itself. These four dangers coincide and seem to form something of a new *syndrome* of causes. This cluster of dangers appears to be shared with other high-tech disasters. It has not before been recognized in the considerable literature on accidents and their causes. Besides the *Challenger* disaster the *Columbia* shuttle disaster (Lighthall, 2014a) is another exemplar of this quartet of causes. The most recent and different kind of high-tech exemplar was the financial and credit meltdown of 2008.[6]

These dangers lie in the human understanding and control of complex technology. They are the dangers of human functioning presented by people who are selected for their experience and competence trying, individually and collectively, to respond effectively to an infrequent but inevitable situation in these high-tech enterprises. It is a situation where *new technical information arises during ongoing operations and warns of a dangerous possibly disastrous operating condition affecting the entire enterprise.*

Why, more than a quarter century after the *Challenger* accident and after not only official investigations but also scholarly books and dozens of scholarly articles, should yet another analysis of causes of that accident be published or, if published, be read? The answer is simply that the human roots of this apparently technological disaster are tangled and deep. Its human complexity requires new, more differentiated perspectives and dimensions of analysis to reveal clearly the actual physical and human causes. Vaughan's (1996) study, widely cited and relied upon for an accurate account of both physical and human causes of the *Challenger* accident, was the only study that made extensive use of primary documents. It examined the shaping of the *Challenger* launch decision through a sociological lens. Unfortunately, it is seriously flawed.[7] I examine the deliberations leading to the *Challenger* accident through a macroergonomic lens that combines perspectives from psychology, sociology, anthropology, and, surprisingly, rhetoric and argumentation. This lens is adjustable, providing at one level the verbal contents of an argumentative exchange unfolding among persons with different backgrounds and motives. At a more macroscopic level, it brings into focus varying practices distributed across two collaborating organizations—practices that reflect a dominant underlying, unrecognized cultural value.

Revisiting the deliberations leading up to the *Challenger* disaster at levels not before examined, therefore, reveals entirely new views of the realities at work—at work in that particular fatal event, yes, but much more. We also get a new, ground-level view of naturalistic decision making under stress, of how engineers and managers communicate effectively and ineffectively, and of how a leader's ideology of data and proof can be highly adaptive in one phase of production and a source of blindness in a second phase. Most significantly for high-tech safety-critical projects generally, however, is the discovery in the complexities of the *Challenger* accident of a new syndrome of conditions lying at the center of the *human* causes of not only the *Challenger* accident but of other high-tech disasters also. They are the causal conditions that shape time-pressured assessments of a new danger during ongoing operations.

I have allocated time over more than twenty years to studying the many layers of cause in the *Challenger* disaster, conducting my own interviews early on of major and supporting participants.[8] It should not be surprising, then, that I reveal new views of a high-tech organization at work: how decision makers, in this case engineers and managers, work at cross-purposes, how styles of leadership influence the content of decisions, how collaboration between private enterprise and government can shift from productive to disastrous, and how one basic value of an organization's culture preempts another basic value and creates a dangerous, extreme corporate form of what David McClelland (1953, 1961) called a "need for achievement."

This book's messages of human and technological complexity, challenge, and hidden dangers will be of interest to four groups of readers. First are the managers and engineers—and the students and professors of management and engineering—who are concerned with managing, monitoring, or teaching about high-tech projects such as space exploration; operating nuclear power plants, submarines, or nuclear-waste sites; or conducting deep-water energy exploration. The second group comprises professors and students of social and organizational psychology, of ergonomics, of the sociology of organizations, and of the burgeoning field of the anthropology of organizations. Third are the scholars and professionals who study the human causes of disasters and the officials who investigate disasters. Fourth is the growing group of retired professionals with backgrounds or interests in the underlife, opportunities, or dangers of high technology.

> *[T]eam structure effective for routine operations could break down in non-routine circumstances.*
>
> —Barry Strauch

> *None are more hopelessly endangered than those who falsely believe they are safe.*
>
> —Johann Wolfgang von Goethe

Introduction

Disasters whose causes are as complex as those in the *Challenger* disaster present complications no single discipline can disclose. I can illustrate the idea of multiple layers of (any segment of) reality by a mundane example. If I go through a person's house from attic to cellar without probing closets, bureau drawers, or out-of-sight spaces, I can still find out a lot about the person's outlook, resources, and choices, but if I go through the person's refrigerator, bureau drawers, and closets, I will find very different significant things about that person's outlook, tastes, resources, and habits. Now, if I examine the contents of all the wastebaskets, trash bins, and garbage cans in the house, I see yet another realm of important choices, resources, and habits. More new disclosures of habits, choices, and values will come into view if I listen in on a full day of conversations with this person in this house. Finally, if I go outside the house and examine the neighborhood and town surrounding the house, I will view still other dimensions of the person's life—opportunities, resources, and risks. Each of these levels reveals its own details of the person's past, present, and future. If the person suffers some mysterious calamity in the house, each of these levels of investigation would reveal retrospectively much of importance, some of it crucial, about the cause of the calamity.

Almost any small event or node of human existence arises out of multiple layers of constraints from which it is shaped and leaves multidimensioned footprints of its life—all the more so in the case of a high-tech disaster. I set out in this study to push deeply into the disaster's multiple layers, from the cognitive-emotional reactions of key figures to the organizations and organizational subcultures in which they had become enmeshed.

It quickly became clear that the *Challenger* disaster was preventable—preventable even on the evening before launch. It was not what the sociological literature has come to call a "normal" accident (Perrow, 1984), caused by interacting factors so complicated that they are beyond human imagining before they occur.[9] This disaster was not only imaginable but actually was correctly warned about in an unusual conference hours before the fatal launch—warned about in an evidence-based argument. We will look closely at that prelaunch conference and that argument as they unfolded.

Most of the same people involved in that argument had also been involved previously in highly effective decision processes, both to approve a shuttle's launch and to approve a launch delay to answer a technical question. They had been involved in an uninterrupted string of successful flights, revealing impressive collective competence in this high-tech enterprise, an enterprise holding an enormous number of possibilities for error. What made this set of decision processes different from all the others, and since the flight danger was plain enough to be correctly warned about by technical experts, what factors revealed in my new sampling of layers prevented the warnings from being understood or believed? What on this occasion robbed this group of decision participants of their usual abilities to make an effective collective decision?

No quick summary of the range of findings is appropriate here, but the picture of that disaster has become clearer, more accurate, and more detailed. One major outcome of the study must be outlined here, however. The clearer picture reveals the *Challenger* decision-making dynamics to be a kind of prototype that exemplifies a wider class of complex high-technology, safety-critical decision situations and processes.

This prototype is characterized by four previously unnoticed dangers, dangers to which *all* such otherwise competent, boundary-pushing explorations of uncharted domains may be vulnerable. Other exemplars or close variants of this syndrome of disastrous decision making besides the two shuttle accidents (Cabbage & Harwood, 2004; Lighthall, 2014a, 2014b, 2014c) are the *Deepwater Horizon* oil spill (US District Court for the Eastern District of Louisiana, 2014), the *Piper Alpha* oil and gas catastrophe (Cullen, 1990; Paté-Cornell, 1993), and the financial crisis of 2008 (Jaffe, 2012; McCuistion, 2012). While these dangers occur in the immediate *context* of complex high-technology operations, they are the complicated dangers of *human performance*—dangers in the functioning of people who generally are selected for their experience and competence trying, individually and collectively and in the context of the project's ongoing operations, to assess a complex emerging situation in real time.

The *Challenger* prototype of human failures reveals first, a particularly dangerous, time-squeezed situation of technical discovery, threat assessment, and decision making that I shall refer to as "the *Situation*"; second, a universal separation of two distinct organizational functions—*expert assessment* of technical dynamics by front-line *engineers*, and decision making about the implications of those dynamics by *managers*—distinct functions whose normally effective execution becomes suddenly dangerous; third, a completely unexamined mode of deliberation and conflict resolution whose handling can either protect or poison effective decision making; and fourth, an organizational *culture* characterized by dangerously skewed values.

First, the *Situation*. [10] By the nature of these high-technology explorations, pushing into an uncharted domain, critically dangerous *Situations*, although rare relative to such an organization's situations generally, will nonetheless inevitably arise, created by a surprising moment or degree of technical abnormality judged to be dangerously atypical. Its discovery will appear as a surprise because it follows a span of successful operations. This sudden abnormality will threaten the whole enterprise if its danger is not neutralized. That discovery will trigger conflicting assessments of the anomaly and of its danger. These conflicting assessments are due partly to the ambiguous evidence of possible danger. Some will see the technical evidence of danger, correctly, as incomplete and mixed. Doubting the evidence of real danger embedded in other information, however, they will urge continuation of normal operations. Others, closer to the raw data pointing to the danger, and more sensitive to the anomaly's abnormality, will urge delay or halt of operations until the danger has passed or been removed.

The *hidden* danger here is entirely different from the technical anomaly that the technicians have detected and warned about. The first hidden danger resides, rather, in the *situation* (*Situation*) *in which* the technicians' or engineers' anomaly is discovered and reported. That *Situation* of diagnosis is often especially time-limited, requiring a quick diagnosis and decision while normal operations are continuing. Further, the evidence of danger is incomplete and mixed. Limited time restricts the necessary thought, review of data to sort out where the threat lies, consultation with experts, and communication with decision makers that any effective response requires. Limited time also prevents the gathering of new data. All these restrictions drastically degrade the quality of intelligence and judgment available for accurate assessment of the anomaly's threat.

The second hidden danger always present in high-tech organizational decision making complicates any *Situation*. It is the normal division of expertise and decision-making authority between engineers and managers. Engineers convey to managers their technical observations and interpretations of the high-tech project's ongoing operations. They advise. Managers, however, decide which technical data and interpretations are most significant and what they suggest for action—or inaction. But when technical specialists suddenly report new technical data indicating a dangerous shift in operating conditions, time to understand them is short when the danger is imminent.

Forced to comprehend quickly and to choose between the conditions and causes of past success, on one hand, and a possible new cause of serious failure, on the other hand, managers' experience of past success weighs heavily. The managers' lag in technical comprehension under the *Situation's* new and time-pressured conditions seriously degrades the accuracy of their situation assessments. Managerial lag in technical knowledge, coupled with their responsibility for *deciding action implications* of any technical disagreement, when paired also with the appearance of a sudden *new* technical danger, then, constitutes the second hidden danger in these safety-critical enterprises.

A third hidden danger arises if participants in the process of assessing the safety-danger issue disagree about the technical facts. If they argue over the evidence, they may unwittingly enter a special domain of reasoned thought, formal argument from evidence, about which all participants will likely be totally ignorant. Settling a disagreement by arguing about mixed evidence holds hidden pitfalls. Whenever evidence is mixed, allowing proof of neither pro nor con, what is decided turns solely on the conditions presumed true at the outset.[11] This strange, surprising effect of argumentation itself in a high-tech decision situation under the special circumstances of the *Situation* is told in Chapter 8. Ignorance of the pitfalls of arguing from evidence makes argument a dangerous tool in the hands of the novice.

A fourth danger hidden to participants, and generally to their organization, is the influence of organizational culture. In the case specifically of the *Challenger*, the diffused nature of the shuttle program's dangerous organizational culture became clear only late in my analysis. Beginning as an inquiry into 18 hours of technical deliberations that led to a disaster, this book became in part a portrait of an encompassing ethos. A shuttle culture emerged from the accumulated detail, revealing norms, practices, and priorities that constituted a dangerous imbalance to which similar high-tech safety-critical enterprises have proven to be vulnerable. It is the imbalance between two basic values of any such enterprise: production and quality.

This book is organized in two parts. We first follow, in Part I, the deliberations in their actual contexts, and then in Part II, we consider the causes—first the *how*, then the *why* from the perspectives of macroergonomics, employing concepts prominent in the current literatures on time-pressured naturalistic decision making, leadership, situation awareness, mental models, and cultural dynamics.[12]

One challenge posed by this and other disasters is how high-technology engineers and managers can learn the lessons from these disasters, and from their own near misses. The challenge goes beyond that learning to the organized extension of learning that actually produces organizational cultures and decision-making processes geared to master new frontiers *safely*.[13] To achieve that advance in organizational and cultural functioning means understanding the inevitability of high-tech *Situations* (in the sense I alluded to above and expand on in Chapter 7). In particular, the needed advance at the level of the dynamics between engineers (or technicians) and managers will require effective modes of detecting, then deliberating and deciding about unexpected threatening shifts in operating conditions of the enterprise—conditions in equipment, of personnel, or in the environment. I address the challenge of that kind of organizational preparation in the last chapter. Its daunting dimensions reveal still another danger, a danger conveyed to these high-tech settings by the wider national culture. This danger consists of a void, a void in examined knowledge about communication, decision making, and power dynamics possessed by those who plan and operate these high-tech programs – a dangerous vacuum in face of the otherwise powerful, unmitigated organizational impulse to initiate and sustain production.

PART I

Narrative

PART I

CHAPTER 1.

Events, Participants, an Unusual Race, and Complexities

The observable events preceding *Challenger's* fateful launch were mundane. They centered on a disagreement about whether a sudden change in flight conditions justified a delay of the *Challenger's* impending launch. The facts and argument supporting a delay were presented formally and were refuted. The refutation was reviewed by different officials, approved despite repetition of engineers' objections, and finally taken as the basis for not delaying the launch already in progress.

Synopsis: The Surface Events

About 2:30 PM (EST) [14] on January 27, 1986, news of unusually cold overnight weather arriving in Florida had been communicated to engineers at the Morton Thiokol, Inc., plant in Brigham City, Utah, where the shuttle's booster motors were manufactured. Search for more detailed projections of temperatures at the Florida launch site brought hourly projections of unusually cold air temperature for Florida from noon on January 27 to 2 PM the next day. Launch had been set for 9:38 in the morning of the 28th. Written notes by some participants showed the projected launch-site temperatures: 56 °F at 2 PM on January 27, falling to 33° by 10 PM, reaching 23° the following morning at 8 AM and 26° at launch time.

Allan McDonald, Director of Thiokol's manufacturing of the shuttle's solid rocket motors (the "boosters"), had been assigned as Thiokol's representative at the Florida launch site. Having heard reports of extremely cold temperatures on the 27th, McDonald set about getting hourly estimates of temperatures at the launch site through noon the next day. Around 4 PM (EST) he phoned them to his subordinate, Bob Ebeling, in Utah, expressing his worry. His engineering staff had studied the critical ability of the boosters' O-rings to seal their field joints against hot gas leakage. The test results indicated that cold temperatures like those predicted for launch time would jeopardize the O-rings' capacity to seal the joints. A joint's failure to seal would be catastrophic. McDonald urged Ebeling to organize an engineering analysis and presentation that would substantiate the need to delay launch until joint temperatures were "acceptable."

Thiokol engineers conferred in groups of increasing size and called in Thiokol's vice president of engineering, Bob Lund. Discussion focused on the ways that cold temperature might affect the crucial sealing dynamics of the O-rings. Tables and charts had to be dug out of records. What was the lowest O-ring temperature safely flown? That would provide engineering rationale for a safe temperature limit. Now facts had to be put in some order to present to the NASA officials who were monitoring countdown toward launch. Time was short.

It was 5:30 PM on the 27th by the time Thiokol engineers could give notice to senior Science and Engineering managers at Marshall Space Flight Center in Alabama that they were recommending a launch delay until noon or after to reach O-ring temperatures in the range of all previous flights (≥ 53 °F). Static and poor teleconference reception prevented discussion, so a teleconference with better transmission was rescheduled for 8:30 that evening. The engineers in Utah scurried to complete review of engineering data, preparing charts that would give a sufficient engineering explanation for a launch delay. Meanwhile, the countdown proceeded normally toward launch the following morning.

The evening teleconference discussion linked managers and engineers sitting at three locations: the Thiokol plant in Utah, NASA's Marshall Space Flight Center in Alabama, and the Kennedy Flight Center in Florida. To explain the engineering reasons that a launch delay was necessary, Thiokol engineers faxed diagrams of the boosters' joints and charts of their engineering data from Utah to NASA managers at Marshall and at Kennedy. Presentation of the charts began about 8:45 PM.

Each Thiokol engineer or manager most knowledgeable about the content of a chart explained its contents and import to the other teleconferees. Some charts were complex, some had minor relevance to the engineers' focal worries about cold temperatures, some reported preliminary and ambiguous results, and several put forth quantitative evidence pointing to a degrading effect of cold temperature on O-ring sealing capacity.

Marshall managers began reacting to Thiokol's presentation, however, before the engineers could prepare and fax two final charts. Those last charts laid out the O-ring temperature range in which the Thiokol engineers knew it would be *safe* to launch. They would simply stay within the range of O-ring temperatures safely flown previously, at or above 53 °F.

NASA's manager of the booster rockets, Lawrence Mulloy, refuted Thiokol's data. He had noted that one of Thiokol's own charts showed data indicating to him that O-rings at 30 °F would safely seal the boosters' joints. He also pointed to the fact that Thiokol's own data about occasional bursts of hot gas past the O-rings before they sealed occurred in both a warm flight and a cold flight. On the heels of Mulloy's arguments, Thiokol's senior vice president, Jerald Mason, signaled that the Utah group would sever their connection to the teleconference network in order to caucus.

After Mason reviewed Mulloy's data and arguments and received his group's assent that he had summarized accurately Mulloy's arguments, the two engineers most expert in the boosters' field joint dynamics, Arnold Thompson and Roger Boisjoly, spoke up, elaborating their earlier comments. They emphasized the importance of actual flight data that showed the colder the O-ring was, the longer it took to seal its joint. VP Mason remained unconvinced. Having heard general consent to his earlier review of Mulloy's arguments showing micro-leakage in both cold and warm flights, Mason concluded that Mulloy's arguments refuting Thiokol's own engineers' arguments were persuasive. He asked his head of engineering, Lund, to assume his managerial stance and make a decision about launching. Lund agreed that the relationship between O-ring temperature and O-ring sealing capacity was not conclusive. Reluctantly, he agreed the launch should go forward.

Reconnected by teleconference to the two other centers, the Thiokol vice president in charge of booster operations, Joe Kilminster, read aloud his revision of Thiokol's position, concluding that flight risk was no greater than on previous flights, and recommended launch. [15] When Mulloy's boss asked teleconference participants for comments, there were none. The teleconference ended about 11 PM. At the Kennedy Center, Thiokol's McDonald argued further with Mulloy and Mulloy's boss. He said he would not sign a statement supporting the launch, giving additional reasons why the launch should be delayed. The NASA managers were not convinced. Thiokol's revised rationale for launching was signed and sent by fax to Kennedy and Marshall.

The following morning, after inspections of ice conditions at the launch site concluded that the widespread ice posed no flight threat, all managers reported "go" for the launch. *Challenger* lifted off at 11:38. Seventy-three seconds into flight, *Challenger* suffered explosive disintegration, killing its seven crew members.

To summarize, as an ongoing countdown toward the shuttle's launch was about to be completed, a disagreement arose. It concerned interpretations of engineering facts bearing on the danger of launching. Data were presented and examined, and the disagreement was resolved through argument, counterargument, and official decision. The official assessment that launching held no grave danger was flawed.

A critical fact not mentioned in this description of events is that the side that lost its argument, the side warning of danger, had assessed the danger specifically and correctly. The argument that was accepted as valid concluded that this flight held no more risk than previous flights. The arguments rejecting the engineers' analysis and recommendations prevailed. What could fully account for this false assessment of this shuttle's situation to prevail over assessments of it that were specific, documented, correct, and explicitly warned about?

We must go below the surface to see clearly and fully what *really* happened, *how* it happened, what *caused* it to happen, and the major *significance* of what happened. The complexities of this accident's causes require deep probing of the social, organizational, and psychological forces that caused the flawed perceptions, reasoning, and communication on both sides of the argument.

Participants

Thirty-four engineers and managers would deliberate whether *Challenger's* launch should or should not be delayed because of the recent arrival in Florida of record-breaking cold weather. The issue would be finally decided by the arguments and counterarguments voiced by nine of the 34 participants and most influentially by six of them. Participants were distributed both geographically and organizationally: 15 at Marshall Space Flight Center in Huntsville, Alabama; 14 at Morton Thiokol, Inc., in Brigham City, Utah; and five at the Kennedy Space Center at Cape Canaveral, Florida.

Two active participants on different sides of the issue who would face each other seated at a table at Kennedy were NASA's manager of booster rockets at Marshall, Larry Mulloy, and Allan McDonald, director of booster motors for Thiokol. Mulloy would argue that temperature was unrelated to the sealing of the boosters' joints, and Stanley Reinartz, his recent boss sitting next to him, would agree. McDonald was convinced that cold temperatures could seriously threaten the capacity of the boosters'

Table 1.1. Key Participants in the Teleconference: Positions They Argued, Their Organization, Their Location

Position argued or supported	Organizational membership	Locations of key participants		
		At Kennedy in Florida	At Marshall in Alabama	At Thiokol in Utah
No added risk	NASA	L. Mulloy S. Reinartz	G. Hardy	—
	Thiokol	—	—	J. Mason J. Kilminster[a] R. Lund
Unacceptable risk	NASA	—	L. B. Powers	—
	Thiokol	A. McDonald	—	R. Boisjoly A. Thompson J. Kilminster[a] R. Lund[a]

[a] Kilminster first supported Lund's initial recommendation to delay launch, but after Mulloy's argument and Mason's review, Kilminster and Lund both changed their minds.

All Other Teleconference Participants

L. Adams (N, M), B. Brinton (Th, M), J. Buchanan (Th, K), J. Burn (Th, U, P), K. Coates (N, M), R. Ebeling (Th, U), C. Houston (N, K), J. Kapp (Th, U), D. Ketner (Th, U), J. W. Littles (N, M), J. Lovingood (N, M), W. Macbeth (Th, U), J. Maw (Th, U, P), J. McCarty (N, M), J. Miller (N, M), W. A. Riehl (N, M), B. Russell (Th, U, P), L. Sayer (Th, U), J. Schell (N, M), R. J. Schwinghamer (N, M), J. Smith (N, M), K. Speas (Th, M), L. Wear (N, M), C. Wiggins (Th, U)

K = located at Kennedy in Florida; M = located at Marshall in Alabama; N = employed by NASA; P = presented a chart in the teleconference; Th = employed by Thiokol; U = located at Thiokol in Utah.

crucial O-rings to seal those joints, and he would make several arguments for delaying the launch.

Most actively arguing in Utah against the cold O-rings' capacity to seal the joints was Roger Boisjoly, Thiokol's engineer most expert in the physical dynamics of the boosters' joints. The other Thiokol engineer at Thiokol's plant in Utah who was fully informed about the effects of temperature on the O-rings' sealing capacity was Arnold Thompson. Thompson had supervised experiments at Thiokol that showed how O-ring sealing capacity became degraded as O-ring temperature dropped from 100° to 75° to 50°. Boisjoly and Thompson in Utah would point out and then emphasize to other participants the O-rings' vulnerability to cold temperatures.

A Thiokol executive who played a key role in discussions at Thiokol was its general manager, Jerald Mason, who reviewed aloud and agreed with many of Mulloy's arguments against the danger of cold O-rings. Mason recommended that the launch proceed. McDonald's immediate superior, Joe Kilminster, would first support the engineers' move to delay the launch but then would find Mason's review convincing. Kilminster would compose Thiokol's final rationale for launching.

Robert Lund, Thiokol's Vice President of Engineering, actively organized Thiokol engineers' assembly of engineering data, charts, and reasoning. He composed the conclusions and recommendation charts that would support the engineers' view that the launch should be delayed until O-ring temperatures reached or exceeded 53 °F. Hearing Mason's summary of Mulloy's arguments against Thiokol's initial argument to delay the launch, Lund recognized that the engineers could not prove the O-rings would fail to seal. With deep ambivalence, he reversed his original stance and recommended that the launch proceed.

Finally, NASA's George Hardy, in Marshall's Science and Engineering Directorate, responded to Thiokol's presentation arguing for a delay, saying simply that he was "appalled"—an unusual comment for one known to be cautiously judicious.

These participants were the ones who immediately influenced the course of deliberations. One other participant whose influence on the deliberations was pervasive but obscured was Dr. William Lucas, Director of Marshall Space Flight Center. He was personally absent from the deliberations, but his influence was evident in the participation of several who were active.

These key participants are listed in Table 1.1, which indicates the positions they argued, their organizational membership, and their physical location. None of these participants could have been certain that the dangers some of them feared would actually lead to disaster.

The nature of that evidence brings us now to details of an unusual nonhuman race whose contesting elements and forces would be known by a few almost completely, by others mostly, and by many incompletely. While participants' knowledge of safety and danger would vary widely, the degree of confidence in what each believed he understood would be uniformly high. The few who did understand the actual danger best would succeed in focusing the attention of all participants on *some parts* of the evidence. In order to understand their deliberations, we must understand the elements and forces of that nonhuman race as well as the site at which that race would take place.

The Race: Dynamics in the Boosters' Field Joints

The deliberations and debate that unfolded the night before the *Challenger* launch concerned what would happen in the field joints of the *Challenger's* ignited booster rockets. Dynamics of the field joints of the ignited boosters involved structural parts, temperature, gas pressure, and timing. All are important to understand in order to follow participants' deliberations and argument. At issue in the argument was the speed of high-pressure hot exhaust gas compared to the speed at which a blocking agent (an O-ring) would block its path.

The exhaust gas and an O-ring became contestants in a race discussed by the participants on the night of January 27, 1986, the eve of the *Challenger* launch. The gas and the O-ring had competed in the race in each of the previous 24 flights, but this time, the loser in all the earlier races would win. The winner in this day's race would be the penetrating force of the dangerously hot gas from the boosters' ignited fuel. The issue in arguments bearing on this race was whether the hot gas would breach, or the O-rings would seal, openings between two steel walls in each of the booster's three joints. Full escape of that extremely hot (5700 °F) gas through any of the twin boosters' six joints was known by all to bring explosive disaster. If the O-rings sealed the joints first, as they had in every previous race, the O-rings would prevent the destructive escape of the hot gas. The loser in this January 28 race, just this once, would be an O-ring in a rocket's field joint that would fail in its usual protective, blocking role.

First, a simple fact that created the conditions of the race: The giant booster rockets could not be manufactured as a single unit. Each booster had to be made in four cylindrical segments, illustrated in the scale model of Figure 1.1.[16] The booster segments ranged in length from 26 ½ feet to 42 ½ feet, and when they were assembled into a complete booster rocket, each booster stood as high as a 16-story building. Each segment was 12 feet 5 inches in diameter and 39 feet in circumference. The four segments of each booster had to be joined together not at the Utah plant where they were manufactured and filled with their solid fuel, but close to the site of shuttle launching at Cape Canaveral in Florida. Shipped by rail from Morton Thiokol's plant in Utah, the booster segments were joined in the giant Vehicle Assembly Building at the Kennedy Center launch site. The segments were "stacked" vertically, one on top of another, beginning with the "aft" segment (Figure 1.1). After the nose and tail components were added to the four assembled segments, each completed booster was attached to the shuttle's giant external fuel tank for flight.

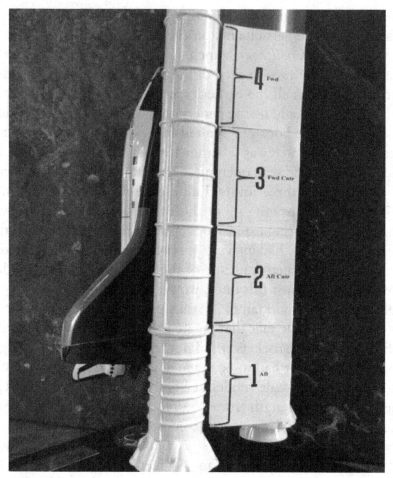

Figure 1.1 Scale model of the shuttle showing the four segments of the booster and the locations of the three field joints between the four segments.

Where each of these booster sections was joined to another, that joint became the site of the race. Because each of the shuttle's two booster rockets had three field joints, every shuttle launch set off six of those races, all taking place where one segment was joined to another.[17] To understand how the top rim of one booster segment became joined to the bottom rim of the segment that was stacked on top of the first, look at Figure 1.2.

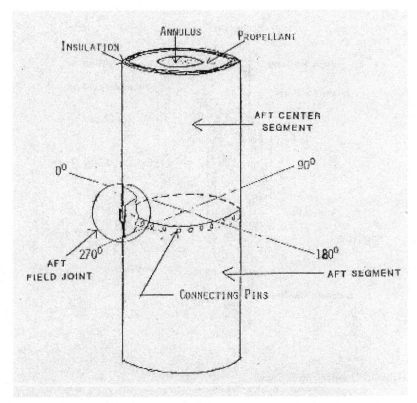

Figure 1.2 Detailed image of the aft field joint of the right hand booster rocket.

The upper rim of the bottom segment had been milled into a U shape. Into the U-shaped lip was fitted the bottom lip of the segment stacked on top. The cylinder's U-shaped lip, pointing skyward, was called a clevis, and the tongue-shaped rim of the segment above, fitting down into the clevis, was called the tang.

A more complete picture of the tang-in-clevis joint, Figure 1.3, shows how protective putty was distributed in the field joint and how the joint's primary and secondary O-rings were positioned in their grooves behind their putty barrier. The trick in these field joints was to make that tang-into-clevis joint tight, sealed securely enough to keep hot (5700 °F) high-pressure (1,000 pounds per square inch, psi) gas from contacting and

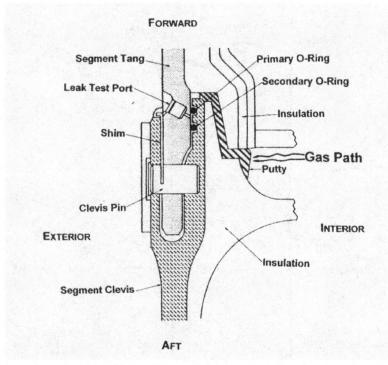

Figure 1.3 Details of the field joint.

completely destroying the steel joint. The joint was designed to be protected against the hot gas by insulating putty (see again Figure 1.3) that filled the space between the insulation lining of the segments being joined. The putty was designed to seal against even mere contact of the hot gas with the O-rings.

Several conditions could compromise the putty's protection of the O-rings, however. One or more air pressure sources in the joint as it was assembled and tested could cause air to push upstream into the putty, toward the fuel inside.[18] Sometimes the air forced upstream as two booster segments were joined (or leak-tested) would cause only bubbles in the putty. Occasionally, however, the amount of air forced into the putty would find its way all the way through the putty barrier, bursting its bubble and making a hole *through the putty* (a blow hole). That hole later provided a possible path for hot gas from the ignited booster to blow back *downstream* through the blow hole. The gas would then reach the O-ring itself. Gas contact with an O-ring might be extremely brief, just pushing it into the gap it was intended to seal, or, as we shall see, the gas could erode the O-ring in two ways.

The only way for the ignited boosters' hot gas to reach as far as a primary O-ring was through such a path in the putty. Engineers had been unable to predict when forced air from joining the segments, or from air-pressured testing of O-rings' sealing effectiveness (the "leak test"), would press a gas path through the putty. The essential and unique protection of the putty was threatened, therefore, by normally occurring (even mandated) test processes whose side effects (bubbles and gas paths) appeared erratically and infrequently by causes no one at Thiokol or NASA understood. Safe containment of any hot gas that was able to exploit an occasional blow hole depended entirely on the capacity of O-rings, and most securely the primary O-rings, to seal their respective joint gaps.

The field joints presented a second vulnerability that gave increased advantage to the hot gas in its race. The O-ring had only a small window of time to seal its joint. At the moment the boosters ignited their million pounds of solid propellant, the buildup of pressure inside the boosters by the ignited gases would go through three quick phases: a slow initial phase, a very quick dynamic phase, and a slow final phase. All three together took only .6 of one second—600 milliseconds—the period referred to in the launch deliberations as the "ignition transient." In this .6-second period, the pressure of ignited gases in all directions reached 800–1000 psi. This pressure caused the tang and clevis of the field joints to deflect, resulting in the joint *opening* from .042 inch to .060 inch.[19] The shift between the "static" joint prior to ignition and the joint as it became deflected under ignition pressure in that brief ignition transient period is illustrated in exaggerated form in the contrasting images of Figure

1.4 (A & B). The open condition (Figure 1.4B) shows the gap between the surface of the clevis and that of the now receded tang.[20]

The primary O-ring's normal ability to seal the joint's gap was partly due to the bit of space around the O-ring allowing air to press the O-ring into its gap. The force causing the primary to move into its gap was simply the difference in air pressure, caused by ignition, between the lower ambient air pressure in the joint downstream of the primary O-ring and the air pressure upstream of the primary O-ring suddenly rising because of ignition pressure.

It is also important to note that the position of the O-rings as depicted in Figure 1.4B, in which both O-rings have lost contact with their tang surface, would lead to a scenario of disaster if the insulating putty contained a gas path to the primary O-ring. The *normal* functioning of the O-rings succeeded in sealing this (now further opened) gap, preventing gas escape. As shown in Figure 1.4B, the hot gas has a free opening to surge past *both* O-rings, precisely the disaster that had been prevented up to the *Challenger* accident. The possibility of that actually happening was at the center of the prelaunch debate on the evening prior to launch.

Timing and Spacing

Time and space were important dimensions of change even within the .6-second ignition transient in which the joint opened. Thiokol studies had shown that the course of the joint's opening was gradual and minimal in the first phase, spanning the first .17 second after booster ignition. In the second, very brief dynamic phase, between .17 and .33 second after ignition, gas pressure ramped up dramatically, causing the joint to virtually snap open in .16 second. The third phase slowed the rate of joint opening until it fully opened at .6 second. The opened gap can be seen from Figure 1.4B to be wider opposite the primary O-ring than it was opposite the secondary.[21] The extremely fast rate

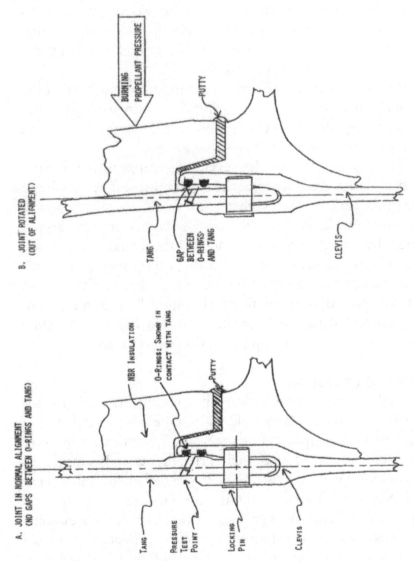

Figure 1.4 (A and B) contrasts the field joint before booster ignition ("Normal Alignment," Fig. 1.4 A) and after ignition ("Rotated," Fig. 1.4 B) showing how the joint opened with the sudden pressure of booster ignition. Fig. B shows a gap between *both* O-rings and the Tang, the disastrous condition that the engineers believed cold O-rings would create.

of opening *after* .17 second meant also that if the primary O-ring had failed to seal for any reason in the first .17 second, the secondary O-ring's gap would so quickly increase in the next .16 seconds that the hot gas could overtake the secondary O-ring. The gas would then win the race with the secondary O-ring and erode or melt everything in its path.

It was thus only in the first .17 second after ignition that the joint had a backup secondary O-ring if the primary failed. Successful sealing after .17 seconds following the boosters' ignition depended on the primary O-ring alone.

The primary O-ring, however, was seated in the farthest corner of its groove away from the gap it must seal, so to achieve a seal, it had to move across that groove.

These two facts—that the gap for the primary was always greater than for the secondary and that the primary was always seated away from the gap it must seal—still presented no obstacles to successful sealing under normal flight conditions. But what constituted "normal flight conditions" as distinct from abnormal and dangerous conditions would become the chief issue in the hours leading up to the *Challenger's* launch.

Two Kinds of Erosion

Flights prior to the *Challenger* had revealed two other kinds of weakness in the boosters' field joints. One was proved safe; the other was known to be very dangerous. The boosters of every flight were recovered after their brief flights and returned to Thiokol for inspection before being refueled for subsequent flight. Six of the initial 24 flights showed evidence of hot gas "impingement" erosion of primary O-rings. In these cases, some of the upstream, non-sealing surface of the primary O-ring had been briefly worn away by the hot gas before it had sealed its joint. Until a safety margin had been determined for impingement erosion, it had worried the engineers, but tests showed that .095 inch could actually be cut out of the non-sealing surface of an O-ring and it would still reliably seal its gap. The maximum depth of O-ring erosion on the six flights with erosion before the *Challenger* had been .053 inch (19% of the diameter of the primary O-ring worn away from the O-ring's upstream, non-sealing surface). That was well below the experimentally determined safety margin of .095 inch (34%). Impingement erosion was a deviation from design specifications and had been scheduled to be corrected in joint modifications already planned. The engineers and managers understood, however, that *impingement* erosion was physically limited and posed no threat to safe flight.

Flight 51C, flown in January 1985, a year before the *Challenger* launch, showed both impingement erosion and a very different kind of erosion. Hot gas from the boosters' fiercely burning solid fuel had penetrated *beyond* the primary O-rings. This "blow-by" of hot gas past the primary O-rings of two field joints eroded some of their upstream surface before the O-rings had succeeded in sealing those joints. As evidence of the length of time (in milliseconds) the field joints had remained open to penetration, black soot was deposited in the O-ring groove downstream of the primary O-ring itself, in the "land" between the two O-ring grooves. For the most severely penetrated joint,[22] soot extended for 110° of the rocket's inside circumference (11.6 feet) and 80° (8.4 feet) in the other joint. The most severely penetrated joint also showed effects of hot gas over 29 inches of the surface of its *secondary* O-ring.

No field joint had ever been penetrated at all, much less to this degree of severity. In addition, the primary O-rings of both joints that had been penetrated had also suffered impingement erosion. The primary O-rings' delay in sealing their joints had allowed time for the hot gas to penetrate both *into* O-ring material and *past* the primary O-rings before they could seal their joints.

Cause: Temperature + Squeeze

What could have caused this number and severity of joint-sealing anomalies on this single flight? Thiokol would need those answers to ensure the boosters' flight readiness of the shuttle next scheduled for launch. After extensive analysis of possible causes, only one remained—the below-freezing weather in which Flight 51C had been launched.

On the day Flight 51C was launched that previous January, and the day preceding it, record-breaking cold weather had descended on the Cape. Thiokol engineers had known that O-rings became hard when cold. They also knew that for the O-rings to function safely, the O-rings had to be squeezed into their joints—just like the washer in a garden hose must be tightened against the house faucet to keep the water from spraying out around the faucet. The O-rings, like the washer in the hose, became somewhat flattened by the tight squeeze, which changed the O-rings' cross-sectional shape from round to oval. That flattening reduced their *sealing widths*.

When the squeezed O-rings at *normal* flight temperatures came under the pressure of the boosters' ignited gas, the field joints would open a gap (between .042 and .060 inches) that would normally be filled by the relatively warm ($\geq$53 °F) O-ring. Being warm, the O-ring would respond to the released pressure on it as the joint opened by recovering most of its diameter. Being warm, it was "resilient" in recovering its sealing width. That recovery of its girth would allow it to stay in contact with the receding surface of the tongue (tang) of the booster's tongue-in-groove joint. The warm O-ring's resiliency in recovering its size when much of its squeeze was released was an essential aspect of its capacity to seal as the joint rapidly opened up about .2 of a second after ignition.

That crucial resilience, the O-ring's essential capacity to regain its size and shape, would become drastically reduced, however, if the O-rings became very cold. The O-rings of the cold Flight 51C, just prior to launch being both squeezed and cold, the engineers understood, would have been vulnerable to this loss of resiliency. Here, then, was the explanation for 51C's many sealing anomalies—the cold temperature robbing O-rings of the resiliency needed to recover quickly their sealing size and shape.

Allan McDonald, booster director at Thiokol, presented that explanation for those anomalies at the flight readiness review (FRR) of the next scheduled flight, 51E, scheduled to fly immediately after the previous January's cold flight, 51C.[23] He had apparently inserted into his presentation the phrase "lower temperatures aggravate the O-ring problem." [24] Larry Mulloy, NASA's booster manager, objected. He said that a single case of unusual O-ring behavior could not be explained by a single occurrence of low temperature. To argue that temperature could have an effect, Mulloy said, Thiokol would have to do research that proved it could do so.[25]

McDonald had to admit that the single instance of a strong connection between severely low temperatures, on the one hand, and severe O-ring anomalies, on the other, was not the kind of proof that would fly with William Lucas, who would conduct the next level of flight-readiness reviews for Flight 51E. McDonald therefore approved removal of his own explanatory phrase from Thiokol's FRR document to be replaced by a softened reference to temperature: "Low temperature enhanced probability—STS-51C experienced worst case temperature change in Florida history."[26]

McDonald and Thiokol's engineers most expert in booster dynamics remained convinced that the cold temperatures had caused 51C's O-ring anomalies. To back up their conviction with some hard data, two of those engineers, Roger Boisjoly and Arnold Thompson, undertook studies of O-ring sealing behavior. They set up a test apparatus that simulated a booster field joint as it opened up under the sudden rise of pressure at ignition—from no pressure to maximum pressure in .6 of a second. The test rig also was set to squeeze an O-ring into the simulated joint prior to the point of the joint's opening. Then O-rings inserted into the test rig were soaked to one of three temperatures: 100 °F, 75 °F, and 50 °F. A series of observations was made with O-ring sealing at each of these temperatures, excluding a number of the sealing dynamics occurring in actual launch conditions. The test was to examine only the effects of temperature on the speed of O-ring sealing.[27]

Results showed a clear relationship between the rate at which an O-ring could seal its simulated joint and the O-ring's temperature. At 100 °F, the resilient O-ring stayed pressed against the receding surface of the tang as the simulated joint opened, leaving no space for blow-by. At 75 °F. the O-ring lost contact for 2.4 seconds, leaving the simulated joint unsealed. At 50 °F, the O-ring did not reestablish contact in ten minutes, at which time the test was terminated—complete sealing failure. The colder the O-ring, the longer it took the O-ring to seal the simulated joint. These findings were communicated on August 9, 1985, in a letter to Larry Wear, Larry Mulloy's immediate subordinate at Marshall Space Flight Center.[28]

Blow-by on a Warm Flight

In late November, a month before the *Challenger* launch, the 22nd shuttle flight (61A) gave Thiokol two more data points that clarified the relation between O-ring temperature and speed of O-ring sealing. Two of 61A's primary O-rings were slow to seal. The booster's exhaust gas had continued to flit past the O-rings of the left-hand center and aft field joints long enough to spread 3.2 feet and 4.2 feet around the spaces between the primary and secondary O-rings of those joints. That was a warm flight, however. The O-ring temperature recorded for that flight was 75 °F.

Did that warm temperature rule out O-ring temperature as a cause of blow-by? After all, the O-rings in the other joints of both the cold flight, 51C, and this one at 75° had all sealed perfectly. Temperature differences seemed to have had no effect on the successful sealing of those joints. Some managers found that fact decisive. Because blow-by occurred in both the warm and cold flights, managers (and some engineers) concluded, temperature had to be ruled out as a cause of blow-by. But when pressed by NASA managers to explain away a different possible cause— for example, the single or combined influence of unevenness of the lubricating grease in the O-rings' grooves, variations in O-ring squeeze, or random imperfections in the O-rings themselves—the managers found the Thiokol engineers agreed that those were possible causes.

Yes, those all could cause blow-by, but their presence did not contradict the role of cold temperature. More than one cause of blow-by was possible. The engineers familiar with field-joint dynamics viewed them as the interplay of many influences. For one thing, although the grease lining the primary O-ring's groove would normally hasten the O-ring's sealing, that same grease when cold would become more viscous. It would now slow the primary O-ring's movement downstream into sealing position. The engineers were convinced that temperature was a factor that could operate *along with* these other impediments. They pointed to both the temperature-sensitive sealing of the O-rings in Arnold Thompson's resiliency experiment and the much greater amounts of blow-by in 51C's cold joints (8.4 feet and 11.6 feet of soot past the primary) than in those of 61A flown at 75° (3.2 feet and 4.2 feet).

By November of 1985, then, the data regarding temperature effects on sealing had become richer, more complex, and more susceptible to alternative interpretations.

The *Challenger* launch, in summary, precipitated another race, a situation this time different. The intricate interaction of forces playing on the O-ring's sealing, with one set of O-rings this time losing their race, reflected six *different rates of change* set in motion by the boosters' ignition:

- The booster joints opening in .6 second in 3 phases of a curve shaped like: ∫, with a slow initial opening followed by a sharply increased opening followed by a short period of slowed opening.

- High-pressure hot gas escaping through a blow hole and into a joint
- Impingement erosion
- A putty bubble's wall giving way to gas pressure—a function of wall thickness
- O-rings recapturing their sealing girth as the joint opened
- The primary O-rings' movement across their respective grooves

Attending to the relations between combinations of these rates and differentiating their significance regarding safety and danger imposed severe cognitive strain on managers when many other dimensions of the shuttle's complexity demanded attention elsewhere. We will revisit in Chapter 7 the issue of high-technology complexity in the decision-making situation.

The record-breaking cold weather at the launch site for Flight 51C, a year before the teleconference, occasioned a new cluster of anomalies in the boosters' field joints. Mulloy cautioned McDonald that if McDonald wanted to argue that cold temperature *caused* a change in O-ring functioning, he had to do the research to provide proof with numbers. McDonald agreed he did not have that evidence, so that argument was settled. Flight 51C's anomalies—greater in number and kind than previous flights, but whose impingement erosion was no deeper than before—were recorded in FRR records as "consistent with erosion data base."[29] Warmer weather soon returned, however. The effects of temperature on O-ring sealing capacity remained a live interest among only the small group at Thiokol whose technical tasks included O-ring sealing dynamics.

4:00 pm January 27, 1986

All of this had transpired in the months after the cold-weather flight of 51C in January 1985. Now, by four o'clock in the afternoon of January 27 a year later, Thiokol engineers had reacted to the news that very cold weather in the teens and low 20s would invade the launch site at Kennedy Space Center. *Challenger's* countdown was at Launch minus 17:38 hours. Thiokol engineers were compiling all the data available on the sealing performance of the boosters' field joints, organizing to present an engineering rationale for Thiokol's delay of the launch.

CHAPTER 2.

Key Concerns and Evidence, Reasoning, and Reactions

About two in the afternoon the day before the *Challenger* launch, Allan McDonald received a call at the Cape from his assistant in Utah, Bob Ebeling, asking McDonald if he had any concerns about an expected overnight temperature of 18 °F at the launch site. McDonald was indeed deeply worried about O-ring sealing at such a low temperature. The threat of cold temperatures had been clear to him for almost a year, since the 15th flight, 51C, the coldest flight so far. McDonald told Ebeling he would call back with hour-by-hour predictions of temperature for the next 24 hours. Then, still early in the afternoon, McDonald conveyed the hourly temperature predictions to Ebeling. He had additional concerns of a different kind, however.

McDonald's Concerns

McDonald knew that to halt the ongoing launch preparations would require a managerial decision. Events and experience had shown McDonald, however, that such a decision could be contaminated by managerial worries about contract renewal quite unconnected to cold O-rings or to flight safety. That contamination had to be neutralized.

The primary physical threat to flight safety, malfunctioning cold O-rings, reflected *engineering* dynamics. If technical engineering grasp of that threat were to be the basis of postponing the launch, the decision to delay had to be, in McDonald's words, "an engineering decision," one based on engineering considerations alone. But what other considerations could there be?

McDonald's position and role at Thiokol were unique. They required that he understand both the engineering details of booster functioning and the management details of securing and holding his company's lucrative contract with NASA, a contract that gave Thiokol a monopoly over booster sales to NASA. It was a contract that, in addition, NASA could split, giving part to one of Thiokol's competitors. McDonald quickly saw how a decision about this launch could become dangerously biased by his superiors' financial and contract considerations, considerations that included the need to meet every launch schedule on time.

Mason's Contract Worry

Those contract considerations had resurfaced recently. Three days before the teleconference, McDonald had participated in a meeting between NASA executives and Morton Thiokol senior management, led by Mason. The subject of that meeting had been under discussion between NASA and Thiokol for some months—namely, the terms of the contract that would govern the purchase by NASA of the next round of booster motors from Thiokol.

McDonald later described to me how those protracted discussions had gone, ending up with an initial triumph by Thiokol—but a triumph mixed with a remaining uncertainty. Some background is necessary to understand his managers' concerns. For a year, NASA and Thiokol had been discussing a proposal based on a decision by NASA to seek a "second source" for the booster rockets, a second company that would compete with Thiokol in supplying booster motors. As McDonald put it:

> [NASA] announced that they were going to seek the potential of establishing a second source for economic reasons, to keep the competition in. And we had done all we could to try to stop that, but we saw it was going

to happen. So they decided that they would ask for a proposal from all of our competitors of what they could build the shuttle solid rocket booster for. . . . We were at the same time getting ready to propose on the next production volume of motors that would not be part of the second source, because it would have obviously taken time to qualify somebody. So for the next few years they [NASA] had no choice but they were going to buy ours. And at that time, their intent was to split the production, so they'd always have two guys [booster manufacturers] in case one guy blew up his plant. And you know, you can't argue with that. So we had some internal management review, and I was party to that, saying, how do we make sure that, one, we get the most of it; two, is there a way that we could still maintain 100 percent of it?[30]

Thiokol's solution initially satisfied NASA. Thiokol offered a *fixed-price* contract, based on the efficiency that they had already developed by being the first to produce the boosters. Competitors, in contrast, would be forced to offer a *cost-plus* contract, because they would be developing boosters from the beginning and would make mistakes that Thiokol had already worked out. Thiokol's fixed-price proposal turned out to be lower than the competitions' proposals. McDonald recalled,

In December of 1985, [NASA executives] had a press conference and said that they'd evaluated all this competition, and that they'd found out it was not economically feasible to establish a second source. We were way under anybody's bid, even on a fixed-price basis, to their cost plus . . . it wasn't even close.

But they later threw in a caveat: "We decided from a national security reason, that we really ought to continue examining this in the future of establishing one [a second source], and therefore, the guideline, which was total cost only, we are setting aside for now." So we won, yet we lost. . . .

Meanwhile, they'd had our proposal for six or seven months. We were supposed to have a signed contract for the next sixty flights or so. We didn't have one, so we tried to say, "Hey, sign the contract, so we can at least get our facilities in place and get our capital money from our company to build this next sole-source batch," because we need to show them [Morton Thiokol superiors in Chicago] we have this [signed contract] to make those kind of investments. . . . And they [NASA] kept stalling. So . . . we didn't have a signed contract; we should have [had] one by the fall of 1985, we still didn't have one.[31]

Mason was caught in a Catch-22. His Chicago boss, U. Edwin Garrison, had promised that Thiokol—i.e., Mason—would deliver boosters on time for every flight, but Garrison would not release the significant funds required by Mason to buy the boosters until Mason had secured a signed purchase contract from NASA.

In April 1985, nine months earlier, Garrison had presented to NASA's highest headquarters level his arguments against NASA seeking a second source. Mason had helped prepare the financial data for that presentation. Garrison's graphics in that meeting had shown Thiokol accommodating not only NASA's past flight rate but also its increased flight schedule rising to 21 flights in 1988 and 24 flights per year through 1992. He had argued that, with its years of rocket-making experience and its routinized production facility, Thiokol had proven that it could meet that schedule with costs "decreasing as production experience builds and flight rates increase."[32] Mason's managerial task, he knew, was to protect the impressive profits that Thiokol earned from its booster monopoly.[33]

That was where those "management" matters lay when McDonald received Ebeling's telephone call asking for more temperatures. Mason's conflicting contract predicament was part of McDonald's context when he called Ebeling back and cautioned him that the decision must be "an engineering decision." An "*engineering* decision," in contrast to one dominated by management's contract concerns, would weigh the question of safe O-ring temperatures independent of contract questions, focusing instead on the physical effect of temperature on field-joint dynamics. The O-rings of Flight 51C, a year earlier, had been 53°. The O-rings to be flown the next day would be only 29°, far more compromised. The data on temperature influences on O-ring plasticity and shape retention that the engineers had collected called for delaying the next day's launch—a launch delay Mason would want to avoid if he possibly could do so. A delay would both invalidate Garrison's promise and underscore NASA's need to pursue a second source.

Realizing full well the power of senior managers to make a decision in response to continuing pressures to meet NASA's flight schedule, especially while facing further delay of a signed contract, McDonald urged Ebeling specifically "to make sure that he had the vice president of Engineering [Bob Lund] involved in this, and all of his people."[34] The engineers would have to put together a strong, data-based rationale for a delay— and it would have to have the managerial and engineering clout of Bob Lund behind it.

Earlier the same day back in Utah, the engineers, along with McDonald's managers, Ebeling and Russell, had been in high gear: gathering in groups, discussing engineering details of field-joint functioning, recalling the O-ring temperature of Flight 51C at launch (53 °F), and reviewing the effect of temperature on O-ring sealing.[35] They conferred with McDonald's boss, Joe Kilminster, who invited Bob Lund, engineering vice president, to join them. It was at this point that Ebeling called McDonald, asking for more temperature data.

In summary, McDonald voiced four warnings in that conversation: (1) the cold temperatures were very serious and must be a central focus; (2) the decision must be an *engineering* decision based on calculations and charts, not a program management decision;[36] (3) the vice president of engineering, Bob Lund, must be involved; and (4) an engineering recommendation was required that identified a specific temperature acceptable for launching. McDonald also said he would set up a telephone conference between Marshall and the Utah group in which they could present their calculations supporting the launch delay. [37]

By this time, about 4 PM on the 27th, the expanded group in Utah moved to Thiokol's management-information room, where notes and charts could be written on the marker boards, and where Thiokol teleconferences with NASA took place. The group would present from this room to NASA's booster group at Marshall the engineering basis for a delay in Tuesday's launch.

At the Kennedy Center, McDonald initiated arrangements for the teleconference linking the Utah group to the NASA group at Marshall. McDonald's O-ring temperature concerns were conveyed to the deputy manager in Marshall's shuttle projects office, Jud Lovingood. Lovingood had been conferring with Marshall's chief engineer on the boosters, James Smith, who had already heard concerns about the cold-weather launch expressed by Keith Coates, who had "worked the [booster] motors . . . from almost day one."[38] Coates and Smith expressed doubt to Lovingood that the boosters were formally qualified to temperatures in the 20s.

Lovingood tried including the deputy director of Marshall's Science and Engineering Directorate, George Hardy, in a conference call, but the hookup at Hardy's home was poor and his responses became garbled. Nonetheless, the hour-and-a-half conversation with the Thiokol engineers had conveyed their doubts. Lovingood's notes written on the day of the accident indicate that Marshall "should delay the launch until noon or afternoon" of the next day and that "their concern was based on previous erosion experience from the January 1985 launch [51C] at which O-ring temperature at launch was calculated at 53 °F. Specifically, they were concerned about O-ring resiliency at low temperatures."[39]

Lovingood had had difficulty following Thiokol's discussion in more detail because he did not have the charts that the engineers were referring to. He directed Thiokol to specify "the criterion for launch in terms of O-ring temperature, considering the projected overnight temperature," and urged that they "crisply" define their position using charts and make their recommendation. He indicated that they would have to reconvene for a full teleconference with clear telephone lines at 8:15 PM, an hour and a quarter later.[40]

Lovingood's final directions revealed how he construed the upcoming teleconference. He thought of it as an in-house, Marshall-type flight-readiness review, suggesting that "this be a Center-only meeting, involving Lucas and Kingsbury [head of Marshall's Science and Engineering Directorate]." They would "plan to go to Level II [the next higher level of NASA supervision at Houston's Johnson Space Center]—if MTI [Thiokol] recommended not launching."[41]

Keeping deliberations about the boosters' flightworthiness restricted to "Level III" (ie, Marshall and associated contractors) reflected Marshall's responsibility for all engineering aspects of assembling and testing the booster rockets, but it also reflected Marshall's distinctive culture, developed by Marshall's director, Dr. William Lucas. Lucas's culture at Marshall demanded that all technical questions regarding the boosters' assembly and flight readiness be settled in-house at Marshall, free from bureaucratic supervision from above. Officially, however, to exclude Johnson Space Center managers, Marshall's supervisors, from any significant flight deliberations during launch preparations violated NASA authority and explicit reporting policy.[42]

The Engineers' Embedded Argument

By 6:00 or 6:30 PM, the group at Thiokol, with discussions facilitated now by Engineering VP Bob Lund, had reviewed all the pieces of evidence related to the functioning of the O-rings. They also included incomplete data from a study not yet completed, a normal practice in Marshall's formal flight readiness reviews. Strong consensus had developed among the engineers that cold O-rings would make the boosters vulnerable to gas leaking through a field joint. All understood that anything beyond minute leakage could lead to catastrophic failure of a booster—and therefore destruction of the shuttle—so all agreed that the next day's launch should be delayed. The basic argument justifying a delay in the launch was supported by five facts that the engineers believed outweighed all the others they had reviewed.

First, successful O-ring sealing of the boosters' field joints is an absolute requirement of any safe launch. Second, O-rings of Flight 51C, the coldest O-rings safely flown so far (53 °F), showed the greatest number and severity of field joint anomalies from any flight, especially the greatest extent of sooted blow-by. Third, the evidence for the degraded sealing capacity of cold O-rings is not only quantitative but comes both from experiments and from comparing the joint leakage produced by warm (75°) and cold (53°) O-rings in actual flights. The latter comparison revealed that cold O-rings sealed the joint more slowly, leaving the joint open longer, than did the warm O-rings. Fourth, the O-ring temperature expected at launch time would be 24° colder than 51C's cold O-rings, and the O-rings would be correspondingly slower to recover their sealing size and catch up to the opening joint's receding surface. One or more of the field joints would therefore be open longer than for that earlier cold flight. Fifth and finally, cold, slowly sealing O-rings, combined with unpredictable timing and degree of hot-gas penetration of the joints' insulating putty, would delay joint sealing. Sealing might not occur in the first phase of the ignition transient, when the joint had not yet opened; it could be delayed into the phase from 170 to 330 milliseconds, where even the secondary O-ring, normally best positioned to seal, would be unlikely to seal the joint.

The engineers' conclusion: These considerations argued for delaying the upcoming launch until O-ring temperatures had all warmed to a temperature at or above the coldest O-ring safely flown so far, 53 °F.

The foregoing was the substance of the justifying argument, logically connecting the facts and their implication. The Thiokol group assumed they must provide an argument as justification for their recommendation; however, most construed their situation as supplying the justifying engineering facts as both necessary and *sufficient*. They did not construe their situation as having to *persuade*. The Thiokol group had no sense that their engineering rationale for postponing the launch might be rejected by an official at Marshall. They assumed that they were the most authoritative source of technical expertise (though it is unlikely that they would have used that phrase), speaking for the manufacturer of the boosters, and if a manufacturer did not want its shuttle element to fly under a certain condition on the basis of its engineers' analysis, no user of the product would oppose it.[43]

Thompson and his colleagues were announcing flight *un*readiness of the boosters under the current unusually cold conditions and were prepared to prove that the boosters (and O-rings) were ready for safe flight *if flown with O-rings at or above 53°*.[44]

Coupled with this implicit outlook—that they were simply reporting the engineering basis for recommending a launch delay—was an explicit sense of urgency. Time allowed only for reporting from available records or from new charts hastily written. It did not allow for careful ordering of the records for presentation or for review and refining of language. NASA had to be shown the necessity of interrupting the launch process in time for the reasons to be heard and understood, and then conveyed to leaders for a decision. Boisjoly later expressed to the Commission the time pressure felt by the engineers:

I must emphasize this. We had very little time to prepare data for that telecon.[45] When it was decided in a
group in our conference room that we would take a
systematic approach and assigned certain individuals
certain tasks to prepare, we all scurried to our individual locations and prepared that information in a timely
manner. That is why the charts for the most part are
hand printed or handwritten, because we didn't have
time to get them typed.[46]

The teleconference connection between Thiokol, Marshall,
and Kennedy was completed shortly after 8:15 PM. The first set
of Thiokol's 13 charts, however, was faxed to the other centers at
8:28 PM, *before* Thiokol's conclusion and recommendation charts.
Thiokol's presentation began about 8:45.

NASA engineers and managers had seen launch count-
downs interrupted before. Most interruptions occurred because
a computer signal indicated that some established limit had been
violated. It could also be a notice from someone monitoring an
environmental flight condition (like clear weather at an abort
site) that was violated. All of these conditions came under the
category of a launch commit criterion (LCC)—a known condition required (or prohibited) in advance for launch to take place.
Many LCCs had been established over the course of previous
launches—for example, the prohibition of launching with wind
speeds at the launch site faster than 15 miles per hour. NASA
teleconference participants had all gone through many delays of
the just preceding flight (61C), one for 18 days.[47]

Those at Marshall who had been called in to participate
must therefore have approached the teleconference with a mixture of skepticism and hope. Which LCC would Thiokol engineers identify as having been violated? And how quickly could
the problem be fixed? For some, like Mulloy, their expectancy
would include intense scrutiny and commitment to see the next
day's launch through unless the data against it were very clear.

Whatever the questions or expectations any listener might have, everyone at Marshall and Kennedy was looking for Thiokol to present a persuasive no-go fact about the shuttle or flight conditions that was both new and a threat to safe flight.

Teleconference Charts and Comments

The Thiokol engineers presented 13 charts of findings and diagrams to illustrate their comments, described by number below. Though all charts will be described, only those charts that reflect important support for or counterevidence against the engineers' arguments and recommendation to delay *Challenger's* launch will be presented in figures and commented on. The *engineers'* outlook in assembling evidence, however, had been established in previous FRRs, as will be detailed in later chapters. That outlook required them to present *all* the evidence available concerning any issue. The questions in focus for them concerned O-ring properties, dynamics, and sealing performance. Some of the complete evidence to be presented, then, would relate to O-ring properties irrelevant to the engineers' intended argument and warning.

1. The participants' first focus (Figure 2.1) was Thiokol's chart 1-1, labeled "History of O-ring Damage on SRM Field Joints."[48] Participants at all three centers would immediately recognize this chart as one they had seen at FRRs before. Not only was the chart not new, but also, its focal subject, O-ring *erosion*, had been repeatedly discussed in FRRs. The O-ring erosion featured in this chart, *impingement* erosion of primary O-rings, had been found by studies to have been well below engineers' empirically derived safety margins, their bread-and-butter safeguards against danger, so the main body of this chart offered only familiar and reassuring figures, not any new data, much less data proving a need to interrupt a launch in progress.

The footnotes of the chart, signaled by the double and triple asterisks, also referred to familiar facts. These facts, however, signaled serious danger, namely the escape of hot gas *past* an O-ring.

		Cross Sectional View			Top View		
	SRM No.	Erosion Depth (in.)	Perimeter Affected (deg)	Nominal Dia. (in.)	Length Of Max Erosion (in.)	Total Heat Affected Length (in.)	Clocking Location (deg)
61A LH Center Field**	22A	None	None	0.280	None	None	36°-66°
61A LH CENTER FIELD** (4FT)	22A	NONE	NONE	0.280	NONE	NONE	338°-18°
51C LH Forward Field**	15A	0.010	154.0	0.280	4.25	5.25	163
51C RH Center Field (prim)***	15B	0.038	130.0	0.280	12.50	58.75	354
51C RH Center Field (sec)***	15B	None	45.0	0.280	None	29.50	354
41D RH Forward Field	13B	0.028	110.0	0.280	3.00	None	275
41C LH Aft Field*	11A	None	None	0.280	None	None	--
41B LH Forward Field	10A	0.040	217.0	0.280	3.00	14.50	351
STS-2 RH Aft Field	2B	0.053	116.0	0.280	--	--	90

*Hot gas path detected in putty. Indication of heat on O-ring, but no damage.
**Soot behind primary O-ring.
***Soot behind primary O-ring, heat affected secondary O-ring.

Clocking location of leak check port - 0 deg.

OTHER SRM-15 FIELD JOINTS HAD NO BLOWHOLES IN PUTTY AND NO SOOT NEAR OR BEYOND THE PRIMARY O-RING.

SRM-22 FORWARD FIELD JOINT HAD PUTTY PATH TO PRIMARY O-RING, BUT NO O-RING EROSION AND NO SOOT BLOWBY. OTHER SRM-22 FIELD JOINTS HAD NO BLOWHOLES IN PUTTY.

No new data relative to 51-L

1-1

Figure 2.1. Thiokol's chart 1-1, a chart previously presented in FRRs to review, not the "blow-by" danger of focal concern to Thiokol's engineers (relegated to asterisks ** and *** footnotes in this chart), but rather impingement erosion, a factor engineers and managers had found from recent tests to pose no risk to safe sealing of the boosters' joints.

No safety margins had been established for blow-by of hot gas past the primary O-rings. In fact, the *cause* of blow-by in *neither* Flight 51C nor Flight 61A had been identified. It had been officially accepted as posing no serious threat on the basis of several earlier abbreviated instances of it in *nozzle* joints of safely flown shuttles.

A notation on one participant's copy of this chart expressed the probable reaction of others: "No new data relative to 51-L" (the *Challenger*).

2. The second chart (chart 2-1), "Primary Concerns—Field Joint—Highest Concern," all participants had also seen before, again in FRRs (Appendix Figure A .1).[49] It addressed the critical issue of timing. The issue was whether the secondary O-ring (under warm flight conditions) could maintain its backup function for more than 170 milliseconds after the boosters were ignited if the primary had failed to seal before then. Boisjoly presented this

chart, reminding his listeners that if the primary failed to seal the joint, studies had shown the secondary O-ring's capacity to keep up with the rapidly expanding field joint—opening between .17 and .33 second after ignition—had a "reduced probability" of sealing, and after .33 second, the secondary's failure to seal would be a virtual certainty if the primary had failed earlier. The secondary O-ring provided a safety net that could be counted on, therefore, for only the first .17 of a second after ignition. All this, the participants had heard before.

Most positively from the presenting engineers' standpoint was that this was an orderly summary introduction to new facts about to be offered. These first two charts provided important earlier data that, combined with new data, provided grounds for recognizing a new flight risk. For those already skeptical or who were committed to getting this launch off, however, these first two charts gave grounds for doubting Thiokol engineers' sudden new cautions because these first charts lacked any *new* information relating specifically to the next day's launch.

3. Thiokol's chart 2-2 (see Figure 2.2), handwritten specifically for the teleconference, did in fact get down to *new* business. Specifically, it laid out the engineers' primary *temperature* concerns for the field joints of Solid Rocket Motor 25, *Challenger's* boosters. Boisjoly presented this chart also, beginning with a focus on temperature and two other important parts of the engineers' argument. First was the fact that the upcoming flight would fall well outside of the O-ring temperature data base of all previous flights, touching on the traditional engineering concept of a range of values of some dimension of safe, effective functioning of one's product—a range of values, in this case of temperature, one must stay within if one wants to assure safety.

The second argument, besides the fact that the next day's temperature of the O-rings (29 °F) would be much colder than the O-rings' safe data base (53 °F), was that O-rings at that cold temperature were *much slower to seal.* They would therefore allow more time for the joint to open, entering into the ignition transient

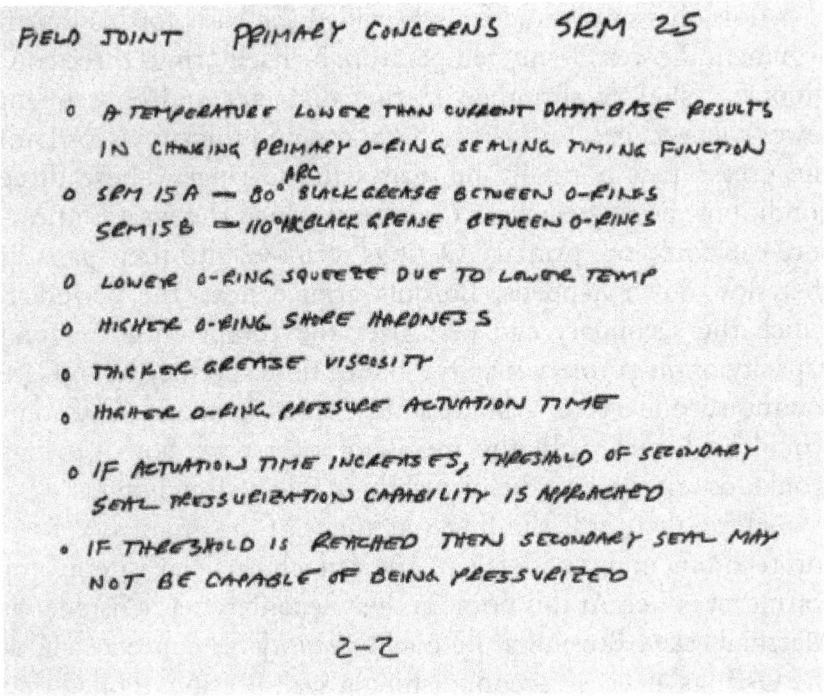

FIELD JOINT PRIMARY CONCERNS SRM 25

- A TEMPERATURE LOWER THAN CURRENT DATA BASE RESULTS IN CHANGING PRIMARY O-RING SEALING TIMING FUNCTION
- SRM 15A — 80° ARC BLACK GREASE BETWEEN O-RINGS
  SRM 15B — 110° ARC BLACK GREASE BETWEEN O-RINGS
- LOWER O-RING SQUEEZE DUE TO LOWER TEMP
- HIGHER O-RING SHORE HARDNESS
- THICKER GREASE VISCOSITY
- HIGHER O-RING PRESSURE ACTUATION TIME
- IF ACTUATION TIME INCREASES, THRESHOLD OF SECONDARY SEAL PRESSURIZATION CAPABILITY IS APPROACHED
- IF THRESHOLD IS REACHED THEN SECONDARY SEAL MAY NOT BE CAPABLE OF BEING PRESSURIZED

2-2

Figure 2.2. Thiokol's chart 2-2, presenting the crux of the engineers' intended argument and evidence, warning against launching with O-rings colder than the "current data base." It notes that sealing with cold O-rings would be slower, bringing later ignition pressure on the O-ring and thus reaching the critical time threshold where secondary O-ring sealing could fail.

period beyond .17 of a second, when the secondary would no longer provide a backup seal.

Boisjoly's third argument, supported by chart 2-2, was that the two joints of the coldest flight so far (51C), from both of its boosters (SRM 15A and 15B), had experienced black, sooty blow-by past each primary O-ring, sooted evidence that extended 80° and 110° of arc around the inside circumference of the boosters' joints.[50] This was a clear indication that those two joints with blow-by had remained open a long time into the ignition transient (ie, into the rapidly opening phase of the expanding joint, .17 to .33 seconds after ignition) before their primary O-rings sealed those joints.

Boisjoly's next three facts provided the basis for his fourth argument. Lower O-ring temperature by itself brings three conditions: a slightly shrunken O-ring diameter and consequent lower squeeze, greater O-ring hardness, and thicker viscosity of the grease that normally lubricates the O-rings. These three conditions, he argued, slow the rate at which the ignition pressure can force the primary O-rings to move into their gaps. If that slow-down happens, Boisjoly argued next, the period in which the secondary can take over the compromised sealing capacity of the primary may run out of time and may be too late for the secondary to seal the joint gap as it opens. The joint would be left *open*. In the metaphor of a race, both O-rings would lose the race to the onrushing steel-melting hot gas.

Here, then, was the first statement of the engineers' basis for recommending a delay in the launch, a delay simply for warmer weather. At this point in the teleconference, a listener at Marshall asked Boisjoly if he could *quantify* his concerns about the O-rings' delay in accomplishing a seal. Boisjoly replied that he had no more quantitative data than he had already provided, referring to the quantified phasing of the ignition transient and the measured extent of blow-by in the two joints of 51C. But all indications, he said, were "away from goodness in the current data base."[51]

Answering in this general way, Boisjoly missed the opportunity to point out the quantitative data of Thompson's experiment, data bearing directly on the influence of cold temperature in delaying the O-rings' sealing.

4. Thiokol's chart 2-3, similar to Figure 1.4 (A and B) of Chapter 1, is not included here. All participants had seen it many times before. It presented a simplified cross-section diagram of a field joint, comparing the joint before ignition with the joint opened (.042 inch to .060 inch of gap) under pressure from the ignited booster. It was otherwise less informative for readers than Figure 1.4 (A and B) – shown on page 23.

5. With chart 3-1, "Blow-By History" (Figure 2.3), Boisjoly described his and his colleagues' concerns about blow-by with cold O-rings. Chart 3-1 presents the contrasting amounts of blow-by of the cold and warm flights (51C and 61A) that had been footnoted by asterisks in his first chart (Figure 2.1). Solid rocket motors 15A and 15B of the cold Flight 51C (with O-rings at 53 °F) had shown sooted blow-by extending 80° and 110° of arc, respectively. In contrast, the blow-by in the two joints of rocket motor 22A of the warm Flight 61A (with O-rings at 75 °F) extended only 30° and 40° of arc.

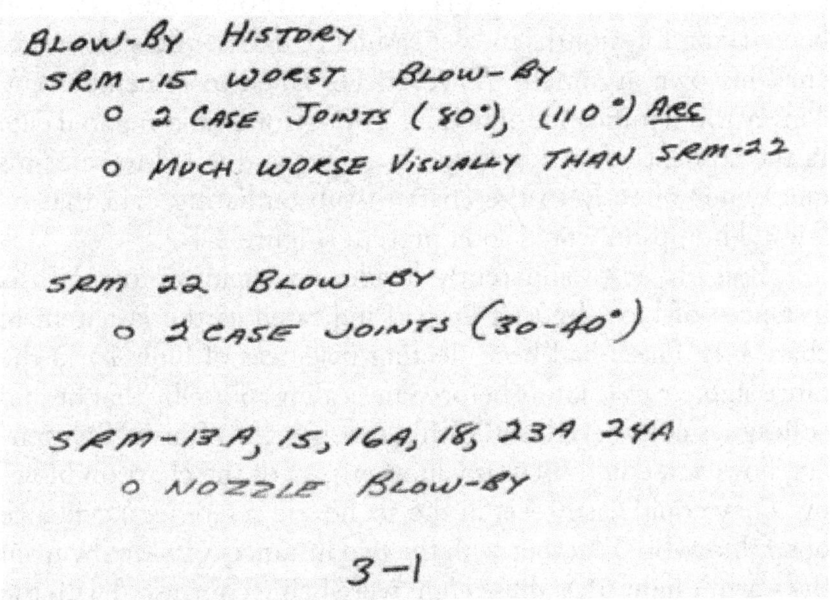

BLOW-BY HISTORY

SRM-15 WORST BLOW-BY

  o 2 CASE JOINTS (80°), (110°) Arc

  o MUCH WORSE VISUALLY THAN SRM-22

SRM 22 BLOW-BY

  o 2 CASE JOINTS (30-40°)

SRM-13A, 15, 16A, 18, 23A 24A

  o NOZZLE BLOW-BY

3-1

Figure 2.3. Thiokol's chart 3-1, focusing attention on the contrast in the amounts of blow-by between the cold flight (SRM-15) and the warm flight (SRM-22), but also including as was normal in FRRs, more complete data, data about blow-by in nozzle joints that could be interpreted as contradicting the Thiokol engineers' warning argument.

Boisjoly was emphasizing both the contrasting *amounts* of blow-by in the two flights and the contrast in the qualities of the residue that had blown by the primaries. The cold flight's blow-by was "worse visually" than that of the lesser amounts in the warm flight. Boisjoly described that worse blow-by as "black just like coal . . . jet black" in contrast to the warm flight's much less blow-by, which showed grayish residue, indicating brief burning at most.[52]

Someone at Marshall stated that they had "had soot blow-by on SRM-22 [Flight 61A's rocket motor], which was launched at 75°." Boisjoly replied, "SRM-15 had much more blow-by indication and . . . was indeed telling us that lower temperature was a factor." Boisjoly was again asked for data to support his claim. He replied that he had none other than what he had already presented, adding that he and Arnold Thompson had been trying for months to "get resilience data."[53] Boisjoly weakened his own argument, however. He failed to remember and convey the significance of his and Thompson's experimental data in the context of his questioner's doubts and failed to refer his questioner directly to the chart of substantiating data that he knew Thompson would soon present (Figure 2.4).

Boisjoly also apparently made no mention of the six instances of blow-by that he had indicated as the last item in chart 3-1. These had been fleeting instances of blow-by in the more stable *nozzle* joints before safe sealing, blow-by that he and colleagues considered well within safe margins. Boisjoly's listeners, however, could focus on another part of the chart on blow-by. They could easily see, in the six nozzle references, evidence of *safe* blow-by. Together with the two instances of blow-by from the warm Flight 61A, these eight were being contrasted with the two joints with blow-by from the cold Flight 51C—eight instances of acceptable blow-by contrasted with two that Thiokol was claiming signaled danger. The only factor noted in this chart that discriminated the safe from the allegedly dangerous blow-by was their O-rings' temperature—but was there any evidence, besides this contrasting amount of blow-by in two cold joints of 51C versus the joints of eight warm flights, that temperature could affect O-ring sealing? After all, in every one of these flights, cold and warm, the primary O-ring had sealed successfully.

6. Chart 4-1, titled "O-ring (Viton) shore hardness versus temperature" (Appendix Figure A.2), showed an array of seven O-ring temperatures dropping in ten-degree units from 70 °F to 10 °F, with corresponding O-ring hardness ratings from 77 at 70 °F to 96 at 10 °F—demonstrating that colder temperatures bring harder O-rings. This chart simply provided quantitative evidence for the assertion on chart 2-2, presented earlier (Figure 2.2), that lower temperatures bring "higher O-ring shore hardness."

7. Chart 4-2, "Secondary O-ring Resiliency," is presented in Figure 2.4. Prepared and reported by Arnold Thompson, it presented the results of Thiokol's experiments measuring the time taken for O-rings at different temperatures to recover their round sealing girth from their squeezed oval shape sufficiently to keep contact with the receding surface of the tang as the joint opened. The experimental apparatus was set to do two things: squeeze an O-ring and release the squeeze by opening the simulated joint at the rate of two inches a minute—a little less than two-thirds the rate at which actual field joints at the secondary O-ring's gap opened from ignition pressure.

Results in chart 4-2 show that O-rings at 100 °F took no time to recover their sealing shape. That is, they never lost contact with the receding tang. At 75 °F, the O-ring lost contact with its tang surface for 2.4 seconds, and at 50 °F, the O-ring had failed to make contact in ten minutes, after which time observation was discontinued.

These straightforward tests of the influence of O-ring temperature on its capacity to recover its round sealing girth and to seal the simulated joint showed clearly that the colder the squeezed O-ring became, the less able it was to recover its sealing girth—a generalization that held for O-rings from 100 °F to 50 °F. Could one expect the same generalization to hold with O-rings at 29 °F, the O-ring temperature expected for the next day's

SECONDARY O-RING RESILIENCY

DECOMPRESSION RATE
2"/MIN (FLIGHT ≈ 3.2"/MIN)

TEMP (°F)	TIME TO RECOVER
50	600
75	2.4
100	*

* DID NOT SEPARATE

4-2

Figure 2.4. Thiokol's chart 4-2 shows the experimental evidence of the strong negative relationship between O-ring temperature and time (in seconds) to recover enough O-ring size and sealing shape ("resiliency") to seal the joint when it opened under ignition pressure.

launch? If so, how long would the next day's O-rings take to recover their sealing girth? These were the questions logically raised by Thompson's chart of experimental findings.

8. The eighth chart, presented in Figure 2.5 (chart 4-3), added sheer completeness of coverage to Thiokol's presentation. Including this chart, however, allowed listeners at Marshall to interpret its notation of "no leakage" at 30 °F as contradicting Thiokol's argument. Listeners were asked by Thiokol's Thompson to disregard its contents. The results reported in the chart reflected unsuccessful attempts to assess joint leakage with O-rings at 75 °F and 30 °F, attempts to assess "incipient blow-by before any joint deflection occurred." The tests were carried out with a "test rig [that] was a solid block of metal which did not have the deflection characteristics of the full-scale joint."[54]

Many listeners apparently heard and understood Thompson's disclaimer of the results at 30 °F on grounds of flawed experimental method. One listener at Marshall, for example, drew a large X across his copy of this chart, explaining later that they were told the "data was incorrect and it should not be considered." [55] The chart's pairing of the phrase "No Leakage" with the two O-ring temperatures of 75 °F and 30 °F, however, would register for Larry Mulloy at Marshall as evidence for doubting temperature as a factor in O-ring sealing.[56]

BLOW - BY   TESTS   (PRELIMINARY)

ARGON		
TEMP (°F)	RESULTS ($^{IN^3}/_{IN}$ SEAL)	
75	No LEAKAGE	
30	No LEAKAGE	
F-14		
75	No RESULTS YET	
30	No RESULTS YET	

4-3

Figure 2.5. Thiokol's chart 4-3, showing preliminary results of tests with argon gas, a chart that could be mistakenly interpreted as contradicting Thiokol's warning about vulnerable O-rings sealing at 30° F, where the chart indicated "no leakage" (in simulated field joints with O-rings at 30° F). Tests with frion gas (F-14), providing a more valid simulation, were still to be carried out.

9. Chart 4-4, "Compression Set—%" (Appendix Figure A.3), provided, for each of three diameters of O-ring, the percent of the O-ring's precompressed diameter that, after being compressed for a given time (varied in the table from 1,000 hours to 70 hours), *failed* to recover when compression was released. None of the chart's information was connected to

temperature, and none was identified with any specific booster's joint or condition, so the chart's information was totally unconnected to the past or future safety or danger of flight. It was, in short, irrelevant to the purposes of the teleconference.

Inclusion of the chart in Thiokol's presentation reflects the haste with which the engineers scurried to provide evidence relevant in any way to O-ring properties or functioning. The engineers' haste was specifically evident in the fact that the order of presentation of the data in the first column of the chart was reversed from the proper order, providing a mismatch to the values in the other three columns. [57] Including this chart in Thiokol's presentation would not only raise questions at Marshall about its relevance but would also create or deepen Marshall participants' doubts about the Thiokol group's argument for delaying the launch.

10. Figure 2.6 (chart 5-1), "Field Joint O-ring Squeeze (Primary Seal)," compared percents of squeeze (and inches) of the primary O-rings in all six field joints (both boosters) of Flight 51C with the percents of squeeze of O-rings in the *Challenger's* six field joints. These data showed that substantial degrees of squeeze, ensuring a safe seal under normally warm flight conditions, were no safeguard against erosion when O-rings were cold, as they had been with Flight 51C (SRM 15A and 15B in Figure 2.6) the previous January. Degrees of O-ring squeeze in the booster joints of the *Challenger* (SRM 25A and SRM 25B in Figure 2.6) were generally somewhat lower than in the earlier cold flight, but *Challenger's* O-rings would be much colder. The implication of Boisjoly's earlier comments and of the data of chart 4-2 (Figure 2.4) was that the next day's booster O-rings, being much colder and much less resilient, would retain their somewhat flattened shape and would have sealing girths reduced 10%–14% more than their condition when warm. It followed from the conditions of squeeze and severe cold, then, that when the joint opened under the pressure of ignited gases, the O-

FIELD JOINT O-RING SQUEEZE (PRIMARY SEAL)

MOTOR	FWD	CTR	AFT
SRM 15 A	16.1 (.045)*	15.8 (.044)	14.7 (.041)
SRM 15 B	11.1 (.031)	14.0 (.039)**	16.1 (.045)
SRM 25 A	10.16 (.028)	13.22 (.037)	13.39 (.037)
SRM 25 B	13.91 (.039)	13.05 (.037)	14.25 (.040)

* 0.010" EROSION
** 0.038" EROSION

5-1

Figure 2.6. Thiokol's chart 5-1 reports per cents (and inches) of primary O-ring squeeze in all six field joints (both boosters) of flight 51C (SRM 15) and the *Challenger* (SRM 25), showing safe-sealing degrees of squeeze under normal conditions, but degrees of squeeze that nonetheless had been compromised by impingement erosion in two joints of the cold flight (51C). The much colder O-rings of SRM 25 would be much less resilient, much more likely to fail to close the gap as the field joints opened under ignition pressure.

rings' sealing capacity would be dangerously compromised by their hard, flattened shape.[58]

11. Chart 6-1, "History of O-ring Temperatures," is presented in Figure 2.7. It reported a mixture of data known to be misleading and data of pointed relevance to the engineers' intended argument. The first four rows of the chart presented temperature data that could be interpreted to contradict the idea that O-ring temperatures below 53 °F posed a flight danger. The first four rows of the chart presented the coldest temperatures of test firings of demonstration motors (DM) and qualification

motors (QM) at Thiokol's Utah test site. Reading across the first row, for demonstration motor 4, the figures 68, 36, and 47 express the temperatures, respectively, of DM-4's solid fuel (its Mean Bulk Temperature), its outside air (Ambient Temperature), and its O-rings. All four of these DM and QM test firings, all with successfully sealed field joints, had O-rings below the lowest temperature (53 °F) of the data base of all O-ring temperatures of shuttles then flown, shown in the fifth row of the chart.

HISTORY OF O-RING TEMPERATURES
(DEGREES - F)

MOTOR	MBT	AMB	O-RING	WIND
DM-1	68	36	47	10 MPH
DM-2	76	45	52	10 MPH
QM-3	72.5	40	48	10 MPH
QM-4	76	48	51	10 MPH
SRM-15	52	64	53	10 MPH
SRM-22	77	78	75	10 MPH
SRM-25	55	26	29	10 MPH
			27	25 MPH

6-1

Figure 2.7. Thiokol's chart 6-1 reported temperature data of DM and QM test flights known to be misleading (see text), mixed with pointedly relevant data about the cold and warm flights experiencing blow-by (SRM-15 and SRM-22), accompanied by corresponding data from the *Challenger*, with its dramatically lower O-ring temperatures.

The temperatures of Rows 5 and 6 of the temperature data referred to the booster Flights 51C (SRM-15 with blow-by and O-rings at 53°) and 61A (SRM-22 also with blow-by and O-rings at

75°). The listing of these two flights without their associated *amounts* of blow-by, however—80° and 110° of arc of blow-by for SRM-15 versus only 30° 40° of blow-by for SRM-22—undercut the engineers' attempt to show how temperature affected blow-by. Without those contrasting amounts of severe blow-by for SRM-15 versus the mild amounts of blow-by for SRM-22, the added juxtaposition of the temperatures of *Challenger's* O-rings failed to highlight the intended but implicit question: "If we got such an increase of blow-by from 75° to 53°, how much increase will we get tomorrow at 29° or 27°, and how will we know whether that increase is safe or dangerous?"

Immediately after chart 6-1 was presented, McDonald broke his silence. He pointed out that the temperature data from the demonstration and qualification motors would not at all apply to issues of O-ring *sealing*. The insulating putty of all those test motors, he pointed out, had been scanned for bubbles and blow holes, which had been "manually filled prior to the static test." Because all pathways for the test motors' hot gas to reach the O-rings had been *manually* blocked, their safe sealing could not be interpreted as the *O-rings'* ability to seal off the test motors' hot gas.

McDonald's rejection of the four test motor results as invalidated by that putty packing meant that those first four rows of data provided no evidence of the O-rings' ability to seal off the boosters' hot gas in those test firings, much less in an actual launch or flight.[59] Although McDonald's disclaimer of the misleading test motor results did warn against concluding anything about cold O-rings' protective capacity, it is not known how many at Marshall understood his discounting of the data.

12. The next chart, "Conclusions" (Figure 2.8) was presented by Vice President of Engineering Bob Lund. It summarized seven points whose bare wording would have been expanded in Lund's presentation but whose written content was a less than cogent summary of the engineers' case against launching in cold weather. In the chart Lund first attempted to explain why blow-by had shown up in

CONCLUSIONS:

o TEMPERATURE OF O-RING IS NOT ONLY PARAMETER
 CONTROLLING BLOW-BY

 SRM 15 WITH BLOW-BY HAD AN O-RING TEMP AT 53°F

 FOUR DEVELOPMENT MOTORS WITH NO BLOW-BY
 WERE TESTED AT O-RING TEMP OF 47° TO 52°F

 DEVELOPMENT MOTORS HAD PUTTY PACKING WHICH
 RESULTED IN BETTER PERFORMANCE

o AT ABOUT 50°K BLOW-BY COULD BE
 EXPERIENCED IN CASE JOINTS   or 75°
      Also Experienced at 75°

o TEMP FOR SRM 25 ON 1-28-86 LAUNCH WILL
 BE 29°F   9 AM
    38°F   2 PM

o HAVE NO DATA THAT WOULD INDICATE SRM 25 IS
 DIFFERENT THAN SRM 15 OTHER THAN TEMP.

Figure 2.8. Thiokol's "Conclusions" chart summarized a number of considerations that could enter an argument against launching (see text), but that were couched in dispassionate engineering discourse rather than as an argument. Note the scribbled comments by participants at Marshall countering the engineers' argument by indicating that blow-by also occurred with O-rings at 75° F.

both warm and cold flights. He was cautioning, without using these terms, that cold O-ring temperature was a *sufficient* cause but not the *only* cause of blow-by. The next point simply was a reminder that Flight 51C, with the coldest booster motor flown with O-rings at 53°, had blow-by.

The next two points acknowledged that test motors "with no blow-by" had O-ring temperatures colder than 51C's O-rings (from 47° to 52°) but that those motors "had putty packing" and that their "better performance" resulted from that preflight *putty packing*, not from O-rings sealing off the test motor's hot gas. The fifth point referred to Thompson's experimental finding that O-rings at 50° had failed to seal in his test rig; therefore, under actual flight conditions, blow-by "could be experienced in case joints . . . at about 50 °F."

Just at this point on one of the copies of the conclusions chart, two participants had written corrective comments. One wrote just underneath the fifth point, "Also experienced at 75°."

Another participant, evidently leaning to the left to write his comment on the chart, wrote "Or 75°," emphasized with double underlining. These two comments expressed the view that blow-by had happened irrespective of O-ring temperature. Neither comment addressed quantities of blow-by, however.

The conclusion chart ended by stating that the O-ring temperatures at the next day's launch would be 29 °F at 9 AM but 38 °F at 2 PM and that the only data differentiating the next day's booster motors from the cold SRM-15 motors would be the next day's much colder temperature.

13. The final chart (Figure 2.9), also hand printed and presented by Lund, was titled "Recommendations." This chart presented a stark contrast with those before it. Discussion and charts before this one focused on flight risk and dangers—O-ring erosion, blow-by, reduced O-ring sealing girth from squeeze and cold temperatures, cold-induced grease viscosity, and so on. With the first line of this final chart, however, came not more proof of danger but a condition required for *safety*. The boosters' O-rings "must be ≥ 53°F at launch." This statement exactly reflected McDonald's pre-teleconference warning to Ebeling that the Thiokol group must "come back with a recommendation for an actual temperature that we would recommend for the launch."

RECOMMENDATIONS :

° O-RING TEMP MUST BE ≥ 53 °F AT LAUNCH

  DEVELOPMENT MOTORS AT 47° To 52°F WITH
  PUTTY PACKING HAD NO BLOW-BY
  SRM 15 (THE BEST SIMULATION) WORKED AT 53 °F

° PROJECT AMBIENT CONDITIONS (TEMP & WIND)
  To DETERMINE LAUNCH TIME

Figure 2.9. Thiokol's Recommendations required launch only within the database of safely flown O-ring temperatures (≥ 53° F.). This chart emphasized the invalidity of the O-ring temperature data from the developmental motors (see text), and concluded that the previous coldest flight (SRM-15, flight 51C) best simulated the safe O-ring temperatures for the *Challenger* flight.

The final line of the chart specified the method for determining time of safe launch. The hour at which that combination of factors would produce an O-ring temperature of at least 53 °F was the hour recommended to launch. The chart further indicated that the safe launch temperatures of the test motors inaccurately represented safe flight temperatures. The best simulation, in contrast, is provided by *all* the booster O-ring temperatures of all 24 preceding safe launches, the coldest having O-ring temperatures of 53 °F.

Two Reactions

George Hardy, deputy director of Marshall's Science and Engineering Directorate, and Larry Mulloy, Marshall's booster rocket manager, both responded to Thiokol's presentation. Hardy firmly believed that the secondary O-rings provided reliable backup if the primaries failed. The secondary O-ring was positioned right next to the gap it was intended to seal, pressed there during booster assembly by the leak test. Hardy reasoned that as soon as any gas blew past the primary, the secondary would be pressed into its gap and seal the joint. In his view, the field joints were self-sealing, exactly as designed: Any unwanted escape of gas past the primary would press the secondary into service.

If Boisjoly had heard any such view expressed, he would have quickly pointed out that Hardy's self-sealing scenario would hold with warm O-rings but might well not happen with cold, deformed, non-resilient O-rings. Hardy's scenario for joint sealing, expressed before actual causes of its failure were known, was the view that led him to discount Thiokol's version of malfunctioning O-rings. [60]

As to Thompson's data about the degrading effect of cold temperature on O-ring resiliency, Hardy simply rejected its validity. If secondary O-rings actually behaved the way Thompson's O-rings at 75° had behaved—so slowly sealing that they allowed 2.4 seconds to elapse before sealing—then, Hardy reasoned, half the boosters already flown would have blown up, and Thompson's data must therefore be disregarded. The secondary O-ring could be relied on to function if needed. Hardy's misreading of Thompson's experimental results, addressed later, allowed him to dismiss Thompson's chart (Figure 2.4) as simply irrelevant.

Mulloy's response to Thiokol's presentation was both more emotional and more systematic. His response to Lund's final chart, calling for launch time to wait until the O-rings reached 53°, was surprise and exasperation. To adequately understand both his emotional response and his more measured, analytical response, we must trace another bit of history. This history is about the culture of work and precision at Marshall, about the leadership and commitments of Marshall's director, Dr. William Lucas, and about the ramifying effects of an inventory error made under Mulloy's supervision.

CHAPTER 3

Mulloy's Experiences, Organizational Culture, and Arguments

Thiokol's sudden move to delay the launch posed special difficulties for Mulloy, Marshall's booster manager. As Thiokol's engineers had presented their charts and explanation for why *Challenger's* launch should be delayed, it had become clear to Mulloy that they were actually thinking that O-ring temperature affected sealing. That was shocking to him. That issue had been settled a year ago, he thought. It was clear to him, further, that their data not only did not "hang together" but actually contradicted their claim. He could never justify halting a launch on this basis.

Mulloy's experiences with actual or threatened launch delays had prepared him to be critical of any claim that this shuttle should not be launched on time. Four strands of experience had emerged from Mulloy's past encounters with "delay" and from his immersion in Marshall's local culture. These four experiential histories would prime Mulloy's emotional response and shape a counterargument to Thiokol's call for a delay.[61]

1. *Marshall's Engineering Standards.* Mulloy had already had to deal with McDonald's inadequate explanation a year before of the two instances of blow-by and other anomalies, where McDonald saw the cause of Flight 51C's anomalies as that flight's low temperature at launch. Thiokol's explanation had not met Mulloy's standards of "credible quantitative engineering analysis or test data."[62] Mulloy had already witnessed one attempt by a Thiokol engineer to offer an explanation that fell short of the standards demanded by Dr. William Lucas. The experience was described by the engineer himself, Roger Boisjoly:

I have been personally chastised in Flight Readiness Reviews at Marshall for using the words "I feel" or "I think," and I have been crucified to the effect that [that] is not proper presentation. Because "I feel" and "I accept" are not engineering-supported statements but they are just judgmental. And so when people go in front of Dr. Lucas, they know full well that if they use words like that or if they use engineering judgment to try to explain a position that they will be shot down in flames. And for that reason, nobody goes to him without a complete, fully documented, verifiable set of data.[63]

Thiokol's McDonald on another occasion, noting trepidation on Mulloy's part in providing engineering reasoning that would meet Lucas's standards, described his own experience of Lucas's standards of analysis and argument:

I was even warned by Larry Mulloy: "We don't want to talk to him about that because he'll eat you up," and I said, "No, I don't think he will, because I know what we are talking about." . . . We were having problems with, for instance, burns in the rubber from methyl chloroform—[which] we use for a solvent—was actually burning some of the rubber, and our conclusion was go ahead and fly it, but it was causing these colored spots . . . on the actual insulation.

And I said, "No, I think I understand that, and I think I understand the chemistry," and he [Mulloy] said, "You well know, he's a chemist, and a physical chemist, and . . . he'll eat you up." . . . And I went to give that presentation to him and had all the right answers, and he said, "Well, I think we understand the problem and I agree with you."

But the problem was, I also saw him [Lucas] tear a guy from Rocketdyne on the main engine problem, and just, I thought very unprofessionally, just destroyed the guy, in front of this big group of people, because he couldn't answer some of the questions in the detail that he [Lucas] thought he should be able to do.

And so his intentions, I always thought, were very good, he was very thorough, but what happened with that kind of an attitude is that people were reluctant to bring anything of controversy unless they knew it to the detail. And these kind of things, most time, you don't know the detail. You finally get to a point, and say, "That's the best I know. My engineering judgment." And Roger's right, he said, "The things he would jump on!" You know, "Well, I feel this," or "I think maybe," and he'll say, "Where's your hard evidence and facts? I didn't ask for what you think. I want to know what you can prove to me." . . . That was Lucas's focus and direction, and his intent was absolutely right. The manner in which he went about it was absolutely wrong.[64]

Mulloy had learned two lessons from such experiences: First, you had to probe all engineering explanations to see if they met Lucas's standards of "credible quantitative engineering analysis or test data," and second, if you yourself failed to meet those standards, you, too, would be "shot down in flames."[65]

2. *Launch Delays.* Mulloy's experience under Lucas had etched deeply NASA's launch schedule. Speedily identifying and solving problems of readying boosters to meet NASA's increasing launch schedule held high priority:

If we were going to delay a launch because we had an unresolved problem, he [Lucas] wanted to be sure . . .

that we really need the time. . . . You go in and say, "I'll have an answer in three weeks," and he'll say, "Why can't we have it in one?" Well, you can. You work everybody on weekends and disrupt families. . . . He didn't believe in taking three weeks to do something that could be done in a week—just because somebody has a trip planned to Europe or something like that. [Lighthall: What do you lose if you don't meet the schedule?] . . .You're contracting to carry a pay load. . .Putting up a communications satellite, the impact of putting it up a month from now instead of a month earlier is one month of not being able to use the satellite . We sign *up* for that [Program Operating Plan]. We make a commitment that says, "We're going to support these launches on this schedule." Failing to support those launches on schedule is a failure of the organization to deliver on its promises. It's commitment.[66]

Getting each shuttle launched on time was more than an end in itself. The delay of one launch often meant that the next shuttle had less time to prepare, which could force a delay of its mission. Future space experiments and observations were limited by restricted windows of opportunity. Delays in missions resulted in lost opportunities all along the line, degrading NASA's reputation in Congress and losing revenues from its payload customers.[67]

To be the person responsible for delaying a launch was something all managers at Marshall feared. Six years after the *Challenger* accident Mulloy expressed to Vaughan (1996) this managerial fear as a need to avoid being "the lightning rod":

You always went to those [Flight Readiness] reviews hoping that somebody else would have a worse problem than you did so that it wouldn't be your problem that held up a launch. We project managers joked among ourselves about it. We called it "being the long pole," the lightning rod, the one that absorbed all the attention and electricity, so to speak, by having the problem that delayed the launch.[68]

3. *Flight 61C's Unnecessary Delay.* Mulloy had himself been the long pole. One month before the teleconference, he had attracted a good deal of Lucas's critical attention. Fourteen seconds before ignition of the motors of shuttle Flight 61C on December 19, 1985, its launch was aborted because of a malfunction of an integrated electronic assembly (IEA) of Flight 61C's right-hand booster. This was the first time a launch had been aborted by a failure of one of *Marshall's* shuttle elements. Because the elements in question were boosters, the failure was Mulloy's responsibility.[69] The abort led to a three-week delay in the launch. A delay of that length caused by someone at Marshall was exactly the kind of embarrassing, black-mark event that Lucas felt deeply.

Lucas had struggled mightily to ensure that the Marshall Center reviews he personally chaired would unearth any defects of shuttle elements being readied for launch. How had this defect in a Marshall shuttle element gotten by both Mulloy's earlier review and Lucas's own Marshall Center review? Lucas was not one to keep his feelings to himself. Mulloy heard Lucas's displeasure. Intense investigation in the next ten days, ordinarily the period of Christmas break, finally identified the cause as a faulty control card. It fell to Mulloy as booster manager to find and explain the cause of the malfunction. He reported initial and then more complete findings of the cause in a set of FRRs of Shuttle 61C leading up to its finally successful launch on January 12, 1986. The trouble was caused, it turned out, by a shortage of electronic control cards, parts ordinarily procured by Marshall. Organizationally, that shortage was caused by a failure of someone under Mulloy's supervision to monitor and maintain the required supply of control cards. The shortage of cards had become the occasion for a one-time substitution of a different brand of control card, one, as it happened, that had not been tested and approved.

That substitution, the fact that it caused the failure, and the aborted launch and delay became Mulloy's mistakes to correct. He had to determine the cause of the launch abort, had to explain it to higher management in subsequent FRRs for 61C, and, of course, had to explain how the repair with new cards had been tested and would function reliably. That explanation was reported to the usual gathering of engineers and managers, including Lucas, at 61C's next FRR.

In the backwash of that lapse, delay, embarrassing public explanation, and Lucas's ire, Mulloy faced yet another embarrassment. That small substituted part, causing the delay of 61C, had produced a critical memorandum from a director higher up in the NASA hierarchy.

4. *Protecting In-House Control.* That memo, from Johnson Space Center, threatened both Lucas's sense of control and his public face of professional competence. Lucas's whole pattern of management bespoke a deep sense of personal responsibility for achieving success, a managerial, supervisory success as perfect as humanly possible. It meant personal, hands-on control and a scrutinizing supervision to assure competence. Applied to Lucas's Marshall Center, it also meant close attention to meeting the flight schedule. Regarding the world beyond Marshall, Lucas's need for complete success meant achieving and protecting his own and Marshall's reputation for excellence. This protective part of Lucas's outlook meant, among other things, that all problems in the functioning of any element for which Marshall was responsible must be solved according to Marshall standards, yes, but also solved *in-house*, by his own engineers and managers. Larry Mulloy expressed this in organizational terms:

When something came out of the Center, he [Lucas] wanted to be sure that, you know, things going to *his boss*, essentially the Level I managers, he wanted to be sure that he [Lucas] approved of it. He didn't want to get blindsided by some problem that he heard about from Level I. That was sure death. . . . Passing open-ended problems up the line was not a good thing to be doing.[70]

Lucas abhorred professional incompetence. He pointed it out wherever he saw it and criticized those in whom he perceived it.[71] Finding out from an official *outside* of Marshall that a mistake had been made *at Marshall* showed incompetence at Marshall. "That was sure death."

The controlling and personal-responsibility dimensions of Lucas's outlook impelled hands-on intervention that reached down deep into the detailed functioning of his Marshall organization. An example was reported by McConnell (1987, p. 107):

On a warm afternoon Dr. Lucas glanced out of his ninth-floor office window and saw two engineers in shirt-sleeves, pitching horseshoes on the shady lawn below. He immediately summoned a subordinate and demanded an explanation. "Those men are on their lunch hour, Dr. Lucas," the man is reported to have replied. "They've finished eating, and they're just relaxing." "If they've finished eating," Lucas is said to have retorted, "they can get back to work."

As it happened, the substitution of the faulty part that Mulloy had to correct prompted an embarrassing complaint by Lucas's superiors at Johnson Space Center.

Six days before the *Challenger* teleconference, Mulloy, Reinartz, and Lucas received an official criticism—"reprimand" captures the tone. An administrator at NASA's Johnson Space

Center, Arnold Aldrich, pointed up "lessons learned" from an official review of the many delays of Flight 61C that had immediately preceded the *Challenger*. Here was a public notice from outside Marshall presenting evidence of incompetence at Marshall. The first two paragraphs of the memorandum were addressed to Marshall's booster project office under Stanley Reinartz, with copies to Mulloy, Lucas, and others.

Its "lesson learned" was a discovery the Johnson Center had made about how Reinartz's office—clearly Mulloy, as Reinartz had only recently been appointed to head that office—had used a "piece part substitute" (the one Mulloy had had to explain) that had caused a malfunction and unnecessary delay in launching Flight 61C. The memo noted that the false-signaling effects of that offending part had previously been warned about "several years earlier." Reinartz's office was directed to review the "formal closeout paperwork for this issue" that had been "communicated throughout the [Space Shuttle] system and to "identify reasons why [Reinartz's booster project office] did not react appropriately."[72] Lucas would have been furious that his managers had left him open to such a rebuke.

With the appearance of this criticism (exactly the kind Mulloy felt was "sure death" for Lucas) just six days before *Challenger's* teleconference, Mulloy had an official reminder of the recent embarrassing situation he had had to go through to explain how the false signal halting 61C's launch had been caused and how he had corrected it. He would now also have to participate in reviewing his and subordinates' responsibility for missing that important "paperwork," causing an unnecessary delay in that launch.

We can summarize the four themes of Mulloy's pre-teleconference experience with delays. First, he had seen the fate of anyone whose explanations failed to meet Lucas's demanding standards of proof. One got "shot down in flames"—in public. Mulloy had also personally experienced Lucas's demand that the flight schedule be met and that those under Lucas had to be prepared to sacrifice their own personal plans in order to meet that schedule. The consequence of causing a delay was to experience being the long pole. For Lucas, any delay in the launch schedule was personally painful, and he passed the pain along.

Even more painful, however, was to fail in one's own supervisory duty to ensure that no *unnecessary* delay happened, to cause a delay out of *negligence*. Mulloy's approval or failure to prevent substitution of a faulty control card caused an unnecessary delay in Flight 61C, the flight immediately preceding *Challenger*. Finally, he had had to suffer, and had caused Lucas to suffer, a recent rebuke and embarrassment sent by superiors at the Johnson Space Center. The memo questioned why a substitute part had been used despite an earlier memo warning that the part had been found defective. For that very recent mistake and public rebuke, Mulloy would have felt Lucas's anger and embarrassment.

This history of Mulloy's experiences had left him with a clear operating rule for handling any action or condition associated with the booster rockets that even hinted at a launch delay. The *necessity* for that delay would have to be proven by a coherent argument based on quantitative evidence that was complete and convincing. In short, Mulloy's rule required that he support only arguments for delay that Lucas would approve of and that would avoid all pain. That rule would hold no matter whether someone was arguing for or against safety or danger.[73] Any argument that failed to fit his rule Mulloy would argue against, because it would fail Lucas's test and, if accepted by Mulloy, would promise pain from Lucas. With this rule and critical outlook, Mulloy was primed to address any argument Thiokol might offer for delaying a launch.

An Organizational and Leadership Context of Safety

Any response Mulloy, or indeed anyone else at Marshall, might make to Thiokol's case for a launch delay would be shaped by the type of engineering argument that Lucas had required of *all* who worked at Marshall. That was the result of more than the force of Lucas's personality and values, however, as strong as that force was. It was also because Lucas had *institutionalized* his outlooks and values by creating a new decision-making unit that he had personally inserted into the safety system that NASA already had in place.[74]

Before Lucas's appointment as Marshall director, NASA had instituted a series of Flight Readiness Reviews (FRRs). At each point where a shuttle "element" was constructed or assembled with other elements—the orbiter, boosters, external tank, etc.—a supervisory review was held in which the element, alone and as assembled with other elements, was presented by its manager to other managers and engineers charged with a critical review. The review task at each stage was to scrutinize the element for all engineering details, all glitches and anomalies discovered from assembly or from the immediate past flight. The sole aim of each review was to test whether those charged with the review could prove that the vehicle at that stage was ready for flight. The reigning assumption of these reviews was always that the vehicle in preparation was not flight ready until proven so.

NASA's system of reviewing the safe functioning of its space vehicles was composed of five stages of review before William Lucas became Marshall's director. The first was conducted by the private contracting manufacturer, a technical review to verify that it had met all of NASA's specifications for its particular shuttle element. NASA itself then held its own four levels of FRR. Level IV, NASA's first review of each shuttle element as received from a private contractor, was followed by a review of the element as fully assembled, and then again as units functioning together (Level III). These Level IV and III reviews were conducted by managers at Marshall. Next, the Level II review, verifying completion and integration of the shuttle and mission as a whole, was conducted at the Johnson Space Center. NASA's final, official FRR (Level I) verified that all previous certifications of readiness had been signed off and that flight readiness of the shuttle was complete.

Into this series of FRRs Lucas inserted his own stringent Marshall Center review. Lucas's deeply felt responsibility for assuring technical competence to ensure safe readiness dictated that he personally construct an organization that would bring a high and consistent level of technical competence to Marshall. It was Marshall's responsibility to carry out complete and final technical vetting of each shuttle as "flight ready."[75] Lucas assumed personal supervision of that effort. He saw to it that the Marshall Center Boards, as they came to be called, were carefully prepared and executed with a keen eye to instilling in all members of his organization his own standards—standards of professional engineering, of quantitative analysis, of technical knowledge and discourse, and of tightly reasoned argument. Any conclusion must be based on quantitative data one could readily cite.

To further this end, Lucas soon approved a preparatory FRR, a "pre-Board" review. The sheer energy and penetration of Lucas's punitive mode of conducting his Marshall Center FRR had caused Mulloy and his boss, Stanley Reinartz, to add their own preparatory FRR, a rehearsal as it were, before going onstage for Lucas's demanding show.[76] Any loose ends remaining after Mulloy's Level III FRR would be assigned an action item for the relevant people to clear up. Just as Lucas cringed at the possibility of being blindsided by a Marshall error or criticized by his bosses at Johnson, so his subordinates had internalized that same fear from him. Their weapon against being caught wanting from above was this added FRR process led by Reinartz and Mulloy. It created an opportunity to actually test for and correct weaknesses in an organized way and further contributed to Lucas's own goal of instituting technical competence at Marshall.

Lucas became at Marshall not only its director and chair of the Marshall Center FRR Boards, but also Marshall's teacher and examiner. He made sure his people knew what they were supposed to do, knew the right way to do it, and then did it.

Although he would never have thought like an anthropologist, what Lucas's deep, indeed fierce, commitment impelled him to do and to sustain at Marshall was to create a *particular Marshall culture*—a culture tightly tuned to Lucas's own engineering standards of what constituted "professional" conduct. That required developing a very particular set of norms, practices, ways of thinking, and rituals that members would enact and take for granted as a way of life. His immediate tools for this task were humiliation for deviations, as already noted — and a cash bonus for praiseworthy performance.[77]

While he could exercise his demanding leadership at any moment and directly from his office, as the horseshoe players in their lunch break could attest, the main venue for hammering home his many required dimensions of professional thinking and conduct was his Marshall Center Board FRR. He and chosen managers and engineers at Marshall made up the examining board for a flight's shuttle elements. He and they would probe the presentation made by the Marshall manager in charge of, for example, the booster rockets (Mulloy), and any additional explanations that might be offered by a member of the contractor's team, like Thiokol's McDonald or, as we have seen, Boisjoly ("shot down in flames").

The quest of Lucas and his board of questioners was always the same: proving each component of the shuttle "flight ready," proving all threats to the shuttle (as space hardware or software) neutralized or removed. Any anomaly discovered in a shuttle's assembly or from a past flight had to be explained in detail, and its correction had to be proven effective—again, by credible quantitative engineering analysis or test data.

Lucas's added reviews and his own demanding style, standards, and probing for flaws reflected the fact that the FRR system of achieving flight readiness at Marshall was the last detailed technical review the shuttle would receive. Once certified as ready by Lucas's Center Board, a shuttle was universally regarded as ready for space flight. This was true despite the fact that Marshall's (Lucas's) declaration that a shuttle was "flight ready" occurred from ten days to three weeks *before* actual launch or flight conditions for that shuttle could be known. The Marshall declaration of flight readiness meant, therefore, that the shuttle was ready to fly only under flight conditions expected or already encountered in previous flights. The possibility that flight conditions posing a danger to flight might arise *after* a shuttle was fully certified by Marshall as "flight ready" had either not occurred to anyone or had been dismissed. It reflected an organization-wide confidence in the FRR process to ensure safe flight, confidence bolstered by an uninterrupted string of 24 successful shuttle flights. Yet flight conditions could change after Marshall found a shuttle "flight ready."

Returning to Lucas's expanded system of FRRs, his near obsession with detail and quantification had five positive effects on the quality of deliberations about flight readiness. A sixth effect was dangerous.

Lucas's FRR Culture: Six Dimensions

1. *Detailed Completeness.* Participants at Marshall came to understand that they had to include in any FRR presentation all details of their analysis, no matter how small or peripheral or contradictory. Even if you had hard evidence showing that a threat to flight safety, like O-ring impingement erosion, was well within safety margins, you had better include a description of both test and test results in your presentation, or be prepared to provide it when challenged. It was the tiny details that Lucas would question, maybe because he thought the matter was crucial or maybe because he wanted the person reporting to understand the importance of detailed preparation.

2. *Specifications as Primary.* All shuttle elements were required to meet specifications established either as part of the original design or through research analyzing previous shuttle

flights. Any deviation from those specifications had to be proven both necessary and safe with substantiating data. Knowing those specifications and being familiar with what had, and had not, been established as safe changes in them was only prudent if one wanted to avoid Lucas's sharp tongue.

3. *Demanding Standards.* Lucas's demanding standards of data and of coherence in reasoning led all who would make a presentation at Lucas's Center Board to prepare thoroughly, to rehearse what they could say in response to questions they imagined he might raise. Mulloy expressed the inner voice of fear when he warned McDonald, "He will eat you up," and only someone who, as McDonald said, "had all the right answers" would dare express his view in Lucas's FRR or, as will be clear below, in any FRR leading up to Lucas's Center Board.

4. *Intense Probing.* Mulloy's "he'll eat you up" reflected the critical and detailed probing that characterized Lucas's FRRs, a questioning of explanations and assumptions that prepared any would-be presenters at an FRR to answer the question "How do we know that?" Answers in FRRs at Marshall were not to be taken at face value. They were to be probed. It was only through probing that Lucas could unearth any dangerous detail.

5. *Cascading Effects.* These four characteristics of Lucas's mode of inquiry and verification gave positive strength to Lucas's Center FRRs. Further, those strengths—and weaknesses (see below)—cascaded down the organizational ranks below Lucas. That was the way Lucas's personal commitments and style had become a living part of Marshall's organization, amplifying Lucas's face-to-face influence. Mulloy's own FRR of booster rockets would be prepared with Lucas's demands in mind to make sure that when Mulloy brought the boosters to Lucas's FRR, nothing had got by him that would allow Lucas to eat *him* alive.

Similarly, when Mulloy then deployed his own critical standards and probing questions in his own Level III FRRs, his subordinate, Larry Wear, would also see the necessity of internalizing Mulloy's standards. He would also to some degree adopt Mulloy's own adaptation of Lucas's style in his own Level IV FRR. Finally, as preparation for presenting Thiokol's booster motors to be reviewed in Wear's Level IV FRR, McDonald and his boss, Joe Kilminster, would conduct their in-house review of their boosters with much the same critical, probing standards as they could expect up the line from Wear to Mulloy to Lucas.

6. The Delta Distinction and Policy. The delta policy was that each FRR would review only issues or anomalies that had *not* been settled before. The delta idea referred to a distinction between new anomalies that needed investigation and anomalies that had already been found or corrected to be innocuous ("dispositioned"). Anomalies showing up in postflight inspections, like O-ring erosion, led to investigation (or actual changes) that either eliminated them or discovered that at their most threatening level they posed no threat to flight safety. The evidence of an anomaly's correction, once affirmed in an FRR, was then regarded as case law, so to speak, a body of established knowledge that could now be taken for granted. The delta policy was regarded simply as providing a useful distinction between what was known and settled and what still had to be investigated.

The delta practice held a hidden danger, however. Flight conditions could change after a shuttle was certified as "flight ready," so an anomalous condition found innocuous earlier and considered as settled could change *after* FRR certification but before the flight's launch. That changed condition could pose a real threat to that shuttle (or to one flown later). Thus, under new flight conditions, an earlier "innocuous" anomaly could become dangerous to a flight already certified as "flight ready."[78]

Mulloy's Primed Response

The day before *Challenger's* launch, listening critically to Thiokol's argument for delaying the launch, Mulloy was primed by Marshall's culture of proof and by his recent embarrassing experiences with launch delays.[79] Could Thiokol's data and interpretations presented this late in launch preparations persuade Mulloy of the necessity of a delay? He quickly concluded they could not.

Seeing Thiokol once again trying to argue that temperature was a serious threat to O-ring sealing, and using that as a reason to delay this launch, Mulloy's first reaction was disbelief. In June, six months earlier, he had found McDonald's and Boisjoly's argument about cold temperatures affecting O-ring sealing to be speculation only. It did not hold water. There had been blow-by in the nozzle joints of at least two other flights by that time, both in warm weather! Cold and warm temperature did not co-vary with presence and absence of blow-by. That issue had been settled in his mind by conclusions reached in the FRRs following Flight 51C. If he were to take their claim seriously, it would mean no launch should take place for months! "My God, Thiokol," he exclaimed, "when do you want me to launch, next April?!"[80]

Mulloy needed to see if Thiokol's management agreed with or perhaps were caught off guard by their engineers' reasoning. He asked Thiokol's senior manager of their boosters, Joe Kilminster, for his view. Kilminster replied that, based on the engineering recommendation, he could not recommend launch.[81] Mulloy then said he had a different view and offered ten points of rebuttal. The counterargument based on these ten assessments of sealing dynamics led him to conclude that the operating "risk recognized at all levels of NASA management is applicable to 51L [the *Challenger*]."[82]

Mulloy's Counterarguments

Of Mulloy's ten points of argument, the first two and the last two are noteworthy, two (the fifth and eighth) state facts that all participants would agree with, and the other four relate to O-ring impingement erosion that all participants understood to be already well within safety margins and posing no threat to safety.[83] Mulloy's first two points, however, provided his basis for directly contradicting Thiokol's claim of a major threat: unusually cold O-rings.

1. "Blow-by of O-rings cannot be correlated to temperature—STS 61-A had blow-by at 75 °F [while STS 51-C had blow-by at 53 °F.]."
2. "Soot blow-by [past] primary O-rings has occurred on more than one occasion, independent of temperature."

These points simply restated the conclusions that Mulloy had reached the previous June, but Thiokol's evidence seemed to him more than merely confused and contradictory. In it, Mulloy found further proof of his own conclusion that blow-by had no relation to temperature. Thiokol's chart 3-1 (Figure 2.3) listed *six* flights whose nozzle joints showed blow-by evidence—all flown with *warm* O-rings.

Mulloy's assessment was selective on two counts, however. First, by attending to the data on nozzle joints, Mulloy ignored the known fact that blow-by in nozzle joints was much less significant than in field joints. Nozzle joints had a much more secure positioning of the secondary O-ring and were much less subject to joint rotation than the more vulnerable field joints— and the Thiokol engineers were not worried about the nozzle joints. Second, he ignored or discounted the large *quantitative differences* in blow-by in the field joints, also shown in chart 3-1 (Figure 2.3), between the warm and cold flights. Thiokol's charts 2-2 and 3-1 (Figures 2.2 and 2.3) together show more than twice as much blow-by in the cold flight than in the warm flight.

It was entirely possible that one set of conditions could lead to the small amounts of blow-by in warm flights and that another condition, like abnormally cold O-rings, could lead to the abnormally large amount of blow-by in cold flights. In any case, Mulloy had dismissed temperature as a cause, assuming that all temperature differences in blow-by were evidence merely of the *presence* of blow-by in both cold and warm flights.

Mulloy's last two arguments present the secondary O-ring as a reliable safeguard against any escape of the boosters' hot gas:

9. "Secondary seal is in a position to seat (200 PSI/50 PSI leak check)."
10. "Primary may not seat due to reduced resiliency—However, during period of flow past primary, secondary will be seated and seal before significant joint rotation occurs."

In both statements, Mulloy's confidence in the secondary O-ring is based on the assumption that the failure of the primary O-ring to seal would take place only "before significant joint rotation occurs." However, the speed with which the primary O-ring would fail to contain hot gas blowing by it depended first on the speed with which the hot gas worked its way through the insulating putty to *reach* the primary O-ring. That, in turn, was mostly a function of the putty's consistency. [84] Since hot gas could reach O-rings only through open blow-holes or by penetrating the upstream wall of a bubble in the insulating putty, and since a bubble (formed from the air pressure created at booster assembly) could vary from minimal bubble to an actual blow-hole through the putty, the speed with which the hot gas could penetrate the putty varied accordingly – and unpredictably. Putty under normal temperature conditions, with no bubbles or blow-holes, prevented *any* hot gas from reaching an O-ring, an infinite delay.[85] So a minor bubble, providing a resistant but penetrable layer of putty could delay penetration – long enough for the joint to open up even the small amount needed for hot gas to blow by the secondary O-ring.

Between the variations in thickness of the putty barrier and variations in the speed of actuating the primary O-ring and its sealing of its gap, considerable (and unpredictable) variations in the time lapse between ignition and primary blow-by were possible. Slight variations in putty consistency would add even more variability to the speed (or delay) of hot gas penetrating it. Virtually all of that variation would be (and had been) compensated for with warm O-rings whose shape, hardness, and resiliency had not been compromised. Cold O-rings, however, rendered any delay in the movement of the primary O-ring downstream next to its gap dangerous, dangerous because in that delay period the joint would be opening. The secondary O-ring would no longer be able to seal the gap that had widened too far for the cold and squeezed O-ring to seal. The delay need be only .2 second—into the second, rapidly changing phase of the ignition transient—for the sealing capacity of both O-rings to be threatened under the severely cold conditions of January 27–28, 1986.

Mulloy's focus on the O-rings' physical location and normal speed of seating was thus blind to the possibility of delayed gas penetration and blow-by due to the interacting complications of putty bubbles' varied size, putty density variations, O-ring squeezing, and cold temperature.

Mulloy's four images of the O-rings' sealing dynamics, denying any combined role of cold and squeezed O-rings with putty variations, were vulnerable to other possible arguments. McDonald, Boisjoly, Thompson, and others could now respond to Mulloy's reasoning. They could give emphasis to the several charts of evidence ignored by Mulloy, both experimental and from actual flights, sketchy as the evidence was, that showed O-ring temperature as differentiating quantitatively between effective and degraded sealing capacity.

At the Thiokol plant in Utah, Senior Vice President Mason quickly took charge. He asked Joe Kilminster to call for an off-network caucus at Thiokol alone. The argument between Mulloy and Mason's engineers had to be settled—quickly.

McDonald spoke up just before the network connection was closed. Anticipating that Thiokol engineers might be called on to recalculate a safe temperature colder than 53°, he commented that while the cold temperatures would adversely affect both O-rings, the secondary O-ring, being already seated downstream (close to the gap it must seal), would be less affected. He regarded his comment as a hint to the engineers at Thiokol, hoping they might test to find an acceptable lower temperature specific for the secondary O-ring.[86] Rushed to get a word in before Thiokol went offline, McDonald made no more than those two points: cold weather affected both O-rings, but the secondary, in a better position to seal, would be less affected.[87] Many at Marshall would interpret his comment as one of safety assurance, indicating that the secondary O-ring could be relied upon and, therefore, that McDonald's comment favored launch.

Kilminster's call for a "five-minute" Thiokol caucus began a new phase of deliberations at all three centers. We begin the next chapter with deliberations triggered at Marshall, then turn to a debate between McDonald and the two Marshall managers, Mulloy and Reinartz, at the Kennedy Center. Finally, we trace how the engineers' argument was reconsidered back at Thiokol in Utah, the review that led to the launch decision itself.

CHAPTER 4

Reconsideration, Resistance, and Decision

Thiokol's call for an off-line caucus freed participants at Marshall and Kennedy to consider how Thiokol might respond to the conflict that Mulloy's rebuttal had created. It would take only a half hour of separate caucus discussions at the three centers to bring Thiokol's resolution of the conflict back to the reconnected teleconference. We now look in on each of those half-hour caucus deliberations.

At Marshall

Some participants took a bathroom break. Others speculated about Thiokol's response. One discussion considered using some arrangement of heat blankets to keep the joint in its normal temperature range.[88] Others considered it likely that Thiokol would recommend a delay until the boosters reached (their understanding of) the lower-limit qualification temperature of 40 °F.

One engineer at Marshall who often disagreed with Thiokol engineering's judgments, Luther Ben Powers, expressed agreement with their reasoning. He and other colleagues at Marshall's structures and propulsion laboratory understood the vulnerability of cold O-rings because of loss of resiliency. When Powers's supervisor, John McCarty, asked him for his views, Powers said he agreed with Thiokol's position:

> I said, "Well, hey, I support the contractor 100 percent."
> . . . [I] talked a little bit with Smith and McCarty about,
> you know, my position was not to launch. . . . Mr.
> McCarty did not commit to any position. . . . Mr. Smith
> was not able to get a recommendation out of him.[89]

Powers's agreement with the Thiokol engineers' assessment and recommendation, although unambiguously voiced by him, was thus never communicated to Smith, much less to George Hardy. In any event, Hardy's strong views of the joint's self-sealing nature and his dismissal of joint temperature as irrelevant would probably have led him to dismiss Powers's comment.

Hardy's own response to Thiokol's presentation was first to say he was "appalled," but then he commented that he would not recommend launch if Thiokol recommended against it.[90] As the senior member of Marshall's Science and Engineering Directorate present, Hardy had to prepare to halt the launch preparations. The External Tank was scheduled to be fueled in the next few hours, and phone calls would have to be made to halt fueling if the launch were to be postponed. Hardy spent most of the caucus time pondering the implications if Thiokol returned a recommendation that the launch be delayed. He had to plan who should be called and what the contingencies might be. Those matters would have prevented Hardy from any polling he might otherwise have initiated to obtain members' assessments of the launch situation.[91]

At Kennedy

McDonald had decided before the caucus that it would be fruitless to try to underscore or sharpen Thiokol's argument during the teleconference. His best chance for delaying the launch, he thought, was to argue the case directly with Mulloy and Reinartz. Their views would determine NASA's official judgment. First, however, before Thiokol could go off line to caucus, McDonald quickly tried a verbal signal to his engineering colleagues in Utah to focus their re-thinking on the *secondary* O-ring's temperature limits. He did so by commenting on how the secondary O-ring, in contrast to the primary, was seated next to the gap it had to seal – an indirect hint to find a new temperature limit for the secondary that would still require a delay.[92]

With the teleconference line closed for Thiokol's caucus McDonald turned to Mulloy and Reinartz with two arguments. He told them he did not believe that every component of the solid rocket motor was qualified to 40 °F. He based that view on his experience as Thiokol's manager of the lightweight boosters being readied for test at the Vandenberg Air Force site in California. Mulloy replied that the 40° figure was the lower limit only of the mean bulk temperature (MBT) of the solid rocket *fuel;* the 40° did not refer to the whole rocket. McDonald thought that "ridiculous," since the mean temperature of the massive solid fuel could not possibly change more than a few degrees even with extreme changes in the surrounding temperature. The two debated some more, and Mulloy soon made it clear that he was convinced that the 40° figure referred to the MBT alone.

McDonald's second attempt to delay the launch was to suggest that the launch be put off just the few hours until late in the afternoon when the outside ("ambient") temperature was predicted to reach 48°–50°. He figured the O-rings would then have recovered more of their resiliency. He was told, however, that that launch window had earlier been ruled out when the MMT had learned that a late-afternoon launch would mean the shuttle would meet unacceptable weather conditions at one of its emergency transatlantic landing sites. At that point Joe Kilminster came back on the teleconference network to announce the results of Thiokol's deliberations.

At Thiokol

At the start of Thiokol's discussion, Jerry Mason took charge. The company's managers and engineers were seated around the big table in its conference room, the room where the engineers had earlier put together their presentation for Marshall. Mason's decision situation now was complicated.

Recall Allan McDonald's description of Mason as being caught in a Catch 22. He was caught between, on one hand,

NASA's delay in signing a contract and its talk about seeking a second source for booster rockets and, on the other hand, his Thiokol superiors in Chicago requiring him to have in hand a signed contract from NASA before the Chicago office could release funds for Thiokol to buy the next round of booster casings.

Mason had helped prepare a Thiokol corporate presentation of financial and production arguments against NASA's seeking a second source for boosters, arguments presented in March 1985 by Mason's immediate superior in the Chicago office, U. Edwin Garrison, president of Thiokol's Aerospace Group. Garrison had presented his arguments at the highest NASA level, to James M. Beggs and others at NASA headquarters.

An important theme of Garrison's argument was how Thiokol had always met, and would continue to meet, NASA's flight schedule. He had presented graphs showing how Thiokol would accommodate not only NASA's past flight rate but also its increased flight schedule—rising to 21 flights per year in 1988 and 24 flights per year through 1992. Thiokol would meet that launch schedule, he had argued, with costs "decreasing as production experience builds and flight rates increase."[93]

This corporate promise to NASA bound Jerold Mason to meet every flight deadline, but meeting that commitment would be impossible if NASA continued to hold off signing the booster contract. That *signed* contract was necessary for buying the next round of boosters, a purchase necessary for Mason to continue providing boosters to NASA on time. In a postaccident interview, I asked McDonald why he thought Mason might lean toward launching when the company had so much to lose if things went wrong. He said Presidential Commissioner Richard Feynman had asked a similar question:

"Why would your own management reverse a decision of your engineers after they [managers] apparently endorsed the original one? Why would they need to do that, knowing full well that if they were wrong, it could be pretty bad for the company pump?"

And I said [to Feynman], "Well, I'll give you my opinion. . . . It was the green ball theory." . . . [R]ecognizing the fact that we didn't have a signed contract, and that . . . they [NASA had] decided even though it wasn't cost competitive to establish a second source [for purchasing boosters], they were going to go ahead and pursue it anyway for national security reasons. . . . I recognized those two facts, and I said, "What do you have when you have a green ball in your left hand, and a green ball in your right hand?" He said, "I don't know." I said, "Well, it's complete and absolute control of the jolly green giant."

Put yourselves in the general manager's [Mason's] position of the company, and sitting there that night, hearing the reaction from his customer [NASA] who hasn't given him a signed contract and should have, who still hasn't decided whether to establish a second source or not, but had decided he's going to pursue it further. I said, "Are you going to get up now and make him madder than he already is [by disrupting an ongoing launch]?" Now that's my personal opinion, and that's the green ball theory.[94]

In this analogy, Mason was the jolly green giant and NASA had gripping control of one "green ball" by withholding a signed contract. Mason's superior, Garrison, withholding funds for Mason to buy the next round of boosters until Mason *had* a signed contract, was the other power holding testicular control. The separate demands by NASA and Garrison together had put the squeeze on Mason. The immediate path for Mason's fiscal relief (worth tens of millions of dollars in profit to Morton Thiokol) was for Mason to make sure he did everything to fulfill Garrison's assurances to NASA and to do nothing to prevent meeting NASA's requirements.

Hearing Mulloy's rebuttal of his engineers' presentation, especially Mulloy's argument that disposed of temperature as a cause for alarm, had given Jerry Mason the opening he needed to force a positive, more optimistic look at the data from the perspective given by Mulloy, NASA's own booster manager. Mason spoke first. He began by summarizing Mulloy's counterarguments. He summarized each of Mulloy's points: "Let me see if I understand what Mr. Mulloy said," securing agreement from his colleagues that he had heard Mulloy's arguments correctly.[95]

By summarizing Mulloy's arguments rather than attending to the arguments of Mason's own engineers, Mason conveyed the impression to Russell and others that he had been persuaded by Mulloy's arguments. Mason readily accepted Mulloy's dismissal of O-ring temperature as a relevant factor.[96] He could readily accept Mulloy's arguments, not only because they solved his contract dilemma but also because he had his own distinctive engineering understanding of O-ring sealing dynamics.

Mason's conception of the sealing problem had four parts.[97] First, he minimized the importance of the evidence of blow-by of Flight 51C in two ways. He had understood that there had been blow-by in only one joint of 51C, not the two joints in which blow-by had in fact occurred. In addition, he had reasoned that because only one of 51C's joints had evidenced blow-by, it was best considered a random occurrence. His comforting conclusion that blow-by was random, thus dismissible, would have been strengthened by his conception of blow-by.

Second, Mason thought of blow-by only in terms of the fleeting occurrence that had been detected in several joints, blow-by allowed in the milliseconds before the (warm) O-ring had time to move fully into the gap of its joint. That harmless pre-sealing blow-by was his model for all blow-by. For Mason, erosion was much more concerning than blow-by, precisely opposite from the view of his most expert engineers, Arnold Thompson and Roger Boisjoly.[98]

Third, Mason's interpretation of the engineers' argument about the phased timing of the ignition transient reflected an important gap in his own understanding: "The engineering people . . . were saying we're going to be outside of our data base to go colder than 53°, and we're concerned about whether the O-ring will move fast enough to seat and seal before the joint opens up . . . not knowing exactly how long it would take for the O-ring to move into position."[99]

Mason's conception of the joint dynamics focused on the primary O-rings' physical movement across its groove. His conception of joint dynamics did not include a delay of hot gas penetrating the insulating putty. That delay in actuating the primary could be long enough for the secondary O-ring's gap to have expanded wide enough for hot gas to blow by both the primary *and secondary* O-rings. In Mason's mind, "blow-by, by itself, was not a failure mode, however; it must lead to O-ring erosion" to cause failure.[100]

Danger of erosion, Mason considered remote, however. He misinterpreted experimental results that had shown that the safely allowable degree of *impingement* erosion of O-rings was about three times greater than the worst erosion observed. While that had been demonstrated to be true for impingement erosion, no such tests had been run on blow-by erosion (which the engineers often called "by-pass erosion," emphasizing the flow of gas *past* the O-ring, eroding its sealing surfaces). Mason interpreted all references to "erosion" as referring to the kind that had been proven safe: impingement erosion. For Mason, therefore, "erosion" had been proven safe.

Finally, Mason had heard Boisjoly's discounting of the abortive experiment with argon gas—reported in Thiokol's chart 4-3 showing "no leakage" at 30 °F—yet Mason nonetheless felt that the argon gas test provided some credible evidence that the O-ring would seal the joint's gap, a conclusion that Boisjoly would have disputed, had Mason voiced it at the time.[101]

Mason's conception of the joint's sealing dynamics—that O-ring temperature was irrelevant to its sealing capacity, that blow-by was dangerous only if erosion occurred, that erosion had been proven safe, and that the argon experiment suggested that O-rings would seal at 30°—provide a case study in how technical information becomes filtered and transformed as it moves from new engineering data upward through the ranks to managerial usage. These filtered interpretations had "worked" for Mason for the first 24 flights. They left Mason confident that his engineers had it wrong, confident that the flight should go forward. Reaching this final understanding, he could feel he had also escaped a sure threat to Thiokol's single-source contract to provide all of NASA's boosters.

As Mason summarized Mulloy's arguments for his engineers and managers at Thiokol, engineering supervisor Arnold Thompson became more aware that his own understanding of the joint would have to be expressed more forcefully, particularly regarding the effects of temperature on the O-rings' resiliency. Before Mulloy had begun to present his contrary reasoning, Thompson had been assuming that Thiokol's rationale for a delay would simply be accepted by NASA.[102]

Well before this teleconference, however, Thompson had been concerned about the O-ring's capacity at various temperatures (its "resiliency") to recover its full diameter after being compressed and then released when the booster joint opened after ignition. Earlier in the teleconference, using his chart 4-2 (Figure 2.4), he had presented the basic data showing degrees of O-ring resiliency as dependent on O-ring temperature.

Thompson, listening to Mason's listing of Mulloy's points, sketched on his pad a graph showing the markedly different slopes of recovery of the O-rings at 100°, 75°, and 50°—recovery of their diameters from their "squeezed" state in the joints. Thompson knew with more certainty, he thought, than anyone else in the room that because the joint's gap opened dangerously wide only a third of a second after ignition, as Boisjoly had earlier explained,[103] the O-ring's sluggish resiliency rate of sealing the joint at 75° (2.4 seconds) was only an eighth of the speed required (0.3 seconds) to be even minimally safe. Or, to put it the other way around, the speed with which the gap between tang and clevis opened after ignition was more than eight times faster than Thompson's measured speed with which the O-ring at 75 °F could recover enough of its pre-compressed diameter to keep up with the opening gap in the joint. But that January morning the O-rings would be 46 degrees *colder*. Like his experiment's O-rings at 50 °F, these O-rings would fail altogether to seal the opening gap!

Thompson was ordinarily very laid back, often late to voice his view in a meeting, but now he felt urgency. As he listened to Mason, he felt an earlier frustration with the lack of management support for efforts being made by a task force to understand the instances of blow-by and O-ring erosion. Erosion and blow-by had been limited so far, but the engineers were still unable to predict where erosion might occur.

Thompson had earlier written a memorandum for his boss to send up the line in which Thompson turned the heat up to get management action. He had his experimental results on O-ring temperatures staring at him, telling him that they now could show yet another vulnerability of the field joints. In his memo, he indicated that further flights should stop until the anomalies in the field joints could be eliminated. That memo had been sent the third week of the past August. Jack Kapp, his boss, had told him he, Kapp, could not send the memo up the line to his boss; Thompson should tone it down. Kapp asked Thompson if he would hold off for two more flights before recommending that flights be stopped in favor of a new design of the joints. Thompson had reluctantly agreed.

He rewrote his memo, tossing the first one into the waste basket. Thompson's revised memo that Kapp did send along to superiors opened with "The O-ring seal problem has lately become acute." It then recommended "that the near-term solution [slightly thicker O-rings and shims inserted to increase O-ring "squeeze"] be incorporated for flights following STS-27 scheduled for the 24th of August [1986]." So Thompson gave the program two more flights beyond the 25th flight, the *Challenger*.[104]

Thompson had been shocked when Mulloy had claimed there could be no correlation between blow-by and temperature."[105] A sense of alarm grew sharper when he saw that Jerry Mason had simply reviewed with approval Mulloy's objections. He now had his chance to speak directly to top management. He just had to seize it.[106] Mason's acceptance of Mulloy's reasoning led Thompson to do something quite out of character for him. He got up out of his chair and went down the table to where the senior managers were seated. Leaning in between Mason and Lund, he placed his pad with the graph he had sketched on the table.[107] He pointed out the very different slopes for the O-rings' response rates at the three temperatures, arguing that the O-rings were, indeed, temperature sensitive.[108]

Thompson's own recollection of his explanation is full of technical detail. He often expresses it in telegraphic engineering language, but one point he made was that the strong trend of relationship between O-ring temperature and O-ring sealing time that he was able to show was from only simple linear fits to the data, not the more precise curvilinear plots. These simple linear descriptions were only gross representations of what surely were much more alarming curvilinear functions. But even the gross linear functions definitely showed O-ring sealing to be temperature sensitive.

Thompson saw, however, that he was not getting through to Mason. He looked up at Mason's face and saw only stern, unresponsive silence.[109] Thompson returned to his seat, feeling helpless and put off by Mason, a man whom he knew personally outside of company life.[110]

Angry at Mason's apparent incomprehension of the situation, Roger Boisjoly saw that he too had to do something to get through to Mason. He also got up out of his seat and walked down the table, positioning himself between Lund and Mason. Boisjoly had photographs of the results of blow-by, pictures of the disassembled joints of the boosters that had been retrieved after the cold flight, 51C (SRM-15), and of retrieved boosters from the warmer flight, 61A (SRM-22). He thought the photographs could make more graphic his earlier teleconference comments comparing the two flights:

> I grabbed the photos, and I went up and discussed the photos once again and tried to make the point that it was my opinion from the actual observations that temperature was indeed a discriminator and we should not ignore the physical evidence that we had observed.
>
> And again, I brought up the point that SRM-15 had 110 degrees arc of black grease [blown by the primary O-ring] while SRM-22 had a relatively different amount, which was less and wasn't quite as black. I also stopped when I couldn't get anybody to listen.[111]

Boisjoly argued that cold weather was the most probable cause of the blow-by of 51C's O-rings a year earlier and that they had never tested boosters or joints at the cold temperatures (29 °F) expected the next day. Mason replied that they had also experienced problems with warm motors as well as cold motors, that there did not seem to be any relation of temperature to problems with the O-rings. Boisjoly countered that cold weather would make the O-rings slower to actuate.[112] He emphasized the point that the flight the previous January, 51C, "was the coolest motor we've ever fired and substantially the most damaged," and that the scheduled launch of the *Challenger* would violate that envelope by 24°, that such a launch would take them "far out of our data base."[113]

Mason's reply emphasized "extensive tests [that engineering had run] to show that we can take quite a bit of erosion."[114]

Despite Thompson's and Boisjoly's clarifications, Mason had interpreted their comments to be about O-ring "erosion." He asked Boisjoly and the engineers whether they were sure they were keeping separate in their minds the *general* desirability of making the joint better from the *specific* matter of whether cold temperature was an important factor. Mason was aware of the penchant for engineers, as a matter of an engineer's slant on occupational life, to put their minds toward improving the functioning of whatever contraption they were currently working on. Boisjoly replied that many of these factors could not be quantified but that they were all "in the direction of badness."[115]

From Mason's point of view, Thompson and Boisjoly were simply dragging the discussion on, going over data already presented, data that also did not square with the success history of shuttle flights. Further, Boisjoly and Thompson were the only ones in the room now giving voice to the data and reasoning that Mulloy had argued against. Other engineers and engineering supervisors among the group actually agreed with the urgency and interpretations being given by Boisjoly and Thompson but remained silent, unable to expand on what Thompson and Boisjoly had already pointed out.[116]

Mason had heard enough. NASA was waiting. He made reference to part of Allan McDonald's last comment in the teleconference, made just before they had gone off the network, namely that while the primary O-ring was positioned in its groove away from the joint's gap, the secondary O-ring would be in a favorable position to seal its gap.

Mason then reframed the discussion. He indicated that all the engineering data and concerns had been reviewed, and now it was time for a management decision. On the basis of all of the evidence, he felt they should go ahead and launch.[117] His demeanor was confident. This despite the fact that two of his engineers most intimately knowledgeable about joint dynamics had been at pains to explain that his engineering view did not accord with theirs.

Jack Kapp's commission interview described well what others corroborated about Mason's next steps:

> And then he [Mason] turned to Mr. Wiggins, and he said, "Cal, how do you feel about it?" and Cal says, "I agree with that." So I presume that Mr. Wiggins's mind was changed because he immediately had concurred with that [initial engineering] decision. . . . Then Mason turned to Mr. Kilminster and he says words to the effect, "Joe, how do you feel about it?" And Joe indicated in some manner that he felt it was acceptable to fire. And so there were three of them that in very short order were in concert that we should fire. Then he turned to Bob Lund and he said, "Bob, what's your position now?" Bob was very, very hesitant. I sat across the table from him, and I could see the agonized look in his face. And he [Lund] looked around the table. . . . My feeling was that he was kind of feeling, "Has anybody changed? I'm really on the hot seat here."[118]

Larry Sayer, Thiokol's director of engineering design and Lund's immediate subordinate, described Lund's situation and quandary:

> Mason said that he felt that under the conditions that we had discussed and with the . . . statements that Larry Mulloy had made, and we certainly could not disagree with what Larry said, that he would recommend we launch. And then he turned to Cal [Wiggins] and asked Cal. He turned to Joe Kilminster and asked him. . . . Cal said, "I recommend a launch," so Joe Kilminster says, "I recommend launch."

He turned to Bob Lund, and Bob sat there for several seconds kind of shaking his head, and I could feel that he was in a very tough position and one that he was very uncomfortable with. He turned around and looked at the people that support him ... putting the engineering data together, and no one said anything. . . . I think he was really looking for help: "Can we, is there anything else we can do [from] an engineering point that would make our original recommendations strong enough that we could stand behind that?"

And at that time, as I recall, Mr. Mason said, "Now, Bob, you take off your engineering hat and put on your management hat. We've done all we can do from an engineering point, and now we've got to make a tough decision, and as a manager we've got to do that." . . . .

As I recall, what he [Lund] said was, "Wishy-washy Lund," and "I recommend that we fly." That was a comment that was characteristic of Bob. If he got to a point where he changed his mind, he'd always say, "Wishy-washy Lund," and off he went.[119]

The Final Rationale

As Thiokol's executives came to their decision to fly, Kilminster outlined a revised rationale to proceed with the launch. Once the telecon connection was restored with the two other centers, Kilminster conveyed the decision to proceed, reading the rationale from his notes. He was asked by either Mulloy or Hardy to put the decision and rationale in writing and to sign it. The resulting revised rationale for launching is given in Figure 4.1.[120]

Kilminster's chart and its underlying logic are organized around a bad-news/good-news format, one that says, in effect, yes, it's raining, but we have a raincoat and umbrella, and besides, we've got our old reliable Chevrolet to take us where we want to go.

Lines 1 and 4 through 6 of Figure 4.1 provide grounds for *delaying* the launch because of negative effects of temperature, but Line 7 offers reassurance, the good news from Mason's point of view—referring to the experimental excision from an O-ring of .125 inch of the O-ring's diameter which had nevertheless sealed its simulated field joint. This test was offered as evidence of a safe margin of *impingement erosion* a little more than three times the amount experienced on the previous January's flight of 51C (at 53 °F).

Line 8 presents the old reliable Chevrolet: the secondary O-ring. It will seat even if the primary does not. Then Lines 9 and 10 tell why the secondary will seat. It will be successfully actuated by gas pressure before the joint's rotation begins. Successful sealing by the secondary O-ring is further ensured by its favorable "outboard" (or downstream) position, which "minimizes sealing time." Line 12 states the official Thiokol conclusion that the *Challenger* flight will be no different from the previous January's flight, 51C (SRM-15).[121] None of Kilminster's revised rationale considered the evidence of blow-by as related to temperature.[122]

With his written summary of Thiokol's rationale, Kilminster signaled that he was ready to reconnect to the teleconference, and all three centers went back online. After Kilminster reported Thiokol's revised reasoning and conclusions, Stanley Reinartz asked over the network if anyone had any further comments. No one responded. Then someone at NASA asked for a written, signed copy of Thiokol's revised rationale and conclusion, to be faxed to Marshall. Mulloy asked that a copy be sent to him at Kennedy.

At Kennedy, McDonald knew he had one more chance to get Mulloy and Reinartz to see how they might justify postponing the launch. He said he would refuse to sign Kilminster's document,

MTI ASSESSMENT OF TEMPERATURE CONCERN ON SRM-25 (51L) LAUNCH

1. Calculations show that SRM-25 O-rings will be 20° colder than SRM-15 O-rings

2. Temperature data not conclusive on predicting primary O-ring blow-by

3. Engineering assessment is that:

    4. colder O-rings will have increased effective durometer (harder)

    5. harder O-rings will take longer to seat

        6. more gas may pass primary O-ring before the primary seal seats (relative to SRM-15)

            7. demonstrated sealing threshold is 3 times greater than 0.038 in. erosion experienced on SRM-15

    8. if the primary seal does not seat, the secondary seal will seat

        9. pressure will get to secondary seal before the metal parts rotate

            10. O-ring pressure leak check places secondary seal in outboard position which minimizes sealing time

11. MTI recommends STS-51L launch proceed on 28 January 1986

    12. SRM-25 will not be significantly different from SRM-15

Joe C. Kilminster, Vice President

Space Booster Programs

MORTON THIOKOL, INC [MTI]

Wasatch Division

Figure 4.1. Facsimile of Thiokol's revised rationale for launching the *Challenger* (51L).

voicing his uneasiness. He could understand how, early on, officials could "sign on" to qualification temperatures of 40 °F to 90 °F, even though he did not believe those applied to the O-rings. However, having officially signed on to those qualification limits, he said, he did not see how NASA could launch outside them.

McDonald issued a warning to Reinartz and Mulloy that "if anything happened," he "sure wouldn't want to be the person who had to explain to a board of inquiry why it was all right to launch at a temperature below that at which the system was qualified to."[123] Neither Reinartz nor Mulloy responded. Mulloy had already discounted McDonald's understanding of qualification temperatures.[124]

McDonald argued further that if the low temperature alone was not enough reason for delay, two additional considerations could be added.[125] McDonald had obtained detailed information on the extreme weather conditions being experienced by the ships deployed at sea to recover the booster rockets. The recovery ships, he advised, were in an "absolute survival mode in 30-foot seas," which may have damaged some of the ships' recovery equipment. It was unlikely that recovery of the boosters could be completed. In addition, McDonald had learned that ice had formed at the launch pad and that it did not seem "prudent" to launch under those unknown conditions. McDonald recalled, "I was told that these were not my problems. . . . I responded that maybe one of these problems was not being considered sufficient to cancel the launch, but that all three of them combined should be more than sufficient to delay the launch. Mulloy and Reinartz indicated that they would pass this information on in advisory capacity."[126]

Mulloy and Reinartz did report up the line the dangerous recovery-site conditions and ice concerns in a telephone call to Arnold Aldrich, chair of the MMT. They omitted mentioning to Aldrich the teleconference presentation, however. They made no mention of Thiokol's charts and its initial recommendation, of Thiokol's caucus and reversal of the original engineering recommendation, or of Mulloy's and Reinartz's local conversation with McDonald. Although failing to inform Aldrich of these events clearly violated a NASA program directive,[127] Reinartz and Mulloy had categorized the teleconference and caucus discussions as "Level III concerns." No change had been made in the launch schedule, and the question of temperature had been officially settled at Level III; therefore, in Mulloy's view, nothing pertinent to the next higher level (Aldrich's level) had occurred in the teleconference.[128]

The launch countdown and preparations for launch continued through the night of January 27 and morning of January 28, 1986. After final assessments of ice conditions at the launch pad, shuttle *Challenger* was launched at 11:38AM. Seventy-three seconds into its ascent, *Challenger* began to disintegrate, eventuating in the deaths of its seven crew members. The immediate physical location of malfunction was the aft field joint of the right solid rocket booster, which had failed to seal.

With NASA's acceptance of Thiokol's rationale and reversed recommendation, my narrative about the decision participants' situations, deliberations, and commitments comes to an end. The narrative of this and the preceding chapters—as close as I can come to a critical, balanced, and inclusive reading of the primary documents and interviews—tells the significant contents, patterns, and directions of individual and collective thought about the realities that cold weather had in store for these participants and for the shuttle as launch decision time approached on the eve of January 27, 1986. Part I's micro-history of the deliberations now shifts to Part II's analysis.

Part II examines deliberation itself for what it can teach us about how those engaged in safety-critical decision making struggle to read reality correctly. We will see how they initially succeeded at the level of the engineering group but failed disastrously at the level of organizational decision making. From the standpoint of recent research in macroergonomics, I examine how participants experience and assess situations. We see how important new dimensions of distributed deliberations arose in this case of organizational decision making—*conflicting* situation assessments, *conflict resolution* through formal argument, and two successive *phases* of deliberation that presented starkly *different objective situations* of deliberation.[129] Finally, we see how a particular mode of deliberation, coupled with conditions altered in specific ways, might have prevented the accident.

Part II begins by identifying eight conditions that together vastly complicated the decision process and the situations to be assessed by participants. Examples of such complications are then followed by considering how "situations" require differentiation, both objectively and subjectively, and how those differentiations were reflected in the situations of key actors in the decision process.

PART II

Analysis

CHAPTER 5

Distributed Decision Making: Organization, Role, Person, and Situation

The *Challenger* case reveals a level of complexity in high-tech time-pressured decision making that is surprising even now, a quarter century after the disaster, and after its seemingly exhaustive scholarly analysis. The sealing dynamics of the field joints when the boosters were ignited, though themselves complicated, could in essence be captured in the simple metaphor of a race between two contestants, hot exhaust and O-rings. But the forces shaping the decision to launch or delay the launch defied simple encapsulation. That decision entailed eight conditions:

1. Persistent evidence of unexpected structural stresses—benign, apparently dangerous, and truly dangerous—straining a still experimental technology.

2. Time-limited, safety-critical decision making about a sudden new intensity of a danger that some argued was real, others argued was not.

3. A distribution among decision participants of complex information variously understood and interpreted among them, information distributed as well between participants and artifacts (charts, diagrams, written statements).

4. A mode of decision-making thought that had been consistently adaptive in the first phase of flight preparation but that shifted with terrible effect in the second, deadline-driven phase of decision making.

5. Deliberation about whether to reverse an ongoing action, currently in the last hours of its implementation—questioning a default decision already vetted.

6. Several key decision makers holding competing priorities, who enacted different professional roles across geographically distant locations, who were distributed across different levels of decision-making power, and who were employed by two different kinds of organization with objectively different primary missions — a public government agency and a private profit-making organization.

7. Inter-group and interpersonal *conflict* among decision-making participants in which, with a correct awareness of a dangerous situation, a small group found themselves in conflict with managers in both organizations regarding an objective situation of danger.

8. The process by which the conflict between the engineers and the managers was resolved was one of formal argument about the meaning and implications of the objective data.[130]

Adequate treatment of decision making of this degree of complexity and novelty requires some adjustment in current conceptions of decision-making "team"[131] and of "situation" and "situation awareness"[132] in time-pressured,[133] safety-critical decision making. Now we must include both *conflicting situations* and *conflicting assessments* of a given situation. Consider, for example, just the complication of two different kinds of organization as key elements in the decision making.

Neither NASA nor Thiokol had a single task or faced a single objective situation. Both had two basic missions. One was to carry out an ambitious schedule of space experiments that required placing satellites in orbital space—*task* priorities. The other was to keep the humans doing the space work safe—a *person* priority. Putting one of these two missions first in priority could easily limit success in the other. The faster pace of scheduling missions could shortchange safety, and caution to ensure safety could slow the rate of missions. Both of these purposes, the work schedule and safety, were constrained, in addition, by the not unlimited resources available and by the unknowns of space flight. Both of these missions and the potential for conflict between them were a chronic part of the objective decision situation that once again arose on the day and evening before the *Challenger* launch.

Another objective complexity in this decision situation was that the consequences of the imminent launch were in open dispute. Whether that imminent action was safe or dangerously risky was a question actively debated by the participants. What actually was *the* situation of the shuttle about to be launched, the situation facing the organization members charged with deciding the issue? One objective situation was that this debate had to be settled by successfully arguing for a reversal of the ongoing action, or the ongoing action would carry the launch to completion. Inevitably, at least one of these two basic missions, production or safety, was going to give way to the other, given the mutually exclusive choice between continuing the countdown and delaying the launch for safer weather.

In the next chapter, I will consider the internal and external market forces set in motion by the collaboration of the two major organizations involved, NASA and Thiokol. They combined the very different missions of a democratic government and a private, profit-seeking company. The present chapter focuses on the general nature of two very complex domains of decision making: objective situations and subjectively construed situations. First, consider the task of understanding "situations" in the case of this accident.

Understanding Situations

It is clear from the narrative in Part I that there were many situations *construed* by various key participants. Only a *subjective* assessment of the available objective data, critically analyzed and evaluated as it might or might not be, was available to each participant to characterize the objective outcome of launching the shuttle. But the shuttle's *objective* situation was not the only situation facing some of the key participants. If we want to understand the participants' various assessments and responses, we must therefore allow our analysis to focus on *both* the subjective and the objective – both the situations (plural) they were construing and responding to, the ones produced by their own before-the-outcome assessments, *and* the objective situation (as we now, after the fact, know it) that would arise if the ongoing launch process were carried to completion. Both subjective situations as assessed and the objective situation that would eventually be produced by the decision must therefore be examined focally in any effective postaccident analysis of decision making.[134]

Two further complications will become clear, however. First, participants can be confronted with two *objective situations simultaneously*, each demanding the participant's attention, each holding important consequences. The demands of these two situations can also seriously conflict with each other, one situation reducing or even distorting the participant's attention to the other situation. Once we understand the participant's objective situations as the participant comes to understand them, we are in a position to see how those understandings did or did not fit with the eventual objective situations confronting the participant and did or did not warrant the participant's decisions and actions.

Second, we can then also know how a participant's subjectively *construed*, before-the-fact, situations *blocked out or distorted* his or her awareness of the actual, post-decision realities. That understanding, in turn, can lead us to explore how the participant's "false" situation assessments became shaped, perhaps even primed, by earlier events and by a competing situation.

By keeping in focus key decision participants' actual construals of their situations in high-tech, high-pressure settings, we can become more aware of the otherwise hidden origins of both the situation assessments that turn out to misconstrue the actual situation and the hidden origins of correct situation assessments. Knowing the origins of both is required to devise corrective measures for more accurate assessments of such situations in the future.

Objective Situations

We now focus first on the origins of a correct awareness of the launched shuttle's situation—an awareness shared by a group of Thiokol engineers and managers. It was an awareness of the shuttle's objective launch and flight situation, the major objective decision situation facing the *engineers* as launch temperatures became known. This close look at how a Thiokol group of engineers arrived at their correct construal of the *Challenger's* dangerous situation may reveal some general preconditions for arriving at an accurate awareness of such situations.

The Thiokol group's correct understanding of the shuttle's (and crew's) objective launch situation had two parts. The first was that launching with the boosters' O-rings at 29 °F would incur unwarranted and dangerous risk, including the very real possibility of catastrophic loss. The second was that the launch should not take place because it would be well below any previous flight-tested safe O-ring temperature. We now know that their knowledge was not complete, that they did not know of the dynamics of post-launch wind shear or of all the variable protective properties of the insulating putty; however, the engineers' awareness of the shuttle's situation as unusually risky and possibly disastrous *because of the O-rings' vulnerability to cold temperature* was correct.

What was the origin of their correct understanding? It had four sources, and the combination of the four constituted a fifth. At least eight months before the teleconference, shortly after discovering Flight 51C's unusual number and configuration of blow-by and erosion anomalies, the Thiokol group concluded that Flight 51C's atypical outcome must have had an atypical cause—something new or some new combination of old conditions.[135] The first hunch was that the unusually cold weather leading up to 51C's launch could be the cause, but other possibilities had to be examined. Exhaustive tracing of each step in the assembly and testing of 51C's boosters turned up nothing that could have accounted for 51C's new pattern of combined anomalies. That was the second origin of the group's correct awareness of 51C's situation—they could rule out that whole set of possible causes of its unusual anomalies.

They understood that the O-rings of 51C, squeezed into their joints, would have been cold, so also nonresilient ("hard"). But how could cold, squeezed O-rings bring the O-rings in two joints to perform so poorly? Arnold Thompson's experiment gave the answer, showing how variations in *O-ring* temperature from 100° to 75° to 50° affected the time it took for O-rings to seal, revealing a measurable loss of O-ring resiliency. Only warm, resilient O-rings would be able to recapture most of their pre-squeezed diameter, enabling their regaining size to follow the opening joint. Colder O-rings lost that resilience sufficiently to delay recovery of their sealing size before the gap would allow air to breach the simulated joint.

Here, then, was the third important source of the group's correct awareness of the shuttle's dangerous situation, an experiment showing the connection between O-ring temperature and the always vital O-ring sealing performance, particularly the *speed* of sealing.[136]

The fourth support for the group's correct situation assessment came from the quantitative details of blow-by evidence from the earlier Flight 61A, whose O-rings were 75 °F. All but a few teleconference participants at Thiokol accepted Mulloy's interpretation, a more global and glossed view, of the mere *presence* of blow-by in both warm and cold flights. Mulloy and most of his colleagues saw the *presence* of blow-by in both cold and warm flights as proving that temperature had nothing to do with blow-by. That view, however, ignored the differential *quantity* of blow-by between the warm and cold flights, details that had immediately grabbed the engineers' attention. The cold flight revealed more than twice the length of blow-by than the warm flight and showed black, sooted grease. That evidence of delayed O-ring sealing performance under actual flight conditions signaled to the engineers that the cold joints had *stayed open much longer before they sealed* than was true for the warm flight's joints.

The fifth basis for the engineers' correct situation assessment was the fact that these *two contrasting kinds of evidence*, experiment and actual flight observations, showed the *same* effect of O-ring temperature on O-ring sealing performance, namely that as temperatures drop, O-ring sealing takes longer and the joint suffers an unsealed gap. Everyone understood that an open joint, unsealed by both the primary and secondary O-rings, spelled disaster.

In sum, the Thiokol engineers had tested a hypothesized cause of the previous January's unusual booster anomalies against a careful review of the many inspections of O-rings, putty, and joint and had eliminated all but the one possible cause. They had followed that idea with an experiment that showed that *cold* O-rings presented a sufficient condition for blow-by to occur and to delay sealing. Finally, actual flight results from two flights, the only two showing blow-by, had confirmed that cold O-rings allowed more than twice as much blow-by as warm O-rings.

In terms of Endsley's (1999, 2000) three stages of situation awareness, the engineers had identified the data relevant to the shuttle's situation, had correctly interpreted its meaning, and had not only projected the future consequences correctly but also had taken action, calling the teleconference, in order to prevent the feared outcome. Both the experimental results and the blow-by findings from the cold and warm flights were presented in the teleconference to the participants at Marshall and Kennedy, including Mulloy and Reinartz, who had authority to recommend a launch delay.

Conditions Preventing Agreement about the Shuttle's Situation

What prevented this correct understanding, an understanding presented by the engineers most expert in the key joint dynamics, from becoming accepted by the Marshall officials? The answer, in brief, is that *both* those delivering the information and those receiving it were seriously hobbled in perception, communication, and argument. They were prevented from accomplishing a transfer of the Thiokol group's correct awareness of the shuttle's situation to the two crucial managers from NASA and Thiokol, Mulloy and Mason.

The Thiokol Group. While the Thiokol engineers and their immediate managers were expert in the relevant engineering dynamics, they were novices in meeting the demands of communication where sharp differences of interpretation and judgment were possible. To communicate their engineering concerns effectively required that they assess and understand correctly their actual *communication situation* with NASA – a situation that demanded persuasion. In that, they failed. Most members of the group seem to have assumed, as Thompson did, that no serious opposition would arise against their reasons for recommending a launch delay. Their assumption stemmed from two understandings. First, Marshall always challenged contractors to prove that their shuttle component was ready for flight, protecting shuttle and crew from flying when they were not ready. On this occasion, Thiokol was claiming the shuttle was not ready to fly, so Thiokol was performing Marshall's usual function. Second, the engineers represented the manufacturing company and would, they thought, be accepted at NASA as being authoritative about the flight readiness of their own shuttle element.

The engineers also weakened their recommendation in two ways. As usual in any flight recommendation, the engineers presented all the evidence they had reviewed, including in their presentation not only their relevant evidence but also some confusing, irrelevant, and contradictory evidence—that is, the complete corpus of data related to O-ring functioning. Further, they allowed the data charts to be sent to the other two centers not in the order that would have framed an argument protecting safety, but merely in the order in which the charts were completed. That misleading sequence of the charts opened wide the gates to interpretation and argument. Had the engineers assumed some NASA opposition to their presentation, they well might have been both intent on highlighting the crucial data and vigilant to include nothing that confused or contradicted their technical argument against launching with unusually cold O-rings.

In summary, the engineers undermined their recommendation in three ways. They misread the communication situation itself as not requiring a persuasive argument; they presented evidence not ordered to highlight their positive recommendation, protecting safe flight by flying only within previously flown O-ring temperatures; and they featured in their presentation irrelevant data, misleading data that contradicted their argument, and data that actually drew attention to evidence they knew to be unimportant (O-ring erosion).

The final major flaw in the engineers' mode of communication came after Mulloy presented his ten points of rebuttal. They failed to refute any of Mulloy's opposing arguments. Even McDonald, facing Mulloy across the table at the Kennedy Center and holding views of launch danger that contradicted Mulloy's view, failed to refute Mulloy's argument. The failure by McDonald and his engineering colleagues to refute becomes even more glaring to us because we know that he and they had quantitative data, both experimental and from flights, to refute Mulloy's first and most damaging assertion: that O-ring temperature could not correlate with blow-by. McDonald did oppose the launch by adding additional arguments of his own, but these were additions, not refutations. Mulloy's flawed argument was left standing. Further, when Mason reviewed Mulloy's points of argument, neither Boisjoly nor Thompson, also sitting at the table with Mason, refuted any of Mulloy's or Mason's statements of engineering dynamics. Nor, indeed, did the others who shared their correct assessment of the shuttle's situation. Boisjoly and Thompson did oppose Mason, but they did so by simply emphasizing and elaborating their previous cautions.

It is clear, then, that the engineers' attempt to convey their correct *technical* understanding became undermined by their maladaptive assessment of their *communication* situation, particularly in their failure to understand that NASA would likely defend their assumption of safe flight. The ongoing launch countdown had resulted from previous FRR certification of the shuttle as "flight ready."[137] To reverse that was to deny the validity of that entire FRR process. Avoiding this dangerous launch would require Thiokol engineers to craft a clear and pointed argument. The Thiokol group certainly had no inkling of Marshall managers' outlook—or of those managers' fear (the long pole) of being responsible for a launch delay without quantitative proof of its necessity.

The engineers were indeed deficient in conveying their correct understanding to Marshall and to their own senior managers. But deficient also was the managers' openness to the engineers' data and warning. Mulloy's, Hardy's, and Mason's prior conceptions, convictions, and interpretive frames blocked a correct understanding of the realities that the engineers were revealing. Instead of listening for, ferreting out, and attending to the engineers' relevant data with the assumption that they might learn something new—that is, instead of being critical *and* open-mindedly searching and analytical—each manager had his own prior understanding as a platform for confidence.

Mulloy. An array of blocking forces—conceptual, interpretive, and emotional—prevented Mulloy from understanding the engineers' valid situation assessment.[138] He had acquired some double-edged conceptions of FRR requirements, a biasing technical conclusion, skewed modes of interpreting joint dynamics and data, and two kinds of situations to avoid. Consider first three general frames that conditioned his thinking.

First, on the emotional side, Mulloy had recently experienced being responsible for the long and unnecessary delay of the preceding flight (61A) and Lucas had hammered home that such delays were not to be tolerated. A chronic fear among Marshall managers was being the long pole, the lightning rod that would attract Lucas's scathing public criticism for any failing. Mulloy had gone beyond that. He had actually made his own boss, Reinartz, and Lucas himself the long pole of criticism from a higher official (Aldrich) at Johnson Space Center. Having thus embarrassed Lucas as well as himself by causing this lengthy delay, Mulloy now was set to make absolutely sure that Thiokol's call for a delay was necessary—that is, conclusively proven as necessary with hard data acceptable to Lucas.

In Mulloy's mind, the basic conditions for an FRR were present.[139] The relevant engineers and managers were on hand at Marshall to assess any issue related to the boosters so the usual FRR procedures and standards would apply. Mulloy had already presented the readiness case to Lucas's FRR weeks earlier, and the *Challenger* had been certified as "flight ready" all the way to NASA's top management. Its launch countdown was going forward. Thiokol would have to either prove some new flight danger or find some deficiency in that earlier, Lucas-tested, certification as "flight ready." Either one would require a very sound case.

What constituted a sound case was also firmly understood by Mulloy. It had to be based on "credible quantitative engineering analysis or test data,"[140] with emphasis on "credible." One of the hallmarks of a sound argument was coherence, a case with no gaps, no contradictions, clear and precise. As in any FRR, a contractor making a case about readiness, or non-readiness, had only two approaches available, in Mulloy's view.[141] The shuttle was either "flight ready" or it was not. The contractor could either prove its case of "flight readiness" by meeting the usual standards, or it could declare, after proper consideration, that it was not ready, that it still had incomplete data bearing on flight readiness. Mulloy reported later that he had been prepared to accept either of these approaches that a contractor's management might take.[142]

He was also prepared specifically on one technical matter. He had heard early indications that the expected cold temperatures would be part of Thiokol's case. If temperature of the joints was Thiokol's issue, then Mulloy's response would be easy and quick—the joint temperatures had already been safely dispositioned in the FRRs for Flight 51E after Flight 51C a year earlier. The issue of joint or O-ring temperature had therefore been settled. Temperature as a nonfactor had become part of delta knowledge: case closed. The data on temperature effects he had seen in the meantime had not in the least changed that judgment.

As the Thiokol engineers explained their charts, Mulloy's skepticism became more pointed. In his view, Boisjoly's data on *blow-by* held no serious threat, since the O-ring *erosion* entailed in that blow-by (in Mulloy's view) was well within its experimentally determined safety margins. The matter of erosion margins had been settled much earlier. Besides, Thiokol's own data showed the presence of blow-by in both the warm and cold flights in which blow-by had occurred, so Mulloy had concluded that blow-by could not be a function of temperature.

In addition, in Mulloy's eyes, Thiokol had presented data that actually proved the joint would seal at 30 °F! Their own chart 4-3 (Figure 2.5) reporting results with argon gas, while labeled "preliminary," still in his view showed sealing taking place at 30 °F. The fact that the data of chart 4-3 had been openly discounted by Boisjoly—the discounting heard by several participants at Marshall and Kennedy—either escaped Mulloy's attention or was dismissed by him. Mulloy regarded the chart's finding that sealing had occurred at 30 °F as important evidence that the joint would seal at that low temperature[143]—contradicting Thiokol's whole case for a delay.

In summary, five factors prevented Mulloy from giving consideration to Thiokol's data and argument. First, he interpreted the situation of Thiokol's presentation as basically an FRR, evaluating a contractor's data in light of the contractor's conclusion. That framing of the teleconference as an FRR brought into focus Lucas's standards of evidence and argument—standards Mulloy would have to meet if he had to take Thiokol's evidence and reasoning to Lucas's FRR. Biasing Mulloy against delaying this launch were four other factors.

This shuttle flight had already been given the "go" by FRRs all the way to NASA's top administrators, including presentations that Mulloy himself had made to Lucas's board less than a month earlier. In addition, Thiokol's engineering data in support of a delay was, in Mulloy's view, a mixture of irrelevant, weak, and contradictory evidence.[144] It gave no clear basis Mulloy could see to justify a delay, an action he was already disposed to avoid because it would again make him the long pole. Third, Mulloy's need to avoid a delay was strengthened by his recent experience of having caused both himself and Lucas the embarrassment of a launch delay that turned out to be unnecessary. Finally, Mulloy was specifically primed to reject any argument for delay based on a supposed risk that a booster's joint would fail to seal because of low temperature. As soon as the Thiokol engineers mentioned temperature, Mulloy examined their data for other weaknesses and fallacies. These five aspects of Mulloy's cognitive-emotional orientation, then, provided Mulloy the lens through which to assess Thiokol's argument.

Mulloy saw where Thiokol's argument was going, with temperature as the supposed threat. He had so many objections, he didn't know where to start. First, their experimental data relating sealing time to three temperatures showed an amount of sealing delay with O-rings at 75° that, if believed, he thought, about half of all previous flights would have failed.[145] He saw that set of data as invalid on its face. Second, what Thiokol was doing in effect was establishing out of the blue a new launch commit criterion of 53° for O-ring temperatures. On the basis of *these* data! The whole thing just did not hang together. His exasperation with the idea that they would want to delay a launch on the basis of this jumbled and contradictory argument, as he saw it, was just too much. "My God, Thiokol," he exclaimed, "when do you want me to launch, next April?!"

After hearing Thiokol's Kilminster say he had to agree with his Thiokol engineers, Mulloy laid out his ten-point rebuttal. His first point addressed the temperature issue directly: "Blow-by of O-Rings cannot be correlated to temp[erature]." He referred to SRM-22, the boosters of the warm flight. In his mind, the fact that both warm and cold flights showed blow-by proved that temperature was irrelevant to O-ring functioning. Mulloy's counterargument put before all teleconference participants a situation assessment that explicitly contradicted the engineers' assessment: This launch and flight would be as safe as any earlier flight.

We now know who had assessed the shuttle's situation correctly and who had not, but how could *they* know who had it right? The engineers certainly had no specific data to show the functioning of O-rings below 50°, much less at 29°. The data presented were certainly mixed, open to interpretation. As James B. Smith, Marshall's chief engineer for the boosters, described the ambiguity years later, "I can't go right [safe] and I can't go left [dangerous]."

The way one can decide an issue for which the data are mixed (proving neither pro nor con) is an important question addressed in legal reasoning. I address that issue and its associated elements of argumentation in Chapter 8. The fact that there are safeguards within argumentation that allow a resolution that would protect safety even in the face of mixed data was not imagined by the participants, however. They became immersed in arguing their specific views about the data, oblivious of forms or pitfalls of argumentation.

No discussion of the conflicting interpretations of the shuttle's situation took place in the teleconference—besides Mulloy's own ten-point rebuttal of the engineers' presentation. The absence of rebuttal against Mulloy's own counterargument was a central part of the argument dynamic and is also a matter we shall examine presently. That absence of rebuttal allowed the crucial first point of Mulloy's ten-point argument to remain unexamined: "Blow-by of O-rings cannot correlate to temp."

Hardy. Hardy, too, had an emotional reaction to Thiokol's data and conclusion: He was "appalled."[146] His technical view accorded well with the ten-point argument that Mulloy was about to spell out. He was convinced that temperature posed no problem for a safe flight. Hardy had the same dim view that Mulloy had of Thiokol's "resiliency" chart of secondary O-ring temperatures and their associated speeds of joint sealing. If the data of that chart were valid, he thought, it would have meant about half of the shuttle flights would have ended in disaster. Besides, he had full confidence in the self-sealing nature of the field joints. Even if hot gas did get past the putty and past a primary O-ring, Hardy was certain the gas pressure would immediately press the secondary into its intended gap, sealing the joint before it opened. Brief blow-by past the primary was just another way the joint achieved a seal by means of ignition-triggered pressure differential. In Hardy's mind, Thiokol's temperature and blow-by arguments simply didn't hold water.

While Hardy was silent during the teleconference about the specific reasoning that gave him confidence, others at Marshall no doubt were confident on similar grounds.[147] It was Hardy, however, who was the senior engineer at Marshall, the person whose engineering perspective had weight and who might have been expected to extract the situation assessment of the Thiokol engineers from their confusing presentation. But Hardy's own confident views and his own narrow reading of Thompson's experimental data blocked any credence he might give to the engineers' views.

Mason. Mason had several grounds for rejecting his engineers' correct assessment of the shuttle's situation. First, he had his own objective situation to cope with, his personal responsibility to Morton Thiokol, Inc., to protect its monopoly and to secure a contract with NASA. To credit his engineers' assessment as valid, he would have to delay the launch, abrogating a prime corporate responsibility by putting his contract and Thiokol's monopoly in jeopardy.

Added to that objective situation for Mason was the objective situation of deliberation and decision making that had arisen from Mulloy's rebuttal of the Thiokol engineers' presentation. Here was NASA's own booster manager who had just now refuted the engineers' assessment of the shuttle's situation. Would he now examine Mulloy's reasoning critically, or would he accept Mulloy's analysis as technically informed, reasoned, and valid? Mason immediately saw Mulloy providing authoritative NASA reasoning for the safety of launching. He now had grounds from NASA's own booster manager for discounting his engineers' reasoning, grounds for dismissing their call for delaying the launch. After reviewing what he had heard from Mulloy, he asked the group whether he had understood each of Mulloy's points. He received confirmation from some members of the engineering group, yet group members' agreement or silence in response to Mason's summary contrasted sharply with Thompson's and Boisjoly's review of their data explicitly warning of the dangers of cold O-rings.[148]

Hearing Thompson and Boisjoly merely expand on points they had already reported in the teleconference, Mason's face hardened.[149] He asked Boisjoly and Thompson if they were not just generally expressing the dissatisfaction they all felt that the boosters' field joint had weaknesses rather than responding to the joints' cold temperature.[150] He referred to tests showing that the O-rings could take more severe erosion and still seal safely. Mason's own understanding of the boosters' field joints was intact: while continuing to show vexing imperfections, the O-rings were still reliably performing their sealing function. Mason announced that he was ready to launch. Securing the agreement of his two program managers, Wiggins and Kilminster, he turned to Bob Lund, VP of Engineering. He told Lund that Lund now needed to take off his engineering hat and put on his management hat.

Mason had succeeded in directing discussion in a way that diminished his engineers' data and concern and avoided the launch delay. An analysis of his influence reveals seven rhetorical moves. First, he listed several of *Mulloy's* arguments out loud, asking if his understanding of Mulloy's points was correct. In doing so, he focused attention on the *accuracy* with which he, Mason, had heard Mulloy's arguments. He did not ask whether Mulloy's arguments were valid. Second, Mason did not voice a parallel listing of his own engineers' points. Third, when Thompson brought the focus back onto the dangerous engineering facts dramatically by physically moving down the table to Mason and explaining what his O-ring temperature implied, Mason responded in silence with a hard stare. After Boisjoly, too, expanded on the nature and implications of the blow-by data from warm and cold flights, Mason dismissed Boisjoly's comments by attributing Boisjoly's views simply to a desire for a generally better sealing performance rather than to anything specifically related to cold temperature.

Mason's fifth move to diminish the engineers' data and concern was to declare that the discussion had gone over the information enough and that a management decision was needed. Mason's sixth move was then to voice personally his company's official decision, a move that could be opposed only by challenging his authority. His seventh and final rhetorical move was to rule out of bounds the only source of challenge that his VP of

Engineering could use: his engineering expertise. Mason cut off any voicing of engineering facts or warnings that Lund, his VP of Engineering, might give by explicitly assigning Lund the managerial role. Lund was to take *off* his engineering hat and put *on* his management hat. Lund had just heard Mason's own enactment of his management role, so he had an immediate model of the right action from his boss.

Mason's management of the conflict between his engineers' data-based warnings and his commitments to company and its monopoly came down to how he would conduct Thiokol's discussion of the shuttle's launch and flight situation. Mason's linguistic and rhetorical moves managed to bring a resolution concluding that launch and flight would be safe. He had protected Thiokol's reputation for meeting every flight schedule. His management of the conflict between his engineers and NASA's booster manager, Mulloy, in their respective assessments of the shuttle's launch situation is a case study of agenda-driven rhetorical management of conflicting views—in this case about a life-and-death matter.

Mason had for the moment managed his objective contract situation. In doing so, he had contributed significantly to an ineffective, indeed disastrous, management of the shuttle's launch and flight situation. Mulloy had managed to avoid the long pole, to uphold Lucas's standards of coherent data. He also had contributed in a key way to ineffective management of the shuttle's situation. He did so by failing to convey even the fact of the teleconference debate to those officially tasked with supervising that kind of deliberation. Outwardly, Mulloy's rhetorical handling of Thiokol's presentation was by straightforward rebuttal. The path by which he arrived at his reasoning and ten arguments, however, involved selective attention and inattention. His pattern of attention and inattention, when compared to the full array of teleconference data and actual explanation of the charts, reveals a prior commitment to the "flight safety" that *Challenger's* FRRs had earlier certified—a certification through a misleading rhetorical discourse, a habit of NASA thought and everyday conversation that miscast shuttles as "flight ready" before any conditions of their launch or flight could be known.

In revealing the objective and construed situations that did shape this disastrous decision, we see not only new complexities in high-tech decision making and not only the importance of analyzing both objective and construed situations on an equal footing. We see also *multiple simultaneous objective situations*, pulling key managers enmeshed in them in opposite directions. When one of those objective situations involves the safety of spaceship and crew and the other involves projection of a lucrative monopoly, basic human values are at issue. However, any choice that must be made between them also devolved to a technical choice first, in recognizing a crucial pattern (in Fig. 2.4) in the mixed data and second, when the choices about data became contested, a choice in framing an argument from one of two opposing presumptions, safety or danger, reflecting opposite cases to be argued with opposite burdens of proof.

Summarizing this chapter's analysis, a number of conditions shaped the course of deliberations. First, the artifacts themselves, the engineers' presented charts, played a distinctive role by mixing together irrelevant, contradictory, confused, and pointedly relevant evidence of flight safety and danger. Inclusion of that mixed data exactly expressed a strong norm in Lucas's FRRs, that all related data be included. Under these decision conditions, however, accurate assessment of that complete set of data charts required the key managers to attend focally to each chart and to interpret and evaluate its data open-mindedly. This required both especially attentive, unbiased mindfulness and flaw-free data interpretation for assessing the shuttle's situation accurately—cognitive qualities that the key managers lacked under the circumstances.[151]

Second, the context of decision making combined three objective conditions. First, the issues were highly technical. Also, lives were at risk, so the stakes were high. Finally, decision making took place while implementation of the countdown toward launch was in progress. Third, participants generally, and those from NASA in particular, approached decision making with distinct, deeply etched images and ideas about proper data and argument. They had not only witnessed or actively engaged in data-based argument supporting the shuttle's "flight readiness"; they also approached this decision with definite ideas of "conclusive proof" and Lucas-required standards of data—ideas that provided a shared cognitive frame for what would count as "professional" reasoning about "flight readiness." For Mulloy and Hardy, it was a frame that primed their increasingly negative perception of Thiokol's presentation.

Fourth was the objective situation of distributed cognition. We see distributed cognition not only extending to artifacts— the graphs, notes, tables, and charts containing participants' decision-making information—but distributed also between decision makers in different decision-making roles: engineers and managers, holding different levels of decision-making power and authority, distributed between two corporate bodies with different corporate interests and commitments.

This more complex distribution of situation assessment and decision participation, together with the contradictory nature of the data, brought the possibility for key decision makers not only to differ in their mental models and situation definitions but actually to hold *conflicting* models and situation definitions. We see here not only conflicting definitions of a single objective and dangerous situation but also the entirely new phenomenon in the decision-making literature: *multiple objective situations* experienced respectively by managers at NASA and Thiokol, each situation not merely taking attention away from the objectively dangerous situation of shuttle and crew but also casting doubt on the existence of danger.

The presence of conflict, in turn, brought the necessity of *conflict management* for a decision to be reached in this high-pressure, safety-critical situation. Among the many possibilities of managing a conflict, we see in this case employment of the kind of formal argument that most participants from Marshall-style flight readiness reviews were familiar with —argument with evidence, conclusion, rebuttal, reconsideration, and revised conclusion.

Fifth and finally, every phase of preparing shuttles and of launching all flights was burdened by a wholly distorted conception of flight safety relative to flight danger, a distorted view of how much was known versus how much still lay hidden to be known. This distorted mis-assessment of space realities in relation to space technology and expertise led to a rate of flights too fast for needed parts to arrive and too hurried for needed analyses to be made. It led to a language and practice of FRRs that declared "flight readiness" before actual flight conditions could possibly be known, a language that denied the frontier-breaking, unique nature of the shuttle program. That naïve overconfidence became deadly. It would become deadly again before the dangers of working in space became more fully recognized.

The *Situation*

Deliberation and decision making were formed by a tangle of situations, subjective and objective. "Complicated" does not quite capture the multiplicity of pushes and pulls playing on the participants—for the most part unwittingly, or at the dim edges of consciousness. One more objective situation, truly beyond their awareness, impinged directly on all of them. It both shaped the direction of their collective thought and drastically, indeed fatally, reduced their individual and collective analytical and evaluative capacities. The preceding discussion has identified individual parts of this added situation, but here I suggest that the parts together constitute the special, separate situation that warrants the label *Situation*. It warrants distinction because it is a particular *type* of situation, a type that has recurred and will recur again.

The *Situation* is triggered by discovery of a threat to the entire enterprise that requires an organizational decision to quickly stop or drastically alter ongoing operations before the operations themselves became threatened. The technical signal of threat is noticed as a threat by engineers or technicians, who monitor the technical functioning and status of the enterprise. These technical specialists communicate the nature and urgency of their discovery to managers who are part of the organization's decision-making process. Time is short. The stakes are high. Information about the threatening condition is sparse and mixed, so contradictory readings of the threatening information are possible, even likely.

The managers who must decide the issue of threat or no threat must, if disaster is to be avoided, correctly detect and frame the evidence of possible danger, but their distance from the frequent shifts in technical data and interpretation leaves them always behind in technical knowledge. That lag is not serious except when the shift in technical data signals possibly imminent disaster. Then, positioned to decide the validity or invalidity of the signal of danger conveyed up from the engineers, they hold a suddenly outdated view of the very dynamics being warned about. But these same managers can also fall prey to two other weaknesses in assessing reality: a bias and a well-known "trade-off."

The confirmation bias, found from research in varied domains of activity, is a person's outlook that the person already understands the new information being presented. It asserts the validity of the person's prior learnings and sets the person to find reasons to discount the validity of new contradictory information.[152] People under time pressure also become the victims of a "speed-accuracy trade off."[153] Being pressed to assess a situation quickly reduces a person's capacity to sort out the significant from the irrelevant, to review considerations, consult with others, or probe alternative interpretations of evidence. Rushing to assess the new threat truncates both length of utterances and clarifications of their content and meaning. Rushing also constricts the number of ideas and experiences retrieved from memory, maximizing retrieval of only the most easily and quickly accessible—which maximizes simple ideas and connections over complex ones.[154] In sum, when faced with a sudden new claim of possible threat, to rely on mental models and schemas normally used in daily operations, combined with limited opportunity to verify one's recalled information, severely degrades the mental effectiveness of decision makers confronting that threat.

Effective managerial decision making regarding the *Challenger's* launch was jeopardized by more than even these biasing conditions, however. Two key decision makers were involved, Mulloy and Mason, and each operated under special additional biasing conditions. For Mulloy, no condition of a shuttle was real until it could be proven so with quantitative data and coherent argument. Emergent new conditions characterized by scanty and mixed data did not alter this iron-clad rule. Because this shuttle had already been certified "flight ready," Thiokol's mixed and jumbled data certainly couldn't prove the danger they claimed to exist.

These particular biasing conditions, important in the *Challenger* disaster, have wider import. Wherever enterprises push into new safety-critical domains, occasions will arise when technicians or engineers will report a signal they take as definite warning of danger. Managers responsible for responding to such reports will also have developed their own images of the kinds and sources of information that require sharp attention. Managers will also have mental models of the kinds and sources of information that they should discount or ignore. In short, they will have their own rules about hard and soft evidence and of important and unimportant sources of technical information. Such managers will also be committed to meeting their production schedules, to completing their ongoing stage of production, and to their usual conceptions and mental models of their technology as safely functioning. As a result, they will likely challenge any claim that calls for an interruption of production, accepting the interruption only if evidence proves that continued production would be dangerous.

Mason's protective situation, too, represents more than a critical part of the *Challenger* disaster. Any executive manager of a private high-tech enterprise like Thiokol, lagging as Mason was in understanding of the technical details at issue, and presented with confused, incomplete, and possibly contradictory evidence of danger, will likely replicate Mason's response in important respects. Faced with conditions that technicians warn about—warnings that, if correct, promise interruption of ongoing production, failure to fulfill production timing promised by contract, and loss of a customer's confidence—such an executive will approach the engineers' warning data with special, goal-oriented bias in favor of continued production and against crediting the danger.

A formal, data-based argument had been pursued, with the presumption that the shuttle had been proven safe to fly and with the burden on those who claimed danger. Given the newness and inherent bifurcation of interpretations between engineers and managers caused by any sudden signal of danger in these kinds of high-tech settings, given the sparse and mixed nature of data bearing on the new danger, and given the inevitability of such new signals from high-technology equipment pushing into uncharted and unforgiving environments—given those conditions of any new warning signal—disagreements about the warning evidence and its action implications will arise. The means by which the conflicting views are finally settled will be a decision either imposed by a senior manager, with all the risks of fiat resolutions, or worked out between managers and engineers by evidence-based argument, with all the risks entailed when formal argumentation is employed by participants uninstructed in the dynamics of presumption, case, and burden of proof.

The foregoing considerations suggest four specific dangers generic to these high-tech applications in these environments. These four dangers combine in a tight chain of events and constitute a generic *Situation* of dangerous diagnosis. Chapter 7 will elaborate how the *Situation* arises and unfolds in these high-tech enterprises as a generic type of dangerous situation:

1. During ongoing operations and after a string of successes, technical experts detect a clear shift in technical dynamics that signals possible danger to the enterprise, a shift whose imminent nature and urgency they quickly communicate to relevant managers.

2. The available evidence regarding the danger suddenly signaled by the technical shift is necessarily ambiguous, mixed, and incomplete, but the signal of the shift and its dangerous import are clear to the most technically informed engineers regarding the new threat.

3. Different degrees of expert knowledge about the technical shift and its dynamics are possessed by, on one hand, managers empowered to decide technical issues and, on the other hand, the expert engineers or technicians who first detect the technical shift.

4. Conflicting views of the shift's evidence and of its interpretation arise and prompt either a briefly informed decision by a single manager or an evidence-based argument in which participants uninstructed in the dynamics of argumentation—not possessing a working knowledge of the nature and effects of presumption, case, and burden of proof—hurriedly argue their views to arrive at a resolution and path of action.

The *Situation* characterized by these dangers is not the situation of the endangered enterprise itself—not, for example, the launch situation of shuttle *Challenger*. The danger of that situation, however dangerous it may be, must be distinguished from the situation in which that danger is detected and diagnosed, the *Situation* in which a decision is worked out in deliberations shaped by the four dangers. This *Situation* brings hurried thinking and communicating about sparse and ambiguous technical information, brings several obstacles to managers reaching adequate understanding of the technical shift and of the enterprise's new situation, and brings two basic alternative modes of settling the safety-danger issue, each of which entails important pitfalls.

Guards against the danger of this *Situation*, against the four dangerous characteristics of *deliberation about* a signal that the enterprise is endangered, come, if at all, through an organization's culture. More specifically, protections may be provided in the many ways the culture ensures, through its structures, norms, and practices, a coequal partnership between engineers and decision makers. Evident in such a partnership are safety roles and practices enacted in frequent and technically informed challenges by safety personnel demanding good evidence of *safety* (not of danger) in each phase of production as well as resources devoted to safety management. The resources for developing and sustaining such a culture are addressed in Chapter 9.

We next consider, in Chapter 6, more precisely how danger came to outweigh safety in the *Challenger* decision. Chapter 7 will consider how a *Situation* arises and develops and Chapter 8 considers how a different kind of argument under different conditions might have prevented the accident. The final chapter addresses needed changes: a wider range of knowledge and new mechanisms for generating site-specific understanding of human performance in these high-tech enterprises.

CHAPTER 6

Production against Safety: An Unbalanced Cultural Equation

This chapter examines how production came to outweigh safety in the *Challenger* deliberations.[155] The chapter has three parts. I first review the influence of internal market forces playing among the shuttle program, Congress, and Thiokol. These forces, affecting Marshall managers and engineers down through the ranks, resulted in pressures toward production that became reflected in an increasing rate of space flights that outran important safety protections.[156] The second section of the chapter examines a counterforce that protected shuttles as safe space vehicles against production pressures. Lucas's personally shaped culture within Marshall, while anxiously vigilant against any launch delay, did develop three safety-protecting norms through his "flight readiness" reviews of the shuttle. The third section considers five conditions that undermined Lucas's safety protections and reinforced the market forces toward production.

Cascading Constraints: Market, Organization, Subculture

Jerry Mason's Catch-22 contract dilemma created by his engineers' move to delay *Challenger's* launch jumps out at us as shaping his assessment of the shuttle's safety. NASA's delay in renewing Thiokol's contract certainly was an immediate cause of his dilemma. But that unsigned contract, with possible loss of Thiokol's lucrative booster monopoly, reflected a more encompassing environment: the complex demands of two markets, an internal governmental market and an external company market. The internal market involved NASA selling its services to the United States Congress. Congress had to decide which of many competing bids for funding should be honored, weighing how much benefit each would confer on the country (and on the reputation of congressional committee chairs). NASA's external market was its purchase of shuttle components from a private contractor like Thiokol. Both internal and external markets induced both contractors and NASA to maximize immediate gain and minimize immediate loss.

The resulting market forces created production pressures for both Thiokol and NASA. One of NASA's selling points to Congress about the benefits of the shuttle program was that the shuttle would become "operational" as a kind of space workhorse. The rate of scheduled flights would increase sharply from nine in 1985 to twenty-four in 1987–1988, two a month, to accommodate both military and commercial interests. NASA was about to achieve that promised rate, it seemed. It would launch two flights in the month of January 1986. Those promises to Congress and the actually achieved launch rates in 1985, however, lagged more than three flights behind the rate promised. This created production pressures on NASA managers at all levels to meet every launch schedule on time.

Pressure to meet schedules was expressed in a number of ways. Supply of parts for the shuttle couldn't keep up with the rate of launches. As a result, pirating of parts from an orbiter not ready for flight to use for another orbiter being prepared for flight had become common.[157]Failure to keep track of a dwindling or exhausted supply of parts had infected management at Marshall also. Mulloy's failure to keep his supply of booster parts sufficient to match the rate at which shuttles were being prepared was reflected in his substitution of the faulty part that caused the long delay of Flight 61C immediately before the *Challenger*. That long delay and the several subsequent delays of that same flight might have been taken as a signal that the launch schedule was too demanding.

In fact, there were earlier signals. Mulloy's investigation of the cause of 61C's long delay, leading to the fact of the substitute part and his report of his findings in FRRs, the failure of Mulloy's office to notice the lack of parts that caused the substitution, Aldrich's rebuking memo noting Marshall's failure to keep track of the memorandum that identified the substituted part as defective— all these together were earlier signals that the rate of building and flying shuttles was too fast for NASA to do within its own resources. The signals went unnoticed, however. No mechanism designed to notice such weaknesses had been created.

NASA's failure to sign the next booster contract with Thiokol reflected not only NASA's concern for national security if something prevented Thiokol from manufacturing the boosters. NASA had also discovered that if it reopened the public bidding for a shuttle component already being supplied by company X, that that reopening could result in company X submitting a less costly contract for that same component.[158] That institutional pressure to keep Congress's confidence, and thus prevent any threat to cuts in funding by Congress, was also reflected in the last paragraph of Aldrich's rebuking memorandum to Marshall and other centers. It noted the importance of the shuttle program being "operational," which, he wrote, meant being able "to safely and consistently launch on time and land on time."[159]

Marshall's director, William Lucas, understood the requirements of schedule. With deep commitment to the space program and to maintaining his own reputation as an effective analyst and manager, Lucas recognized the complexities of preparing shuttles for flight. He knew the military necessity of earth surveillance, understood that it requires satellite cameras placed to travel in certain orbits and not others, and that timing of a space shuttle was dictated by those orbits. To deliver and maintain those satellites in those orbits set hard schedule requirements. He developed the Marshall Space Center as a shuttle-building organization constantly motivated to attain three goals: strictly on-time production, vigilantly scrutinized quality control over the space vehicle, and maximum productivity while controlling cost.

Lucas's own brand of leadership, expressed through his own expanded FRRs and his hawkeyed vigilance and publicly critical manner of conducting his FRRs, generated a cascading mind-set downward through the successive FRRs, coalescing into a Marshall Center subculture whose theme was on time, no delay. Marshall's (Lucas's) salient values, goals, and outlook were internalized by his booster manager, Larry Mulloy. The highest value was on-time productivity, followed closely by Lucas's own brand of engineering reasoning to support shuttle preparation, featuring data and language that must not deviate one iota from precise, complete, quantitative support for any claim. His sharp eye for threats to meeting launch schedules and his humiliating critiques for violations of his version of quantitative engineering evidence (and proper engineering language) became internalized by his managers and engineers.

Also internalized by all at Marshall was that time and effort were resources to be spent productively. Lucas's scrutiny over this third goal was detailed—reaching down even into workers' after-lunch horseshoe pitching—but was reflected also in managers' giving up planned vacations to make sure work was done on schedule. Overtime, when devoted to that purpose, was, for Lucas, return on a cost well spent.

The need to save resources was not Lucas's alone. It also was reflected in the contract negotiations by managers higher up in NASA, those who had to deal more directly with its internal market with Congress. Officials at that level—possibly with the knowledge of Lucas, but possibly not—discovered that one contractor would respond to a threat of competition by submitting a lower cost contract. Both Mulloy's readiness to avoid launch delays and Mason's fear that his engineers were about to cause a delay therefore had the same remote cause: NASA's pressure to increase the flight rate, to meet every launch deadline, and be truly "operational," thus fulfilling both its "can-do" image from its earlier success in lunar exploration and its promises to Congress of the benefits that would come with further space flight.

In summary, Congress had to justify to its constituents the billions it had spent and allocated for the space program. That was an objective situation; congressional members had to be able to show both promise of results and fiscal balance. That situation, in turn, created for NASA a situation of pressure to stay within its budget, to save time and money, to create a schedule that increased in flight rate and fulfilled NASA's promises of "operational" performance. That created a pressured situation for Lucas, which became communicated to all his managers down the line. Pressure to show results to match Congress's budget led not only to pirating of parts to get shuttles ready on time and to managers' cutting short or eliminating vacations; it also fostered NASA pressure on contractors to rebid their contracts at lower cost.

The cumulative constraint of these market pressures situated every decision in a context of meeting the schedule. The *Challenger's* acute situation of danger on January 27 and 28, 1986, arose as a sudden challenge to that chronic on-time production situation. Safety could be protected in this production subculture only where managers built in safeguards that prevented the dominant production impulses from taking over completely. Lucas, for all his faults in managerial style, and despite his commitment to the launch schedule, succeeded in accomplishing that safety protection in his FRRs.

Three Safety-Protecting Practices of Proving Readiness: Lucas's FRRs

Lucas's leadership and the subculture it spawned resulted in highly ordered, tightly reasoned "flight-readiness" presentations of engineering research on each shuttle's structures and performance. Presentations to Lucas's FRRs were characterized by three highly adaptive practices. The regular repetition of these practices reflected their taken-for-granted status as norms. Supporting the norm of *high standards* of data and engineering reasoning ("credible quantitative engineering analysis or test data") was a second normal practice of *probing* evidence and assertions. Lucas's FRRs were adversarial in their critical examination of quantitative evidence with (unspoken) parallels to forms of legal argument structured around "presumption," "burden," and "proof." The third norm was that safety had to be proven.

The review board at each review level played two roles, "defense" and "jury." In every flight's FRR, the reviewing board at each level defended the proposition (and the presumption) that the shuttle was *not* "flight ready" until proven so with hard engineering evidence. The board's role was to question and refute the prosecution, the contractor group, which came prepared to argue that the boosters or external tank *was* "flight ready." The board's challenging probes reflected members' engineering expertise and experience with performance evidence from previous flights. The burden was always on the contractor to prove that its shuttle component was "flight ready,"[160] meeting Lucas's demanding standards of data and reasoning. Moreover, because the NASA review board both conducted the questioning and probing and also decided what the presenting contractor had or had not proved, the cards were stacked against those claiming readiness. Safe, flight-worthy shuttles (flown under normal, expected conditions) were ensured by these stringent guarantors of readiness.

In summary, three safety-protecting norms guided deliberations in Marshall's FRRs. The first demanded high standards of data and reasoning. The second was that all evidence and arguments be subjected to challenge and probing. The third norm, derived directly from the fact of testing a shuttle being newly assembled, was the tacit, universal presumption that the shuttle was not ready for flight unless and until it was proven so, with the burden on the contractor to prove readiness, ie, safety.

These Marshall norms controlled a more general process of *argumentation and proof* about readiness that had been highly effective in protecting safe flight under flight conditions before those arising on January 27, 1986. These norms and the FRR procedures around them applied, however, *only to Lucas's particular FRR context at Marshall*, preparing shuttles as space flight vehicles—"flight ready" only within already expectable flight conditions. In this first phase of preparing shuttles for flight, the FRR phase, time was expandable, not pressed to meet an imminent launch. A crucial element in this first process was Lucas's own very personal, knife-edged control over the course and contents of argumentation.

Production Phase, FRR Leadership, On-time Ethos

That same knife-edged concentration Lucas devoted also to making sure that nothing done at Marshall would cause a launch delay that was not absolutely necessary. Lucas was fully enmeshed in, and actually a key driving force in, promoting the production-on-time ethos. That ethos was further sustained by the pervasive managerial discourse of "operational" flights.

The Marshall ethos demanded both proof of readiness (safety) and launching on time (production), but would Lucas's subordinates internalize both of these norms equally, or would one be given priority over the other? We know the answer from hindsight: Production won over safety. One tilting force was the comparative specificity and immediacy of production over safety. Safety has no specific schedule, no deadlines. Production is all about meeting specific deadlines. The urgency of production was also, in NASA's collaboration with private contractors and in meeting congressional expectations, about meeting commitments of distributed stakeholders. These stakeholders formed a chain down a hierarchy from Congress and its real or imagined constituents down to Lucas's bosses at Johnson, to Lucas himself, then Mulloy, and on down the line—a hierarchical system of demands all with their own expected, sometimes deeply committed time lines.

Lucas's norms protected safety within Lucas's own phase of shuttle assembly and preparation. Lucas, however, had neither authority nor control over the second phase, directed by the MMT at the Johnson Center, the phase of actual *flight*, preparing a safe launch and ascent into orbit. What would it take for safety to prevail if it were threatened *in this second phase* (launch and flight preparation)? Would safety be protected *after* the FRRs had run their course and where Lucas's vigilance would be absent? That question is addressed specifically in Chapter 8. We now move from protection of safety to conditions of danger.

Five Organizational Conditions Undermining Safety

Five conditions, including the first two as noted earlier, set constraints on the deliberations of January 27 and 28, undermining the safety of *Challenger's* flight.

1. Delta Thinking. Part of Lucas's FRR system was the regular practice of finally settling ("closing" or "dispositioning") issues, known as the delta concept. Recall that once an anomaly had been found (or made) harmless and reported as such in an FRR, it became a kind of "case law," a precedent that was regarded as settled knowledge. This outlook and practice failed to recognize that once an anomaly was declared in Marshall's FRR process to be harmless, that anomaly could be discovered to be *a threat* later under different conditions of actual launch or flight. This conditionality of previously "settled" anomalies was nowhere recognized, much less warned against. FRR certification of the shuttle as "flight ready" in Lucas's phase of shuttle preparation was taken as absolute and final proof of flight readiness. Ignored was the possibility of a flight danger arising in the next, post-Lucas, phase of launch and flight preparations. That phase would be led by the MMT, led by Arnold Aldrich at the Johnson Space Center. Following the practice of regarding flight anomalies as settled unconditionally if they had been settled by an earlier FRR, Mulloy would be surprised, and not a little annoyed, when Thiokol raised an issue of O-ring temperatures that an FRR had settled months earlier.

2. *Lucas's Norm of In-house Control.* Lucas's personal need to control his subordinates' outlooks and commitment produced a strong norm of in-house managerial responsibility and control at Marshall. Lucas was acutely aware that when his Marshall Center FRR declared a shuttle "flight ready," that review was the last probing *technical* vetting the shuttle would get. He made sure, therefore, that all issues coming to Marshall about a shuttle component would be settled in Marshall according to his own standards, not passed up the line. This norm contributed to Marshall's effectiveness regarding shuttle preparation by, for example, applying its own high, Lucas-monitored standards to issues that might otherwise have been settled by consultation with less technically informed officials at Johnson.

The immediate tendency of Mulloy and other officials at Marshall to regard Thiokol's teleconference launch objections as a matter to be settled in-house had two results. First, it meant Mulloy would be the pivotal manager to evaluate Thiokol's data and argument. He would bring to the task the particular outlooks he had extracted from his Marshall experience under Lucas, including Lucas's view of what constituted a professional data presentation. Mulloy also brought his fear of being the one to cause an unnecessary delay, his fear of being the long pole.

The second result of the in-house outlook was Lovingood's exclusion of the MMT from participating in the teleconference. Aside from the fact that it violated explicit NASA policy of who (the MMT) should be responsible for handling any post-FRR issue, it also eliminated any influence that Arnold Aldrich, MMT chair, might have on deliberations. As an independent manager of NASA's deliberations, Aldrich would have displaced Mulloy and Reinartz from leading NASA's *Challenger* deliberations about the boosters.

3. *Restricted Time Degraded Thought.* Yet another objective situation arose that could only reduce the effectiveness of deliberations.

It was the situation of the collective deliberation itself, a situation whose effects on deliberation that the participants were unaware of. The restricted time for deliberation and decision both subtracted and added significant force. It was a situation that drastically *reduced* participants' cognitive and communicative effectiveness. In the face of any new, possibly dangerous, flight condition arising during a countdown, the restricted time to diagnose and avert the threat meant reduced scanning of memory, truncated reflective analysis, reduced communication with colleagues, and reduced reconsideration. Simultaneously, however, it meant an *increase* in error.[161] The sheer shortness of time ruled out collecting any new data that specifically addressed the new condition. Deliberation and decision would have to rely on only already available data. That data would necessarily be of mixed relevance to the new condition and would hold ambiguous implications. None of the available data would have been gathered to address a condition so recently discovered in the launch process.

While subtracting intelligence, the countdown situation also added pressure, both urgency and much higher stakes than in any FRR. FRRs allowed time and opportunity to gather any data needed to answer a key question, and if an error were made, time and structured opportunities to correct it were available. While a person's sense of professional competence might be at risk of embarrassment if one made an error under Lucas, no shuttle or lives could be lost. Not so in the MMT phase of production, particularly in the shuttle's two-day countdown. The fate of a shuttle and its crew was irreversible if any flight threat that turned out to be real were not successfully countered. Further, the hour set for a launch brought more than the stress of a deadline. The hour and minute of every launch was announced *publicly* via news media and television to millions of people—and millions of voters. The countdown, then, brought both reduced time with restricted intellectual resources and, simultaneously, greater psychological stress of a public launch decision.

4. Managerial Distance from Technical Discoveries. Deliberative effectiveness was undermined by more than just weakened intelligence and heightened psychological pressure. To these was added another condition that impinged directly on deliberations: a chronic *bias* that NASA and Thiokol managers brought to this time-pressured launch decision.

The managerial bias in question relates to differences between engineers and managers in the immediacy and detail with which each comes to understand the physical *engineering* dynamics of a high-tech piece of equipment like a booster joint.[162] Any *new* properties of shuttle functioning first come to the attention of engineers, who are the ones experimenting, measuring, and comparing performance characteristics. Those new properties subsequently become communicated to managers up the line. As managers make decisions about flight or delay in this launch-preparation phase, they do so in positions removed from any recent engineering data and discoveries.

Managers receive the new engineering warning with a mind-set and their own mental model of each shuttle component already established, an outlook conditioned by a series of (managerial) successes. Suddenly and quickly in this established mental outlook—and, from the managers' perspective, an outlook well tested and adequate —they must evaluate the new technical evidence and its implications.

Under countdown conditions, managers rely on technical communication from engineers. Interpreting the engineers' report of a new, threatening condition, managers will rely also on technical information (previously provided by engineers) about the shuttle's previously successful flights. They will be prone, as Mulloy was, to base their assessments and decision making largely on that already acquired knowledge. That knowledge is more familiar, more cognitively accessible to the mangers than will be the implications embedded in newly presented data. That new data, furthermore, can be presented in abbreviated engineering lingo that is easily misunderstood.

Engineers may therefore have an uphill struggle to infuse managerial thinking with a newly discovered technical dynamic that signals to them a new complication or actual flight danger. On their part, managers will have an uphill struggle to reorganize their thinking to replace their already acquired technical knowledge and mental models of booster joint dynamics with new knowledge they can trust. Time may or may not be available for the managers to accommodate the new technical information being communicated by the engineers.[163]

Added to these normal managerial vulnerabilities, Mulloy and other managers at Marshall Space Center had been primed to meet each launch schedule. They had experienced William Lucas's double-edged influence regarding on-time launching, but also his insistence on quantitative data and coherent reasoning. Meeting every launch schedule on time had left Lucas's managers wary of becoming the long pole and of drawing any conclusion without coherent, persuasive data. Inconclusive evidence of a threat to a safe launch or flight would not meet Lucas's strict standards of proof. If this flight were to be delayed, Mulloy would have to answer to Lucas with that proof.

5. *Vacuum of Attention to Safety.* The fifth force undermining safety was a vacuum, not the presence of pressure toward production but the absence of *independent* attention to safety. Marshall's Office of Reliability and Quality Assurance (MRQA) was responsible for overseeing that the standards of orbiter and booster construction were upheld and that flight preparations protected the safety of persons, flight, and mission. MRQA answered directly to Marshall's head of Science and Engineering. The director of Science and Engineering reported to Marshall's director, William Lucas. MRQA depended for all safety monitoring on just two engineers from a staff of 20, one of whom spent 25% and the other spent 10% on "shuttle maintainability, reliability, and quality assurance" (no mention of safety). These two engineers, like all at Marshall, became subject to the priorities of Marshall's director, Lucas, as Lucas's influence was felt down through the ranks.[164]

The Commission's opening paragraph of Marshall's "Silent Safety Program" reflects that safety vacuum:

> The Commission was surprised to realize after many hours of testimony that NASA's safety staff was never mentioned. No witnesses related the approval or disapproval of the reliability engineers, and none expressed the satisfaction or dissatisfaction of the quality assurance staff. No one thought to invite a safety representative or a reliability and quality assurance engineer to the January 27, 1986 teleconference between Marshall and Thiokol. Similarly, there was no representative of safety on the Mission Management Team that made key decisions during the countdown on January 28, 1986.[165]

These five perception-shaping dynamics—the delta practice of interpreting FRR disposition of any anomaly as absolute and definitive, the settling of all technical issues in-house only, the time-restricted countdown-decision situation, managers' vulnerability to their confidence in their inaccurate mental models, and Marshall's silent safety system—presented dangerous barriers to effective deliberation. These barriers would have tilted Mulloy and Mason toward launch even if they had been otherwise open-minded, but their respective personal experiences and situations could only multiply the force of these conditions, solidifying their opposition to delaying the launch.

In this chapter, I have reviewed three sets of forces shaping the *Challenger* deliberations. First were the cascading effects of internal markets limiting NASA's and Thiokol's resources, triggering contract pressure on Lucas, Mulloy, and Mason. These pressures led NASA to set pressing and unrealistic "operational" launch schedules and, more generally, to establish a thought- and behavior-forming culture at Marshall of making do with less, of stringent in-house control, of FRRs that honored proof by data as imperative and meeting all launch schedules on time as sacred.

The second set of forces shaping the deliberations offered a conditional counterforce to the cascading dangers of marketing pressures. Lucas's FRRs established three safety-protecting norms that were followed consistently: high standards of quantitative data and reasoning, standards maintained through tough probing, and refutation and verification of claims. These norms might have been a source of protection in the second, post-FRR, phase of launch preparation, but participants had learned to generalize and to be explicit about only one of the three norms: Proof lies in the quantitative evidence. The importance of another constant practice in Lucas's FRRs—probing verification of facts and reasoning through questioning and direct rebuttal—seems to have been learned well at Marshall as they addressed *contractors'* evidence, but not learned by contractors regarding reasoning or data offered by *Marshall*. No one had learned the general applicability of the Marshall FRRs' safety-protecting practice of presuming danger and accepting the burden of proving safety.

The final set of forces shaping deliberation were the five perception-shaping dynamics that combined with the market pressures to drastically overbalance deliberations toward production. It was not just the deliberations that were overbalanced toward production, however; reflected also was a subculture driven by a schedule to produce, to launch on time.

Labeling the sequence of reviews to which the shuttle was subjected as "flight-readiness reviews" falsely represented the actual condition of all certified shuttles. Declaring the shuttle program "operational" was another denial of reality. The launch schedule regularly demanded overtime work. It led also to launching a flight before the previous flight's orbiter or boosters could be inspected. Managerial actions that resulted in launch delays regularly led to punishing humiliation. That humiliation, in turn, gave rise at Marshall to managerial fears of being the long pole. Lucas's demand that the horseshoe pitchers cut their lunch hour to get back to work reflected that same time pressure. Finally, the central theme of the ethos that connects these varied organizational events and expressions, the theme of on-time production, was pointedly underscored by the absence of any safety personnel from deliberations about shuttle or launch preparations generally, and notably absent from the *Challenger* deliberations.

The next chapter examines in detail a specific organizational situation that adds further danger to these high-tech enterprises beyond the imbalance described above: the *Situation*. Chapter 8 then explores how both the production-safety imbalance and the dangers of *Situations* can become neutralized by a particular framing and handling of the form of analysis referred to as formal argumentation.

CHAPTER 7

A Situation's Elements, Context, and Development

This chapter begins by briefly recapping the elements of a *Situation*. It then portrays the kind of technological complexity regularly presented by multi-level high-technology enterprises, a portrait of the *chronic context* in which *Situations* arise. We then turn to the chief business of this chapter, an account illustrated by the *Challenger* deliberations, of how a *Situation* develops from start to finish.

Situations comprise five basic elements:

- Origin: a warning of a new technological condition threatening to the entire enterprise
- Evidence: necessarily mixed and incomplete, but containing data indicating danger
- Restricted time: the warning must be evaluated as real or false quickly
- Confirmation bias: managers, who decide such issues, have developed confidence in their "working" models of the technology being warned about and receive the warning with skepticism
- Argument settles the issue: the relevant manager, ignorant or knowledgeable about the power and pitfalls of argumentation, decides the argued issue by a final interpretation of the data.

The High-Technology Context

Revealed in the *Challenger* case and similar high-tech cases is decision making about intricate technical engineering dynamics. One example will illustrate. The interacting forces playing on the O-rings' crucial sealing before any hot gas can escape through the joint, with the O-rings winning their race at 53 °F and above, but losing the race below 30 °F, reflected no fewer than six rates of change set in motion the moment the boosters were ignited:

1. Rate of the joints' opening after ignition in .6 second, with its ʃ-shaped curve of gap opening over time (.6 second), generating three phases of the joint's opening
2. Rate of high-pressure, hot gas escaping through a blow hole and into a joint
3. Rate of impingement erosion
4. Rate of the insulating putty's wall giving way to gas pressure—a function of wall thickness and putty density (both varying in unknown amounts)
5. Rate of the O-rings' recapturing their sealing girths as the joint opened
6. Rate of the primary O-rings' movement across their grooves

Rate 2 was limited by rate 4; experts knew that the maximum limit of rate 3 was innocuous, but some key participants did not; and experts knew rates 5 and 6 were influenced by temperature, but other key participants rejected temperature effects altogether. The significance of all of these rates was how, under *usual* flight conditions, they led to successful O-ring sealing of their joints within .17 second after ignition of the boosters.

This listing of the complexities posed by this single dimension of the shuttle's myriad dimensions of complexity shows the kind of interacting forces and conditions that typify complex high technology's performance in unforgiving environments. Those forces and conditions must become quickly understood by participants in the *Situation's* discovery and diagnosis, understood not only by the technicians or engineering experts on the ground but also by *mangers* at all levels responsible for deciding the issues. These complications must be understood, again, as pertaining not only to the facts but also to implications for safety and danger, understood not only at multiple levels of the organization but also in ongoing real time, before time to decide and act runs out. Finally, the technical specialists who first perceive the danger signals must communicate the signals to managers who are oriented to completing the ongoing phase of operations. Clearly, the *Situation* imposes on participants severe intellectual and social-communicative requirements.

The severe cognitive and communication demands such complexities impose, however, become drastically increased when a sudden new dynamic, like O-ring temperature, has to be integrated into the time-pressured deliberations. In the *Challenger* case, all participants had reached *an* understanding of these six rates, but *correct* understanding was limited to a few who tried to inform the rest.

Many complex high-technology enterprises that push boundaries of knowledge in unforgiving environments will necessarily reach a point where they encounter this *Situation*[166]— enterprises from nuclear power plants and nuclear-powered submarines to deep oil and gas exploration,[167] explorations of pathogenic viruses,[168] and human space exploration.[169]

How the *Situation* Arises

The following concept and model of the particular discovery and diagnostic situation that I am calling *Situation* is drawn from the *Challenger, Columbia* (Lighthall, 2014a), and Near Miss (Lighthall, 2014b) cases, but I abstract them as exemplars of a generic situation that many high-tech safety-critical explorations – and *all* such enterprises operating in new, unforgiving environments — will encounter.

As those enterprises push into untested environments or conditions or use new procedures or equipment they will occasionally encounter new conditions that threaten the enterprise's ongoing operations. A considerable span of successful operations will have created in managers increased confidence that they have instituted sufficient safeguards against known and unknown dangers. Their attention and resources will focus on production volume and efficiency. A special condition arises when, after a period of successful operations, an important stage of ongoing work is interrupted by the discovery of a possible new, serious threat to the ongoing enterprise—a new fact or combination of facts creating a new dynamic that, if not adjusted to quickly, may well cause disastrous cost or loss. All such enterprises will be guided by mission goals to which each newly discovered condition will be judged relevant or irrelevant, threatening or supportive. These judgments of relevance and threat will be made by participants who vary in expertise and in decision-making authority.

The newly discovered changed condition or relation (e.g., unusually cold temperature or an atypical rate of O-ring recovery from squeeze) will be encountered first by one or a small number of technical specialists. They will evaluate the degree to which the new change poses a threat to the enterprise's mission or project. They will then communicate their assessment of the situation's threat to their managers.

The issue of safety or danger of the new discovery will be deliberated with necessarily incomplete, mixed, and unverified evidence by participants both close to and distant from the relevant information. That mixed evidence will generate differences in technical views that will be assessed by both technicians and managers. In these high-tech enterprises, that assessment will often entail some arguing, even intense debate, about that evidence and its implications,[170] arguments that will include at least these five characteristics:

- Implicit or explicit *presumptions about current conditions or dynamics;*
- An assumption of which side of the argument must prove its case: *the burden of proof;*
- High, mixed, or low *standards of evidence;*
- Coherent or inconsistent, logical or illogical *reasoning; and*
- Strong, weak, or absent *probing of evidence and reasoning.*

Participants in such deliberations can develop a configuration of these five dimensions of argument that protects safety, but without specific training are more likely to differ among themselves in their presumptions, their standards of evidence, and their reasoning. In any case, the process of arguing—effectively or obtusely, intrapersonally or interpersonally—will usually be the *final* process through which all data and conflicting assessments are winnowed to yield a final situation assessment, decision, and action.

Resolution of conflicting views of danger by argument from evidence will hold the hidden danger of focusing on the lack of clear proof of *danger*, thereby missing the one form of argument that protects safety. The *protective* form of argument, explored in Chapter 8, is one that (1) reflects skepticism toward confidence in assured success in this high-tech safety-critical enterprise, (2) tacitly presumes danger rather than safety, and (3) seeks renewed proof of *safety* whenever serious evidence arises of a possible danger to the ongoing project.

A new danger arises at the point where both engineering specialists and managers consider together the necessarily incomplete and mixed evidence of the new technical threat. It is a danger not of technological functioning but a danger in human functioning, in how engineers and managers interpret and evaluate new information. The danger is revealed in the different roles, priorities, and situations between managers and engineers. It is engineers or technical specialists who first detect any weaknesses that threaten the enterprise at the technical level of its functioning—illustrated in the *Challenger* case by the engineers' warnings of the dynamics of cold O-rings and in the *Columbia* case by the warnings the day after launch of an unusually large chunk of debris that threatened *Columbia's* wing (Lighthall, 2014a). Managers are distant from those dynamics, attending to other dynamics of resource allocation, on-schedule completion of organizational tasks, and the like. Managers will depend on technicians and engineers to inform them of the technical dynamics.

The details of those technical dynamics are received by managers with minds attuned to their own managerial responsibilities for production and their own mental models of technical dynamics. Managers hear and read the new information in light of these responsibilities and mental models. They evaluate the new information against their mental models of the technology in question and in relation to their production responsibilities. They will be prone to be more sensitive to the *programmatic implications* of the new technical information than to careful scrutiny of the technical details themselves.

Managers at all levels in the *Challenger* case, for example, had built up over an uninterrupted series of 24 successful flights their own implicit, simplified mental models of the joints' functioning, each of which gave assurances that the boosters' joint dynamics had been engineered to work safely. *Columbia* managers had built up mental models of the repeated instance of foam debris as innocuous (Lighthall, 2014a). Some booster joint anomalies had occurred, like O-ring impingement erosion, but had been empirically proven to be well within safety limits. *That* fact, all understood: a shared mental model of impingement erosion.

George Hardy's model of the *Challenger's* timing of sealing was comforting. It ruled out as impossible any hot gas reaching the secondary O-ring *after* the joint opened. Mulloy's mental model of field joint dynamics was that temperature had no bearing on O-ring sealing. Mason's model pictured blow-by as innocuous unless accompanied by erosion. These kinds of errors in managerial models of technical dynamics are probably endemic to managerial life. Hardy's, Mulloy's, and Mason's flawed models of how the O-rings sealed their joints "worked" under *usual* flight conditions. Those fair-weather models had worked for 24 safe flights. Their incompleteness or inaccuracy in details became dangerous only when flight conditions affecting the real dynamics changed.[171]

Tracking sudden changes in technical dynamics and updating participants' mental models to remain in tune with those sudden changes depends on participants' perceptual contact with, or distance from those dynamics. Thiokol engineers were able to track accurately one key shift in the crucial O-ring dynamics — their capacity to seal their joints, their resiliency.

Well before the dynamic conditions of O-ring resiliency actually changed with the much colder weather of January 27 and 28, those Thiokol engineers' mental models had shifted, responding in part to the many anomalies the year before in Flight 51C. Being closer to the data—in fact, having been closely involved in carrying out Thompson's experiment on temperature effects—they could see joint vulnerability to temperature in the future.

Managers' mental models, in contrast, would be out of date and false unless they, too, tracked the O-ring changes in response to changes in temperature. When McDonald's assistant, Brian Russell, sent his memo to Marshall's managers, spelling out Arnold Thompson's experimental data relating O-ring temperature to O-ring sealing time, one major purpose was to bring Marshall managers' mental models of O-ring sealing dynamics up to date with respect to the important temperature effects. Sending that memo describing the effects of temperature on O-ring resiliency turned out to be insufficient to shape Marshall managers' mental models of temperature dynamics. Doing such an experiment and examining directly the soot that had escaped past 51C's primary O-ring, as the engineers had done, can have a strong affect, changing one's model of how temperature affects O-ring sealing. Merely reading a report describing the results of engineers' post-flight quantitative analysis of soot or reading a memo describing the results of engineers' experiment, in contrast, will have a much less pronounced effect, leaving one's prior model largely intact – especially if one is preoccupied with other concerns.

The larger implication here is that managers in these high-technology settings are vulnerable to being out of date, to lagging behind the engineers in their mental models of ground-level dynamics. This endemic managerial distance from shifts in technical dynamics allows false models to be built up and to "work" under usual conditions. Those lagging, fair-weather models that "work" over a span of successes become the basis for managers' confidence. That confidence then becomes a wall against grasping how new conditions can falsify those suddenly outdated fair-weather models.

But it is still managers, even with outdated mental models, who make the decisions about issues raised by new data. Managers, not engineers, settle any disagreements about the validity or interpretation of the data regarding its action implications.

Still another danger of human functioning arises in *Situations*. If the manager who is responsible for the component being warned about disagrees with the engineers, the manager in these high-tech enterprises will likely argue that the engineers' evidence is ambiguous and insufficient to establish danger. The ensuing argument between the manager and the engineers contains, as argument, a danger neither side will likely be aware of. They are ordinarily not educated in the demands and pitfalls of argumentation itself.

Two of the most powerfully shaping forces in determining any argument's resolution are the technological conditions or dynamics tacitly presumed to exist before the discovery, and the side of the argument that is burdened to prove its case (see Chapter 8). The presumed safety or danger of the technical dynamics and the side of the argument that is (tacitly or explicitly) assigned the burden of proof can be absolutely determinative whenever the evidence being argued about is mixed – as it almost inevitably is when a new technical issue first shows itself. This fact, that the form of argument participants happen to fall into can itself determine the conclusion they will reach, will likely be unknown to them.

As in the *Challenger* case, the near miss case (Lighthall, 2014b), and in the *Columbia* disaster (Lighthall, 2014a), managers' initial focus on a sudden warning of danger in the midst of ongoing operations will be to consider whether that danger is real, demonstrable by evidence. If so, they will immediately have fallen into tacitly presuming the project safe unless proof of danger is forthcoming, and those who see evidence of danger will be called upon to prove it. Because the mixed and incomplete evidence will be insufficient to demonstrate danger, they will conclude the situation is safe. Focused on danger, they will likely not stumble onto the fact that the evidence is insufficient also to demonstrate that the situation is safe.

Participants deliberating safety or danger, furthermore, will do so also unaware of the impact on those deliberations of the very situation in which their deliberation is taking place, unaware, that is, of the *Situation* itself. They will be focused on solving the specific new technical issue, concentrating on evidence and reasoning that suggest danger. They are unlikely to attend to the immediate conditions or processes affecting *how* they are collecting and presenting data, unlikely to be aware of the *ways* that constricted decision time blunts and distorts both thought and communication, and unaware of *how* they are hearing and thinking about the issue, and *how* they are communicating— much less are they attending to the effects of such matters as market pressures, leadership style, institutional culture, or the demands and pitfalls of effective argumentation. They will be unaware, in short, that the very process of assessing the technological danger they are evaluating has itself become dangerously dumbed-down, drastically restricted in critical, intelligent analysis and deliberation.

Resolution of the conflicting assessments of the *Situation* will emerge finally one way or the other. One of three outcomes will occur: (1) the supposed danger will turn out to be absent, (2) the danger will be correctly assessed and avoided, or (3) the danger will be misjudged and serious damage or disaster will occur. One result or another will bring the *Situation* to a close, having run its course from the first technician's claim of possible danger to presentation of the mixed evidence of it, to rebuttal with contrary evidence of no danger, to further argument and final assessment by the manager in charge who decides what response will be made to the claim of danger.

These decision-making complexities of the *Challenger*, the near miss case (Lighthall, 2014b), and the *Columbia* (Lighthall, 2014a) will apply, in summary, to all *Situations*: wherever such safety-critical technological enterprises encounter a new program threat during operations, which they inevitably will as they push the boundaries of knowledge, a threat that demands a quick technical assessment and managerial decision. That decision will be based on necessarily incomplete and ambiguous information about which conflicting evaluations of safety and danger will arise. The issue of threat or safety will be finally settled by how managers, ignorant or knowledgeable about the power and pitfalls of argumentation, settle the conflicting interpretations of the technical data.

The *Situation*, in short, is dangerous. Its danger intensifies the dangerous imbalance described in Chapter 6. What hope can there be, then, for long-term safety in these high-tech enterprises? The means to that end will be found in participants' modes and instruments of individual and collective perception, deliberation, and action. That, however, depends on strong, continuous support from an organizational culture very different from those now evident in most complex high-tech safety-critical enterprises that push the boundaries of knowledge. The changes required for a culture of safety to emerge in such enterprises are explored in Chapter 9. We now turn, in Chapter 8, to one absolutely necessary mode of thought and collective deliberation that protects safety in decision making. It will be one necessary part of any culture of safety.

CHAPTER 8

Evidence-Based Argument: Resolving Safely a Safety-Danger Dispute

We now take up the problem of protecting safety when danger is in dispute. This chapter first addresses how good data and analysis fail to protect from error when interpretations of new evidence differ. Next, it considers a solution to this vulnerability: participants frame their efforts to settle their conflicting views explicitly as argument from evidence, a framing that recognizes explicitly the role of presumption and burden of proof. The chapter then examines eight components of formal argument to clarify its complexity as an analytical and evaluative tool. We conclude the chapter by considering how the *Challenger* argument between the engineers and managers, reframed to protect safety over production, might not only have protected safety but also rendered innocuous the flaws in participants' interpretations, actions, and assumptions.[172]

Requiring Good Evidence: Necessary but Insufficient

Participants on both sides of the issue in the *Challenger* dispute shared a belief developed as a central part of Marshall's culture. They had internalized Lucas's insistent idea that any engineering issue of "flight readiness" would be settled by complete, quantitative data—in Mulloy's phrase, "credible quantitative analysis or test data." That belief appears sound, even indisputable, but it is false. More than credible quantitative evidence is required to settle a technical dispute.

Faith in good evidence ignores situations where a decision is required but where evidence is abundant but mixed, that is, where the data can prove neither the danger nor the safety of continuing to operate normally (e.g., proceeding to launch). Testing only the danger case ignores the safety case, and ignoring the safety case turns out to be dangerous.

To make a sound decision when the evidence is mixed and when important values are contested, effective argument must meet two crucial requirements. It must guarantee a decisive outcome despite indecisive data, and it must protect the highest of the competing values in the dispute.

The way of thinking that meets these two requirements also protects against making a serious error or disastrous decision—engineering, medical, environmental, moral, or otherwise. That mode of thinking comes from the discipline of formal argumentation and debate. It has been formalized and institutionalized in the system of legal argument and decision making of the systems of justice in the United Kingdom and the United States.

Underlying these justice systems, providing modes of reasoning through conflicting views and settling them, is the idea that *every conflict in views of evidence reflects also a deeper conflict in values.* Argument over conflicting interpretations of mixed evidence is always also simultaneously an argument, usually unspoken, over which of two conflicting values should on that particular occasion be honored over the other. In legal argument in criminal cases, for example, the focal issue is whether the accused is guilty of a crime, but underneath is the more basic issue of whether the accused individual's liberty will be given priority over the state's need for controlled social order.[173] The legal system establishes *in advance*, for all criminal trials, that the individual's liberty is of higher value than state's power to maintain its social order. It protects this prime value by requiring, before any charge or trial, that the accused be presumed innocent and that the state has the burden to prove the accused's guilt.

In contrast to such decisions about criminal guilt or innocence, the issues of everyday disputes vary in many dimensions (e.g., promising vs. worthless, strong vs. not strong enough, patriotic vs. unpatriotic). Everyday arguments may be framed to protect either of the conflicting values.

Formal argument always starts with a presumption, explicit or implicit, that defines which side of the argument wins if the evidence does not itself point indisputably to one of the two contested views. The *evidence* may be mixed and indecisive, but formal argument still allows a decisive outcome that both sides accept because both sides share a value, outlook, or preference that serves both as an initial assumption and as the default outcome if evidence is insufficient to prove the focal claim.

Assuming, as virtually all *Challenger* participants did, that the shuttle's status as "flight ready" had been already certified, and that such certification was absolute, not conditional, any new evidence suggesting a change in its readiness would have to show convincingly that it was not ready. The shuttle, in other words, was presumed ready (safe for flight), and would be confirmed as ready if the engineers were unable to prove their claim of danger. Such proof depended on convincing quantitative evidence of a failure of some critical part of the shuttle. If the engineers' argument for a launch delay turned out to lack convincing evidence, the situation of no proven danger would be accepted by both parties.

Eight Basic Components

Formal argument has eight basic components: case or issue, two sides of arguing the case — default or privileged side, and burdened side, standards to be met (including data relevance), validation of evidence and reasoning, the body of evidence, values or preferred conditions at issue, and regulating context. To illustrate, consider each component as it figured in the *Challenger* deliberations.

Case. Two cases were considered, the initial one by the Thiokol group alone and the one finally argued in the teleconference. Thiokol's initial case was flight safety, and it specified conditions to be met. Flight safety was the case to prove and could be proved, they believed, if and only if the boosters' O-rings were at or above 53 °F. Because the Thiokol group had no conscious grasp of argumentation, they were easily drawn into the very different case that Marshall participants believed needed proof. At Marshall, because their view was that flight safety had already been proven more than a week earlier by the FRRs, it was flight danger that had to be proven. Flight danger then became the case actually argued in the teleconference, a case that the Thiokol engineers were unprepared to argue.

When we are trying to solve a problem in real time, we can easily assume that if there is no good evidence of danger, we are safe. Circumstances might tolerate that logic, but it is false. The evidence may be insufficient to prove *both* danger and safety, and where the stakes are high, the absence of proof of safety becomes crucial. Safety and danger, therefore, are not opposite sides of the same coin. Instead, they are two different cases, and it makes a difference which one becomes the focus of argument—ie, which one becomes the case argued. When the Thiokol engineers shifted unwittingly from focusing on proving safety to Marshall's focus on danger, the engineers also shifted, unknowingly, from presuming danger to presuming safety. That was itself dangerous.

Default or Privileged Side. When danger became the case to be decided, all participants tacitly presumed that if danger could not be proven, the flight was safe. The engineers were seen at Marshall as challenging that presumption. Danger, then, was theirs to prove. Marshall was burdened to prove nothing, since their case, safety, was already presumed. They only needed to refute Thiokol's evidence. They had the much easier role in this argument, showing weaknesses, casting doubt.

Burdened Side. The burdened side of an argument has the hard task of bringing solid, convincing proof of its case. Because the engineers had no solid data showing how O-rings would perform below 53°, they could present no such proof. Having unwittingly accepted Marshall's presumption that the shuttle would fly safely unless proven dangerous, the engineers were unable to overturn that presumption, so the presumed safety of the shuttle remained as the argument's conclusion.

Standards. The quality of evidence and reasoning from it can dictate the quality of decision. To arrive at a decision that best captures the realities being debated, evidence and reasoning on both sides must meet high standards of relevance, adequacy, coherence, and completeness. Thiokol's inclusion of data was high, honoring completeness, but the quality of participants' sorting of relevant from irrelevant and misleading was low.[174] Mulloy, for example, continued to give strong weight in his assessment to Thiokol's incomplete experiment using argon gas (see Figure 2.5) even after Boisjoly had explicitly disqualified that experiment's evidence of safe sealing at 30 °F as invalid. Hardy's and Mulloy's failure to grasp the clear trend in Thompson's experimental data was another example of a low standard of reasoning.

Validation. The level of standards actually achieved in argument depends greatly on the quality of probing, questioning, and rebuttal brought to bear by both sides to validate each side's reasoning and evidence—including testing of each side's rebuttals. Mulloy probed and refuted Thiokol's evidence, but his own flaws in doing so were never questioned, much less refuted, in the teleconference. His flawed reasoning and conclusion were left unchallenged, allowing O-ring temperature to be dismissed as a causal factor in the minds of all but those from Thiokol already arguing for caution.

Evidence. Persuasive evidence requires that it be based on expert command of details, relevant to the intended argument, presented in a coherent sequence, with data adding up to a coherent meaning with no contradictions, confusion, or ambiguity. Also, when time for deliberation is short and accurate situation assessment is required, data trends and contrasts must be presented with graphic clarity. The engineers presented their data in tables but not in graphs.

The engineers' rushed assembly of evidence to support a launch delay fell short of meeting all but one of these five principle criteria of "solid evidence." The report of their evidence was a fairly complete survey of evidence both pro and con. From the point of view of substantiating Thiokol's case for delaying the launch, its evidence was both incomplete and too complete.[175] It presented no O-ring temperature data below 50 °F, while the key technical issue was O-ring performance at its launch temperature of 29 °F. Thiokol's evidence was also too complete, however, because it also included evidence that could be construed as contradictory.[176] The engineers' chart of argon data (Fig. 2.5) could be construed as contradicting their intended case. The sequence of charted data also began with a chart that *diverted* attention from the intended case, focusing principally on (impingement) erosion. Temperature effects on O-rings and blow-by, the principle dangers, were absent from or obscured in the first chart—and were not presented jointly in several charts. Altogether the jumbled data allowed participants to see what they wanted to see or feared to see – or to examine dispassionately. Thiokol's evidence did contain, however, sufficient data in the mix to support its argument for delay if the argument had been clearer, if the argument had been framed to require proof of safety, not danger, and if conditions had supported mindfulness (Langer, 1989,1997) of participants on both sides of the argument.

Values. Values constitute our mental-emotional commitments, operating in the background, that shape our choices. Values often conflict, however, and in the press of everyday activities, values can become buried, remote, forgotten for periods of time. The moment's choice made in immediate conditions can even violate one's deeper values. That violation can stay hidden for short or long periods. In the press of the teleconference argument, when tacit agreement emerged that committed all participants to testing for danger rather than for safety, their tacit choice of the case to argue also constituted a choice between competing values basic to the organizational mission. They tacitly chose production over quality, getting another flight launched over testing for and ensuring safe flight.

Regulating Resources. Two important resources that regulate argument are time and participants' working knowledge of argumentation. Rushed time degrades all dimensions of truth finding (Fitts, 1966; Hollnagel, 2009; Nickerson, 1998; Wickelgren, 1977). Regulation of the argument—framing the case (safety or danger), monitoring and maintaining relevance, securing opportunity for rebuttal, etc.— comes either from the participants themselves or from some independent authority. That independent regulation—the judge in a courtroom trial supported by opposing side's objections—helps ensure that argument stays on case, is informed by relevant expertise, and proceeds thoroughly and evenhandedly. The teleconference deliberations were rushed by the requirements of launch preparation. The argument's case, presumption, and burden were regulated only by the arguing parties themselves, who were naïve about the components, dynamics, and pitfalls of argumentation. These two circumstances militated against selecting safety instead of danger as the case to be argued.

A Reframed Argument

If participants on each side of the argument had been armed with explicit, practical knowledge of the dynamics of argumentation, could their argument have prevented this accident? Does formal argument itself actually have that kind of power to shape deliberations to favor one value over a competing value? Consider how the *Challenger* deliberations might have handled these elements differently, thereby making a different decision – *all with exactly the same data.*

By framing the *case* to be argued as safety rather than danger, and by *presuming* danger instead of safety, the entire collective effort would focus on proving flight *safety*. That would preserve the presumption, case, and burden of proof of Lucas's FRRs. That framing would protect the highest of the contending *values*, the safety of human life. The same mixed *evidence* would now be a barrier *against* proving flight safety, thus substantiating flight danger. The reframed argument would have shifted the *burden of proof* from the Thiokol engineers to Mulloy and Mason. Mulloy's evidence would be *refuted* by Boisjoly, Thompson, McDonald, and NASA's engineer, Luther Powers. A salient point of their rebuttal would be the complete absence of flight or experimental data bearing on O-ring performance in the range from 50 °F to 29 °F.

Mulloy's attempt to refute the *relevance* of temperature by his argument, which ignored Thompson's experimental data as well as the contrast between amounts of blow-by in the warm and cold flights, would also be countered by McDonald, Thompson, and Boisjoly, supported by Brian Russell. Russell had authored the memo to Marshall that reported Thompson's experimental results showing the close relationship between O-ring temperature and the O-ring's capacity to seal its simulated joint. The much more extensive blow-by in the cold flight than in the warm flight, coupled with Thompson's experiment linking speed of O-ring sealing to O-ring temperature, would establish O-ring temperature as at least a relevant factor.

Mulloy might counter by pointing out that Thompson's data were difficult to believe, that if Thompson's results of slow sealing by O-rings at 75 °F were to be believed, half of the shuttles already flown safely would have blown up. Thompson, Boisjoly, and others would point out that (1) the experiment did not simulate the joint under all hot-gas conditions of flight but only the capacity of O-rings at those three temperatures to recapture their normal dimensions to seal a joint's gap, (2) the relationship in Thompson's data in chart 4-2 (Figure 2.4) was very clear, showing that as O-rings got colder, they were slower to recapture their normal shape and had decreased capacity to seal the joint, and (3) the O-rings' sealing capacity the day of launch, with O-rings at 29 °F, would be much weaker than that for the coldest O-rings (50 °F) in Thompson's experiment (Figure 2.4) and would have an entirely unknown sealing capacity.

Mulloy might still attempt to show that Thiokol's chart 4-3, showing that "preliminary" results with argon gas actually sealed a simulated joint at 30 °F, was evidence that O-ring temperature did not degrade sealing capacity. That view would be rejected by Boisjoly, who would disavow, as he actually did disavow during the teleconference, the argon results as invalid and would point out that the experiment replacing the argon gas with the more appropriate Freon 14 had not yet been set up.

How would Mason then respond to this kind of interchange between his engineers and Mulloy? Seeing Mulloy's arguments directly refuted by the engineers *and* by McDonald, would he still call a caucus? As he pondered calling the caucus, he would now know that McDonald viewed O-ring temperature as a major factor in the O-ring's crucial sealing role and that McDonald actually opposed launch on those grounds.

If Mason did call the caucus, he would have to contend with Thompson and Boisjoly, who would cite McDonald's earlier arguments against launching. Mason would have to reverse the refutations his engineers had already expressed against Mulloy's views that O-ring temperature was irrelevant. In the end, Mason would again have to ask Lund, his vice president of engineering, to put on his management hat. Now, however, Lund would not be ambivalent. Having heard McDonald's on-site views and Brian Russell's comments validating the weakness of cold O-rings and supporting Lund's own earlier recommendation to delay the launch, Lund would respond that no proof of safe launch was possible, that launch should be postponed until O-ring temperatures had returned to their usual, safe range. Providing Mason stayed in the engineers' mode of arguing from evidence, he would acquiesce and recommend a delay. It is difficult to imagine him acting otherwise under those altered circumstances.

Kilminster's subsequent report of this caucus discussion would have an entirely different thrust, justifying a delay of launch on grounds of insufficient evidence to prove safe flight. It would assert that a launch could not be demonstrated safe from vulnerable O-rings performing under temperature conditions not yet tested as safe.

Argument from evidence that is framed to protect a basic value can indeed protect that value if the evidence is presented, examined, and tested by both contending parties through refutation and counter-refutation. [177]

Such argument is always subject, however, to the powerful intervention of a senior manager who decides to disregard the evidence, who allows only preferred evidence to be presented, or who misreads the evidence in favor of his or her preferred decision.[178] Such managers in high-technology safety-critical enterprises do so, however, at great risk to themselves, to others' lives, and to their enterprise. Holding to the discipline of formal argument—framed to protect the highest of the competing values—to resolve technical disagreements provides an important protection against such managerial risks.

The still hidden danger here lies in the fact that virtually all high-technology engineers and managers currently are ignorant of the benefits and demands of, and choices entailed in, formal argument. They are therefore unable to control its protections and pitfalls consciously in *Situations*.

CHAPTER 9

Safety: Vulnerabilities and Protections

This final chapter has four parts. First, it refocuses on the decision *Situation* that arises for any high-tech enterprise that enters new, unforgiving conditions whose properties are known very incompletely. The *Situation's* components are reviewed: the signal of a new threat to the whole enterprise, the inevitability of mixed evidence of safety and danger, the necessity of a quick yet accurate diagnosis, participants' accumulated confidence in the enterprise, and the undermining of decision participants' accurate assessment by restricted decision time. The chapter's second part points up the nature and distribution of five major threats to safety in the ways decision participants in these high-tech enterprises deliberate and decide between the safety and danger of the shifted conditions about which engineers, technicians, or electronic signals have raised warnings.

Part three steps back to consider the underlying source of the threats to effective decision making. It offers the integrating perspective of cultural anthropology to examine the organizational culture that seems to characterize many of these enterprises and is reflected in detail in this book's earlier narrative and analyses. The argument is made that if these enterprises seek more effectively to protect safety their prime task in addressing the whole landscape of these threats must be a reconstruction of their production-dominated culture. A metaphor drawn from our society's wider culture, the metaphor of health monitoring and fitness maintenance, is offered to support new systemic attention to the idea of regular monitoring and maintenance of these enterprises' organizational processes and capacities.

Part four outlines the kinds of new knowledge and expertise that are required for these enterprises to reconstruct their organizational culture sufficiently to protect against the five major threats to safely handling such signs of danger. The chapter concludes the book with wider implications.

A prime goal in this book is to bring into focus one especially dangerous kind of decision situation, the *Situation*. The complexities and time-urgency in this situation severely weaken participants' individual and collective abilities to assess new signs of threat to the enterprise. That sudden, time-squeezed reduction in participants' capacities for analysis and judgment occurs just when safe, accurate assessment of a signaled danger requires maximum perceptual acuity and intelligence.

The *Situation* crops up repeatedly in high technology operations. It arises whenever an enterprise moves into some new frontier: an unchartered environment or a new extreme of operating conditions, or uses complex technology that is new or newly modified. Under such conditions, the forces at work in the new equipment or environment are known only by extrapolating from past knowledge, knowledge gained from a familiar environment or with familiar technology or usage. Forces at work in the new environment, in the new technology, and in their interaction still remain to be discovered.

A *Situation* is actually triggered under these conditions when the warning sign of possible new danger is detected by a specialist (engineer, technician, front-line worker). The immediate danger of arriving at that critical diagnosis is in the decision situation itself, the *Situation of distinguishing* the safety or danger in the newly signaled threat. The number and complexity of the technical and mundane facts that must be considered in that *Situation* of diagnosis can be enormous (Chapters 5 and 7), yet a quick decision is required before the possible threat, if real, will exert its dangerous force.

The combination of complex technological issues, scanty and mixed information about the new threat, and speed required by the danger's imminence will militate against effective, error-free decision making in these enterprises – unless specific protective changes have been made in advance. The need for such changes is reflected in five major conditions that militate against a safety-protecting diagnosis and decision in any *Situation*.

First, the dominance of production thought and motivation over safety, examined in Chapter 6, is widely evident in the causes of these high-tech accidents. An organizational ethos dominated by production renders that ethos dangerous in explorations of these unforgiving, and safety-critical domains. That production ethos must be replaced by an organizational ethos in which safety is reflected in organizational structures, practices, and outlooks.

Safety awareness must be anchored, however, in a sharp awareness of *dangers*, dangers of three kinds. First are the dangers that lie submerged in the new domains of exploration. Second, the high technology demands of those new situations create dangers in the technology itself. Third, and possibly the most important but certainly the most thoroughly ignored in these enterprises, are the new human skills, new dimensions of awareness, and new norms required to guide and control the enterprise's high-tech exploration of the new domain. The cause of pushing these explorations too deep, too far, or too fast always comes down to human failure, failure to understand the fact that deeper, farther, or faster quickly intensifies three crucial factors simultaneously – the operation's unknowns, the operators' ignorance, and the requirement that decision making be swift, accurate, and safe.

The production impulse to go deeper, farther, or faster may initially signal strength, but that is only an early signal. Deeper, farther, and faster always bring actual weakness, vulnerability, ignorance, a time not for pride but for vigilance, for checking one's perceptions, for imagining glitches and their consequences – in short, deeper, farther, and faster brings an occasion to revisit the story and details of *disasters*. *They* can reveal the mistakes in human processes that we must learn from. How these enterprises presently fail to learn from them or succeed in learning from them is a crucial and still unanswered question. *That* they fail in learning the demands and strategies of safety is evident from the frequency of near misses and disaster in these enterprises.[179]

The brute fact that must be underscored here is that to move deeper, farther, or faster reflects production motivation only. Unmitigated, production in these enterprises becomes the enemy of safety.

The second dangerous condition is the gap between those close to the daily technical information about operations and those more distant. Specifically, deciding technical issues is dangerous when managers are responsible for deciding whether complex technical information does or does not require a halt in operations to avert the danger being signaled while, in contrast, the engineers most familiar with the technical information and most expert in assessing their physical dynamics have no authority to decide the danger's threat or action implications. That disjunctive distribution of authority also prohibits those technical experts from inquiring into or evaluating managers' technical understandings before the managers decide the safety-danger issue (Chapters 1, 5, and 6).[180]

That disconnection between expertise and decision making becomes most dangerous in *Situations*. Under those conditions managers' images of technical dynamics, suddenly rendered out of date and discordant by the new technical realities being signaled, easily override the technical readings and interpretations by the engineers most expert. Managers' mental models of the dynamics at issue, having been reinforced repeatedly in normal times, remain in force – unless striking evidence of their incorrectness is quickly presented, easily grasped, and overwhelming.

Organizational change in high-tech enterprises must arrange for role changes in managers and technical specialists that support managerial openness to inquiry by specialists, questioning and verifying the managers' comprehension of the relevant engineering charts, data, and interpretation. More generally, changes must be made to ensure that the working relations between specialists and managers move away from a definition of management as having the most authoritative technical knowledge in any dispute and, instead, defines managers as partners with specialists, partners in collaboration and mutual exchange and authority based not on position but on technical expertise.

Third, all members of high-tech enterprises, particularly managers who are likely to be involved in detecting or interpreting new technical signs of possible danger, will suffer the impact of any *Situation's* distinctive dumbing-down effects on their deliberation (Chapter 7), and therefore will be unaware of the need in that *Situation* for unusual caution and verification of technical interpretations, particularly the interpretations made by those empowered to decide between differing interpretations.

A fourth dangerous vulnerability relates to pitfalls in thinking about how evidence does or does not lead to valid conclusions (Chapter 8). Disciplined forms and processes of thought which protect against the pitfalls are not learned merely by arguing about everyday evidence as proving or disproving a conclusion. The forms and processes that protect against error, protect deep social values, and still guarantee clear conclusions and paths of action have been developed through centuries of legal reasoning and formal debate. They have emerged from the necessity of deciding on an objectively accurate picture of events where the decision has grave consequences for both the individual and society. These *consequential* thought forms and processes are learned through education and disciplined practice. High-tech decision makers, along with most managers and engineers generally, have not had the benefit of that kind of education or disciplined practice. Nor, indeed, has research or theory in cognitive or social psychology about attitude change, persuasion, or logical and illogical thought investigated how, for example, variations in presumption, burden of proof, and framing of case affect the outcomes of argument when outcomes carry varying degrees of value. This vulnerability in how high-tech decision makers face highly consequential decisions about complicated evidence can be mitigated by training and practice. The evidence from disasters, especially clear in the *Challenger* and *Columbia* cases (Lighthall, 2014a), offers curricular material for such education. Arranging for practice in that kind of deliberation and decision making has challenges of its own.

This absence of knowledge of the components and dynamics of evidence-based reasoning is but one case, though an important one, of a wider void, the absence in these organizations of a working knowledge of the human sciences generally. Two examples of the void were evident first, by Marshall managers' misinterpretations of the simple, basic trend in Figure 2.4 showing the clear correlation of O-ring temperature with time taken to seal its simulated joint and second, when the shuttle was officially designated "operational", revealing a distinctly premature confidence at the *organizational* level (a dramatic case of the widely researched psychological phenomenon known as "confirmation bias," see especially Nickerson, 1998).

A few examples at the level of individual cognition will illustrate the gap between knowledge available outside these enterprises and knowledge deployed inside them.

Managers and engineers in these enterprises often work under time pressure. At the same time they must also make accurate assessments of complicated situations. However, they are usually unaware of the dangers that speed brings to accuracy, a connection of opposing conditions long known in educational and cognitive psychology as the "speed-accuracy tradeoff" (Fitts, 1966; Wickelgren, 1977). More speed in performance means less accuracy, more errors. Managers and engineers engage in arguments intended to persuade but rarely have any knowledge of the strategic choices offered in power-dependence relations (Emerson, 1962, 1972) or by differentiated bases of power (French and Raven, 1959; Koslowsky, Schwarzwald, and Ashuri, 2001), not to speak of the widespread ignorance of the power and pitfalls of argumentation itself (Chapter 8). Managers in these enterprises make judgements about evidence that comes across their desks but are unaware of primacy and recency effects (Howard & Kahana,1999), or of the "availability heuristic" (Kahneman & Tversky (1974). Being unaware of these thought-shaping tendencies, participants cannot deploy cautionary and corrective thinking. Perhaps the most crucial failure to transfer external knowledge to high-tech participants inside these enterprises is evident in managers' confirmation bias (Wason, 1960; Nickerson, 1998), a bias known among banking regulators as "disaster myopia" (Guttentag & Herring, 1986; Haldane, 2009). An extended period of time since participants witnessed or experienced an emergency or disaster in their enterprise develops in participants both a strong expectation that operations are successful and a bias against expecting or being sensitive to signs of serious error or disaster.

These few examples of high-tech participants' knowledge gaps merely illustrate. They represent in a very small way the immense accumulation of tools of eye-opening, highly practical, and clarifying thought available from the fields of knowledge outside these enterprises that are needed inside them. Required, then, is correction of this vacuum of knowledge, specifically, creation of a mechanism which over time can bring this outside knowledge inside.[181] I will presently outline the many additional *kinds* of knowledge, attention, and skill required to equip participants in these enterprises with the intellectual tools and perceptual sensitivities necessary to handle the joint demands of production and safety. First, however, we have to stand back and grasp what all these vulnerabilities signal together.

We see human failings at all levels of organizational functioning in handling the normal vicissitudes of NASA's high-tech enterprise and, by extension, in the functioning of other boundary-pushing enterprises:

- individual psychological level – managers' (at Marshall) misinterpreting charted data, focusing on equal *presence* of blow-by only while excluding contrasting *amounts* of blow-by; the decision by a (Marshall) manager to approve the substitution of a defective part for an approved part when the defective part had been warned about earlier
- interpersonal level – subordinates' fear of being publicly humiliated by a powerful supervising manager (the "long pole," being "shot down in flames")
- group level – an engineer communicating to his supervisor his complete agreement with a warning from other, informed engineers, recommending that ongoing production be postponed, and the supervisor's decision not to communicate that agreement to higher authorities; a manager in a different organization telling his engineer that he, the manager, could not pass to higher authorities the engineer's warning that production should cease until demonstrable weaknesses in the product be corrected
- inter-group level — engineers' misconstrual of the degree to which managers in another organization empowered to decided an issue would likely accede to, or oppose a data-supported request for a delay in production
- agency level – an agency's policy (the "Delta" practice at Marshall) whereby all issues of product quality ("flight readiness") that were settled in formal reviews (FRRs) became settled unconditionally rather than settled only conditional upon later review of events that could threaten the product's safety
- inter-agency level – (Marshall) managers' obedience to a higher manager's (Lucas's) requirement that all issues be managed "in house," not referred upward to higher authority (Johnson Space Center); a letter from a higher authority (Aldrich) at a supervising agency (Johnson) rebuking managers in a subordinate agency (Marshall) for ignoring earlier warnings against using a faulty part

that someone at that subordinate agency had approved for use, resulting in a production delay

- organizational level – an organization-wide (NASA's) assumption that its certification (Level I) of a space vehicle as "flight ready" was absolute, not conditional on events occurring after certification, when successful flight might actually depend on events arising after such certification; an organization's (NASA's) declaration after only initial trials (the shuttle's first four flights) that the vehicle was no longer experimental but was now "operational"
- inter-organization level – one collaborating organization's (NASA's) long delay in signing its contract with a partner organization (Thiokol) for additional parts that the partner ordinarily supplied (boosters), parts the partner could not manufacture without that signed contract; an organization's (NASA's) internal market relationship with a parent organization (Congress), leading to overpromises from the organization to its parent organization and to underfunding of the subordinate organization's project by its parent organization; an organization's (NASA's) achieved rate of production as contrasted with the rate it had promised to its parent organization (Congress)

When we examine such an array of weaknesses at levels throughout the organizational collaboration, we want to ask, "What is going on here?" It leads us to consider some set of superordinate or underlying conditions that would cause all of these weaknesses. True, it might be that each of them has its own separate cause, but at the very least the whole array suggests the more pointed question, "How did such a number and distribution of weaknesses arise with no recorded notice taken of them?" The evidence reviewed earlier does show that some of these weaknesses were noticed and that adjustments were made. For example, the shortage of funds and the excessive flight rate were noticed and responded to by cannibalizing parts from future flights to prepare the next flight. Some adjustments were made, yes; but they did not attend to the question, "How come?" Had the organization had the capacity to pursue that question – a curious manager, a group tasked with looking into individual, social, and organizational causes of each launch delay, an office of organizational development — it is likely that these undetected weaknesses would have been mitigated, substantial loss of work and scarce money would have been prevented, and the lives of seven astronauts would have been saved. But these weaknesses remained hidden. They were hidden not out there in space, not in the technology itself, but hidden in the human system.[182] And that brings us to the fifth major vulnerability.

Dramatically missing in this story of human failures is any sign in these enterprises of the impetus that propels all human research: a spirit of investigation, of looking into interpretations and decisions to discover how participants craft them, putting a microscope on human errors to discover their causal networks. NASA did try to *correct* missteps, after the fact. But there is no evidence not only of attempts to discover how and why errors were made through misperception or miscommunication, for example, but also no evidence of any organized capability or leader motivation to do so.[183] Corrective discourse was distinctly engineering, not social or psychological, much less cultural, and certainly not the discourse of investigating human processes.

The conclusion I am led to about this landscape of human strengths and weaknesses adds up to the pervasive influence of a certain kind of organizational culture. Its salient practices, its norms (and norm subverting forces), its meaning systems, and its discourse all spell out a dominant thrust of tightly scheduled production. It is a peculiar kind of production impulse, however. It is one whose gaze is on where it is going but not on where or how it is stepping, attuned to getting it done, however it is to be done, on time. And beneath that time constraint lay a prior commitment to the funding body, Congress, which was sold a program that promised too much but once sold became believed.

The major thrust of action indicated by this *Challenger* story and by the story of other high-tech disasters is that these enterprises must create a safety-protecting organizational *culture*. It must be a culture, however, whose members' abilities to manage and protect safety are informed by knowledge about the full range of human processes, including knowledge and skill in organizational self-examination. To do that, however, will require developing some *organizational structures specifically tasked* to do so, tasked with incorporating into the organization the range of knowledge and skill that has been so far glaringly absent.

The culture required is one that creates and sustains an organization that goes beyond doing. It continually learns from doing, from doing well and doing poorly. It is a *self-reflective, self-monitoring, self-studying* organization as well as a productive organization. That needed range of knowledge and skill, including knowledge about culture itself and about planned change, I will presently address. First, however, we need a metaphor that will capture the principal character of the kind of new culture required to protect safety.

A Metaphor: Monitoring Wellness

Production now dominates most high-tech organizational cultures. However, along with production there exists a minor theme of reviewing causes, of examining disasters, of learning from extreme failures. Just as in the wider culture we do post-mortems of people who have died from mysterious circumstances, so at the organizational level we also do post-accident analyses of every airline crash, and every high-tech disaster. And we examine causes of economic crashes. We can do these post-mortems better, with more depth and scope, but we do regularly analyze them for causes.

Our national culture, however, has moved beyond analyzing extreme failures that cause loss of life. It now also gives widespread attention to individual *health*. Citizens are asked by health organizations to stop smoking, drink alcohol only with moderation, monitor blood pressure, monitor cholesterol levels, have a medical check-up annually or every six months, exercise for physical fitness, follow a healthy diet, protect themselves from the sun, and with advancing age, take cardiac stress tests to examine the heart for pre-morbid signs of weakness or incipient failure. Toward individual citizens, then, our culture has begun to acquire a widespread, institutionalized attitude and norm of attending regularly to our *wellness*. Social-cultural resources have been allocated for extensive research on individuals' *healthy functioning*. We have developed national, state, and local departments of public health to monitor deviations from healthy environments in most places of public gatherings.

We now must take the next step. *We must create organizational cultures that attend to, regularly test for, and promote chronic organizational health and wellness.* Such new organizational cultures would develop analogues to regular check-ups that look for premorbid signs (e.g., near misses), regular programs of exercise with appropriate simulation "drills," and periodic stress tests monitored both for unforeseen dimensions of robust effectiveness and for premorbid signs of failure – effective or failed attention, deliberation, diagnosis, inference, situation assessment, reading or interpreting of data, deployment or bases of power, or communication. In short, we need first, a metaphor that captures, and a discourse that promotes organizational wellness. Second, we need a commitment to organizational wellness that allocates important resources to support regular organizational monitoring, regular organizational exercises, and regular infusion into the organization of new ideas and methods from a variety of outside sources.

To promote such an organizational culture of wellness attuned to safety, protections of at least five kinds are needed.

Each kind requires the recruitment into these organizations of special *new domains of knowledge and expertise*. An organizational culture that promotes *healthy* functioning is one that supports regular importation of knowledge about patterns of effective and ineffective problem sensing, problem communication, and problem solving, to name one dimension of human functioning.

Five Kinds of Protection

1. Protection against an *organizational ethos* that honors production over safety
2. Protection against the dysfunctional asymmetry in technical knowledge and decision-making authority between engineers and managers, an asymmetry reflected in engineers' reluctance to elicit and correct managers' flawed interpretations of engineering data
3. Protection against the *Situation's* dumbing-down of participants' collective analytic powers, deliberation, and communication
4. Protection against technical, evidence-based disputes whose participants are naïve about the forms and dynamics of evidence-based argument and who are uninformed about the power of presumptions and burden of proof to settle disputes when evidence is mixed
5. Protection against the organization's chronic incapacity to identify, learn from, and correct blatant or creeping flaws in its *human* processes—in management processes, in communication in and between its groups and upward and downward across levels of authority, in its cognitive biases, its deliberation and decision making, and its maladaptive use of different bases of power and influence.

Consider each of these five in turn, and examples of the kinds of published expertise already available to begin to address them.

First, the term "safety culture" appears widely in reviews of high-tech disasters, but cultural anthropologists, the professionals specifically educated and experienced in exploring, analyzing, and conceptualizing cultures appear nowhere among those who create, participate in, or investigate high-tech enterprises or disasters. The discipline of cultural anthropology has produced a rich body of practical and theoretical work that is yet to inform most high-tech enterprises—or investigations of their failures. Many high-tech managers and analysts speak of "culture," but none are sufficiently informed to think anthropologically about, for example, the organizational discourse in use (e.g., "flight-readiness review"), the symbols that capture core themes of everyday work (e.g., long pole), the routines and norms that develop, what gets repeated and what gets ignored in daily work, the organization's repeated practices (e.g., Delta), and the organization's deep sacreds (e.g., work schedule). Also, leadership styles reflect a culture's fundamental taken-for-granted values— values that dictate choices between the wanted and the unwanted. I have yet to see an anthropologically informed article that deals with the *creation or analysis* of an organizational culture that produced a disaster or near miss. Such an article would draw upon an extended list of research in cultural anthropology.[184]

As to the second protection required, a more adaptive organizational management of the emergence of a new risk has received enough scholarly attention to produce its own term, "resilience" (see, for example, Woods, 2006) and characterizations of the "resilient organization." Hollnagel (2013a, 2013b), theorizing in the context of air traffic control, offers a new perspective in his draft essay contrasting "Two Safeties." [185] All efforts to infuse resilience into organizational functioning will also depend, however, on creating an organizational culture (the fifth protection) that will *sustain safety-promoting* resilience.[186]

The third needed protection is to mitigate the dysfunctional contradiction between, on one hand, managers' responsibility to decide all organizational disputes, including technical disputes, and on the other hand, the managers' necessarily incomplete, generalized, and only slowly updated knowledge of the technical dynamics being disputed. This contradiction was expressed in the *Challenger* case when Thiokol's Vice President Mason and NASA's Mulloy favored their own (flawed) views of the boosters' joint dynamics over the views of the two most expert engineers.[187] I know of no study that focuses specifically on this contradiction, but the insights and sensitivities required to mitigate it are exhibited in several studies, notably those focused on the bases of social power and power-dependence relations.[188]

Protection against the *Situation's* time pressured weakening of effective analysis and deliberation—reducing participants' grasp of possible dangers, combined with their lack of necessary skills and concepts from the human sciences—is addressed by a volume of research on cognition and judgment under stress, on the effects of restricted time on accuracy of perception (the "speed-accuracy tradeoff"), and on the complexities of "situation" and "situation awareness."[189]

The concepts and processes entailed in the fourth protection, against unsuspected pitfalls of argument about evidence, have been treated by scholars in the law, argumentation and debate, and the social sciences. Understanding evidence-based argument as a form of assessing and reasoning about realities, and especially as a means of resolving a conflict about evidence, is crucial if technical disputes about safety and danger have a chance to protect safety *and* uninterrupted production.[190]

Finally, the fifth protection, against the organizations' chronic incapacity to analyze its own processes, is addressed by an extensive body of knowledge and experience — relating to individuals', groups', and organizations' capacities for monitoring, analyzing, and correcting *their own* collective maladaptive tendencies and practices. Safety and effectiveness are not sufficiently protected by studies like the present one, done by an academic *outside* of a formal organization about processes *inside* a complex organization. Inside learning must also go on. It proceeds by insiders, with the assistance of experienced professionals, studying their own organizational practices and processes. The extensive "outside" body of more generalized knowledge must become complemented by each high-tech organization's more grounded *local* knowledge of its own strengths, weaknesses, and self-correcting powers of its processes.[191]

These five kinds of protection imply for these high-tech enterprises, then, the infusion into their operation of a wide range of new knowledge and skills about *human* functioning. The more than 100 studies that I have suggested in this chapter's endnotes to each of these five kinds of protection give a tangible picture of the dangerous knowledge void that must be filled. The concepts, distinctions, and insights from these varied intellectual domains can strengthen the human functioning shown in the *Challenger* disaster to be so weak.[192]

Even more important, however, these new analytical resources will help inform and create a self-sustaining culture whose processes help prepare participants at all levels to meet the *human* demands of high-technology operations in unforgiving environments.

Reading case histories such as this one can help provide some terms of discourse required to grasp the technological and human complexities of a decision emergency. Reading about these distant events, however, will do little to reorient future action. Reading and seminars are necessary, but direct experience is also required—participation by managers and technicians *in* these high-tech projects *first*, in simulations of conflicting technical assessments under relaxed and time-pressured conditions in which they enact, refine, and practice their respective organizational roles and commitments as managers and technicians, and *second*, as participants in post-simulation *reviews* in which, together, they analyze where their deliberative process was effective and where ineffective in reaching for or actually reaching an objectively correct assessment of a newly discovered anomaly or danger.[193]

This kind of training in safely confronting something new and potentially dangerous is not accomplished in one day's or one weekend's intensive training. These complexities are learned over time. To be effective, furthermore, they have to be learned by the teams of those who normally become involved in an organization's critical online technical assessments and decisions.[194] The training exercises by the officers and crew of nuclear submarines, by the managers and technicians in nuclear power plants, and by surgical teams (see, for example, Edmonson, Bohmer, & Pisano, 2001) provide examples of preparation for unknowns in high-stakes, time-pressured situations,[195] yet even those simulations would require greater complexity to reflect the kind of *Situation* revealed in the *Challenger* decision, with, for example its market forces, its two phases of "readiness," its mixed data, and its conflict between frontline engineers and the managers empowered to decide.

Finally, the Achilles' heel in the high-technological exploration and exploitation of these uncharted domains is not present knowledge or skill in human functioning, as severe as that vacuum is. Models for updating participants' knowledge and skills are available.[196] The Achilles' heel lies, rather, in the willingness of those who initiate and support these enterprises — governments and corporations — to provide not only sufficient resources for participants to do the technical work and make the technical assessments but also resources sufficient to support *ongoing study by enterprise participants themselves* of the enterprise's assessment and decision processes, supporting participants to learn from their doing. Doing the task is a short-term perspective only. Accomplishing this frontier-exploring type of high-tech task focuses on a *doing* that becomes blind to the by now well demonstrated fact that beyond the dangers discovered and managed in early successes of these high-technological programs, further exploration still holds unknown dangers, dangers requiring an attentive, mindful, self-studying search for warning signs.

Still unrecognized unknowns also lie in the sphere of how we actually apply and fail to apply our individual and collective intelligence to the technical tasks of these enterprises and how we actually apply and fail to apply our social, organizational, and economic resources to the perceptual and deliberative processes leading to decisions in these enterprises. Reflexive study of their own processes and planned change by high-tech organizations is still largely uncharted territory. Our society seems to foster this vacuum, being so often focused on doing to the exclusion of examining and understanding the processes of the doing. Organizational self-exploration holds both serious, obdurate challenges and new horizons of insight and achievement.

Acknowledgments

I first must gratefully acknowledge the authors of the most important official source: the commissioners and staff of the five-volume *Report* of the Presidential Commission on the Space Shuttle *Challenger* Accident. I especially commend the decision of Chairman William P. Rogers to conduct an open inquiry and to include all of the Commission's extensive interviews in the public record, open to researchers. Richard H. Gaskins' penetrating analysis, *Burdens of Proof in Modern Discourse*, provided necessary insights into the prelaunch deliberations. Diane Vaughan's analysis, *The* Challenger *Launch Decision*, expanded the *organizational* analysis of high-tech accidents and provided important testimony from teleconference participants.

I want to thank the staff of the National Archives for their help in locating and reproducing the Presidential Commission's interviews of all those who participated in the key prelaunch teleconference. Historians Mike Wright and Bob Jacques also gave generously of their time and gave me access to their rich store of documents and internal memoranda from the Marshall Space Flight Center's archives.

With deep gratitude, I thank two intellectual antagonists in this story, Larry Mulloy and Allan McDonald, both for their generous time and openness in my lengthy recorded interviews of them and for their continued willingness over the years to respond to questions by phone and e-mail correcting my errors. Any errors remaining in my analysis exist despite their best and continued efforts. Allan also agreed to read and comment in detail on an earlier draft, going the extra mile, as is his nature. Roger Launius gave generously of his time from his research and administrative duties at the National Air and Space Museum to provide much-needed focus to the present manuscript after reading a much longer one, and to suggest other readers. Special thanks to Steve Jennings for his close, caring, and articulate editing of the manuscript. I am grateful also to my colleague and friend Dan C. Lortie for his reading of an earlier version.

Thanks also to Roger Boisjoly (1938–2012) for lengthy letters early on and for setting me straight on several matters, and to several teleconference participants for their illuminating interviews: Thiokol's Arnie Thompson and Jerry Burn; NASA's James D. Smith, who also offered subsequent clarifications; and NASA's Luther Ben Powers. For reading early or recent versions of the manuscript, I owe a great debt to Larry Elkins, Sig Mejdal, David Thelen, Stephen Waring, and Bill Wimsatt. Thanks also for help from Joel Maw, Mark Wiley, Moe Tawil, who shared his engineering and managerial experiences from the Apollo program, and Alex Lubertozzi. I am grateful for special encouragement over the years from Walter Feinberg and also from friends in the Harbert men's discussion group and the Park Forest Martini Club. Constance Goldberg has given me a special kind of insight and encouragement that I want to acknowledge with thanks.

I am especially grateful to the following participants in the *Challenger* decision for permission to quote from my recorded interviews of them: Allan McDonald, Larry Mulloy, and James D. Smith. I received three small grants from the Division of Social Sciences at the University of Chicago. I want to give very special thanks also to Megan Weddle, Ray Robinson, Adrienne Miller, and Amber Ortner for shepherding this project, and the editing troops for their close reading and critical improvements of the manuscript.

My last word, of loving gratitude, is to my wife, Maureen Sylvia Lighthall, for her deep and abiding love and for her encouragement, her critical help, her timely, freeing suggestions, and her struggles to improve my writing and to get this story out.

Appendix

The following charts were presented by Thiokol engineers in the January 27, 1986, teleconference and are explained further in Chapter 2. Their information was either better summarized in the text or irrelevant to the launch decision.

PRIMARY CONCERNS -

o FIELD JOINT - HIGHEST CONCERN

   o EROSION PENETRATION OF PRIMARY SEAL REQUIRES RELIABLE SECONDARY SEAL
      FOR PRESSURE INTEGRITY
      o IGNITION TRANSIENT - (0-600 MS)
         o (0-170 MS) HIGH PROBABILITY OF RELIABLE SECONDARY SEAL
         o (170-330 MS) REDUCED PROBABILITY OF RELIABLE SECONDARY SEAL
         o (330-600 MS) HIGH PROBABILITY OF NO SECONDARY SEAL CAPABILITY

   o STEADY STATE - (600 MS - 2 MINUTES)
      o IF EROSION PENETRATES PRIMARY O-RING SEAL - HIGH PROBABILITY OF
         NO SECONDARY SEAL CAPABILITY
         o BENCH TESTING SHOWED O-RING NOT CAPABLE OF MAINTAINING CONTACT
            WITH METAL PARTS GAP OPENING RATE TO MEOP
         o BENCH TESTING SHOWED CAPABILITY TO MAINTAIN O-RING CONTACT DURING
            INITIAL PHASE (0-170 MS) OF TRANSIENT

NO NEW DATA RELATIVE TO 51-L

2-1

Appendix Figure A 1. Thiokol's chart 2-1, familiar to participants from past FRRs, reminded them of the importance of timing and of a quick seal of the field joint by the Primary O-ring. It warns that the Secondary O-ring would provide a back-up seal reliably only in the first 170 thousandths of a second after ignition – only, that is, in the first phase of the ignition transient, but not in a later phase.

O-RING (VITON) SHORE HARDNESS VERSUS TEMPERATURE

°F	SHORE HARDNESS
70°	77
60°	81
50°	84
40°	88
30°	92
20°	94
10°	96

4-1

Appendix Figure A 2. Thiokol's chart 4-1 shows a close relationship of O-ring temperature to O-ring hardness, a part of Thiokol's warning about the relevance of temperature to O-ring sealing: hard O-rings seal slower than normal, resilient O-rings.

COMPRESSION SET (%)

TIME (HRS)	O-RING DIA (IN)		
	.139 ∅	.275 ∅	.295 ∅
1000	8.6	9.6	9.75
500	8.8	10.3	10.52
168	11.8	13.7	13.98
70	12.8	12.7	12.69

$$c = \frac{t_o - t_i}{t_o - t_s} \times 100$$

4-4

Appendix Figure A 3. Thiokol's chart 4-4, shows the per cent of compression of O-rings at room temperature that remains when compression is released – information related to O-rings at normal flight temperatures but unrelated to the engineers' argument about the danger of *cold* O-rings. Note: the order of the figures in the left-hand column, the number of hours of compression, is reversed.

End Notes

1. Shuttle *Enterprise*, the first orbiter built, was moved from the Smithsonian's National Air and Space Museum at the Steven F. Udvar-Hazy Center in Virginia to the Intrepid Sea, Air & Space Museum in New York. The Udvar-Hazy Center became the new home for shuttle *Discovery*, which retired after completing its 39th mission in March 2012. Shuttle *Endeavour* went to the California Science Center in Los Angeles. *Atlantis* is displayed at the Kennedy Space Center Visitor Complex in Florida.
2. Presidential Commission on the Space Shuttle Challenger Accident. 1986. *Report*, Volumes I–V, Washington, DC: United States Government Printing Office.
3. Ibid, vol. I.
4. Ibid, vol. II, Appendix L, L37–L49.
5. When I refer to "engineers" from this point on I mean to include all those who are technically trained to monitor and report on an enterprise's technological dynamic states and changes – engineers, technicians, technical operators, etc.
6. For two accounts of front-line technical experts warning of the disaster, see Jaffe (2012) and McCuistion (2012). See also National Commission on the Causes of the Financial and Economic Crisis in the United States (2011), especially Part One, "Crisis on the Horizon." The BP *Deepwater Horizon* Oil Spill in the Gulf of Mexico in contrast was an exemplar of a warning signaled by display instruments whose information was misinterpreted. See the report, National Commission on the BP *Deepwater Horizon* Oil Spill and Offshore Drilling (2011).
7. See my critique of Vaughan's analysis of the disaster at www.high-techdangers.com .
8. My search of primary documents at both the National Archives and the History Department at Marshall Space

Flight Center includes not only copies of the Commission's interviews with every teleconference participant but also an important Thiokol-NASA contract document as well as inter-center reports calling for and describing corrective steps taken in the wake of an extended and "unnecessary" launch delay of the flight immediately preceding *Challenger*, flight 61C. I also have interviewed key engineers and managers at both Marshall and Thiokol about their participation in the decision and about the boosters' technical dynamics—including phone conversations, correspondence, and recorded sessions at the home or office of both Larry Mulloy and Allan McDonald over many years (10 years with Mulloy, 22 years with McDonald). My own lack of engineering education has been mitigated by corrective engineering guidance by key participants at both Marshall and Thiokol (again, including both Mulloy and McDonald). My account of the dynamics that caused the O-rings' failure to seal the booster's joint is also the only account that is informed by two post-accident investigations reported in Appendix L of Volume II of the Presidential Commission *Report* (see note 4). The results of both investigations, carried out by different sets of engineers independently, agree in their findings—and validate the prelaunch warnings by Thiokol's Roger Boisjoly and Arnold Thompson—that O-ring temperature, not O-ring erosion, caused the booster's joint to remain unsealed for the booster's hot (5700 °F) gases to escape and erode or melt everything in their path.

9. Leaning heavily on testimony from Mulloy and others at the Marshall Space Flight Center, Vaughan (1996, 415) concluded that the *Challenger* disaster was inevitable.

10. "Situation" as I use the generic (nonitalicized) term has three major elements in its simplest form. A tree limb that comes loose and falls with no import to anyone or to any sensing-evaluating agent constitutes not a situation but a *condition*—ie, a limb lying on the ground. It becomes an element in a

situation only at the time it becomes situated importantly—eg, as threat or opportunity—in relation to some sensing-evaluating agent. "Situation" (nonitalicized), then, is defined by a (temporal and spatial) relation joining three elements: a *condition*, a *sensing-evaluating agent*, and a relation between them having some past, present, or future positive or negative *felt import* to the agent. A situation then, distinct from a condition, always entails some agent's evaluative response to a subjectively construed condition. A situation can be objective, subjective, or simultaneously objective and subjective ("accurate" situation awareness in Endsley, 1995a, 1995b, Endsley and Garland, 2000).

11. Where a manager acts alone to decide the issue quickly, he or she maximizes speed over accuracy. By relying on the manager's own powers of perception, analysis, and experience, he or she deploys competencies that, first, cannot match the combined intellectual powers and experience of subordinates and the technical specialists who issue the warning and, second, reflect a manager's occupational bent toward completing production tasks in the face of difficulties.

12. Important concepts are situation assessments and situation awareness (Endsley, 1995a, 1995b, 1997, 1999; Endsley & Garland, 2000); recognition-primed decision making (Klein, 1993, 1997; Lipshitz & Shaul, 1997; Orasanu & Connolly, 1993); conflict management in high-tech decision making (Buljan & Shapira, 2005); functional and dysfunctional leadership styles (Bass, 1998); and "culture" (Abu-Lughod, 1986, 1991; Boddy, 1989; Marcus & Fischer, 1999; Ortlieb, 2010; Shweder, 1991).

13. See Marais, Dulac, & Leveson (2004) for a thoughtful assessment of the strengths and weaknesses of the two most prominent approaches to safety and danger in high-technology enterprises: Normal Accident Theory (NAT; Perrow, 1984; Sagan, 1993) and high-reliability organizations (HRO; La Porte, 1996). Marais and her colleagues find

both NAT and HRO insufficient accounts of the possibilities and requirements for high-tech safety. They present a "system approach to safety in complex systems."

14. Time given is Eastern Standard Time throughout even though key participants were located in Utah's Mountain Time zone. The following global synopsis of events is based on the *Report* of the Presidential Commission on the Space Shuttle *Challenger* Accident, Volume I, June 6, 1986. Washington, DC, hereafter referenced as PC *Report*.

15. See Seife (2003) for a summary analysis of risk assessment in risky settings—in the *Challenger* era and also regarding the *Columbia* accident. See also Paté-Cornell (1990) for more extended analysis of risk assessment in relation to organizational functioning. All technical risk assessments, however, no matter how sophisticated, become filtered through decision-making processes whose vicissitudes under rare (but inevitable) *Situations* (see text below) defy precise quantification.

16. Author's photograph of 1/100 scale model of Space Shuttle *Atlantis* (Toys and Models Corporation). Background is *Out There*, acrylic on canvas, 24" x 36", from the space series by Maureen Sylvia Lighthall (www.maureensylvialighthall.com).

17. Called a field joint because these joints were created only when the booster segments were assembled vertically in the "field," in the giant Vehicle Assembly Building at Kennedy Space Center in Florida.

18. One source of air, the leak test, forced air through the leak test port of each joint (see Figure 1.3) into the space between the primary and secondary O-rings. This would force the *primary* O-ring into its upstream gap, closest to the booster's fuel but away from the downstream gap that the O-ring was designed to seal. That was the bad news. The good news was that forced air from the leak test would also push the *secondary* O-ring *downstream*, closer into the gap it was designed to seal.

Before the forced air from the leak test could push the primary O-ring into its upstream gap, however, some air could pass around the primary, beyond the primary, and *into* the protective putty on the other side, or even pass all the way *through* the putty, creating a gas path (see Figure 1.3) through which hot gas from the ignited boosters could later surge back through and actually reach the O-ring itself.

19. Before booster ignition, the gap in these field joints averaged .004 inch and could vary from less than .002 inch to .020 inch (PC *Report*, vol. I, p. 61).

20. The size of the O-rings shown in Figures 1.4A and 1.4B is also exaggerated. They are too large in comparison to their grooves. A more accurate picture of normal O-ring size in relation to O-ring groove is given in Figure 1.3, but Figure 1.4B does illustrate the fundamental fact that by the end of the .6-second period of rising gas pressure, the field joint opened up.

21. See the discussion and diagrams of the field joint's gap opening in PC *Report*, vol. I, p. 60.

22. The most severe blow-by was in the center field joint of the right-hand booster, while the joint with the lesser blow-by was the left-hand booster's forward field joint.

23. The shuttle hardware designated 51E was shifted out of sequence. The shuttle flown immediately after 51C was 51D.

24. See Vaughan (1996, p. 178), where Vaughan cites pages in the Commission's interview of Allan McDonald as the source of this phrase. I can find no evidence of this phrase on the pages cited or elsewhere in McDonald's Commission interview. The phrase is entirely consistent, however, with the meaning of language about temperature affecting 51C that must have been included in the review of 51C's anomalies, language Mulloy objected to as needing quantitative substantiation for temperature to be accepted as a causative factor.

25. The issue of *causes* for the unique pattern and severity of 51C's anomalies was not pursued further at Marshall. Instead, the *effects*—the two instances of blow-by, the two eroded O-rings, and the heat effect on the secondary O-ring—were all judged to be "within the experience base." That was true only if one ignored the extent of 51C's two instances of blow-by.

26. See PC *Report*, vol. V, p. 908, where the General Conclusions chart of McDonald's August 19, 1985, briefing at NASA headquarters in Washington, DC appears in boldface as referencing a Presidential Commission interchange (p. 846) between Commissioner Kutyna and Mulloy. The phrase was either close to or identical to the one Mulloy had challenged in the FRRs conducted at various levels in January and February of that year: "Data obtained on the resilience of the O-rings indicate that lower temperatures aggravate this problem." Mulloy's response to Kutyna was that he had looked for "the substance behind that [the data presented in Chapter 2, Fig. 2.4, relating O-ring temperature to O-ring sealing time (also, see note 28)], and I can't find it" (p. 846).

27. The simulation excluded the effects of cold grease in the joint, grease that would slow the movement of the primary into its sealing position. The simulation also excluded pressure effects from hot gas.

28. See PC *Report*, vol. V, pp. 1568–1569. Copies of Russell's August 9, 1985, letter went to Mulloy's subordinate, Wear, at Marshall and to Thiokol's Kilminster, McDonald, Ebeling, Brinton, Boisjoly, and Thompson, among others. Thiokol's Russell had responded to a memo from J. W. Thomas at Marshall concerning "Actions Pertaining to SRM Field Joint Secondary Seal." Russell's summary is couched in terms of the secondary O-ring, but both primary and secondary O-rings would be compromised by cold temperatures. Russell restated, then answered, two questions that Thomas had asked:

1. Question: If the field joint secondary seal lifts off the metal mating surfaces during motor pressurization, how soon will it return to a position where contact is re-established?

Answer: Bench test data indicate that the o-ring resiliency (its capacity to follow the metal) is a function of temperature and rate of case expansion ["bulge" and joint rotation]...At 100°F, the o-ring maintained contact. At 75°F, lost contact for 2.4 seconds. At 50°F, the o-ring did not re-establish contact in ten minutes at which time the test was terminated. The conclusion is that secondary sealing capability in the SRM field joint cannot be guaranteed.

2. Question: If the primary o-ring does not seal, will the secondary seal seat in sufficient time to prevent joint leakage?

Answer: MTI has no reason to suspect that the primary seal would ever fail ... after the ignition transient. If the primary o-ring were to fail from 0 to 170 milliseconds, there is a very high probability that the secondary o-ring would hold pressure since the case has not expanded appreciably at this point. If the primary seal were to fail from 170 to 330 milliseconds, the probability of the secondary seal holding is reduced. From 330 to 600 milliseconds the chance of the secondary seal holding is small. *This is a direct result of the o-ring's slow response compared to the metal case segments as the joint rotates.* [emphasis added]

29. PC *Report*, vol. II, H-32, chart 60.
30. Personal interview with Allan McDonald, March 20, 1992, pp. 106–108.
31. Ibid, 107–110. See also McDonald & Hanson (2009, pp. 81–83).
32. See Lindstrom's memo to Lucas, "Subject: Discussion with Jerry Mason," February 6, 1985, announcing that Mason had advised "that Garrison will be visiting Beggs, Heflin, Fuqua, and others re second source," with five of Garrison's

viewgraphs attached (see history archives of Marshall Space Flight Center, Huntsville, AL, drawer 27, folder "SRB 1985"). Garrison's presentation was titled "Is There a Need to Broaden the Industrial Base to Enhance National Security?" and its first point was "Along with other major Shuttle system developers, Morton Thiokol provides high confidence for meeting Shuttle schedule requirements," with a sub-bullet as "All SRM flight set deliveries on schedule."

33. In addition to Mason's need to support his company's explicit stance on meeting launch schedules, Mason had other worries about his engineers' temperature threshold of 53 °F. Thiokol had been developing a lighter-weight booster for Department of Defense missions by the Air Force. Launch facilities had been built at the Vandenberg Air Force Base near Lompoc, California, where winter low temperatures were sometimes in the low to mid-30s. Thiokol's development of the new "filament wound case" boosters had progressed to the point where, at the very time the *Challenger* teleconference was going on, two of the lighter rockets were stacked on their Vandenberg launch pads, ready for test flights. Flights had been scheduled for April or May to be launched from Vandenberg, and the shuttles for those flights were to be refurbished from NASA shuttles flown from Kennedy (personal interview of Allan McDonald, March 20, 1992, p. 18).

Thiokol's Air Force contract for the lighter boosters, allowing for substantially heavier space payloads for the military, brought important profits and prestige to Thiokol, but military planning demanded that space launches be possible at any time, irrespective of season, time of day, or air temperature. Mason, or anyone in his corporate position, could only have sharp anxiety about certifying his company's rockets as usable only at or above O-ring temperatures of 53 °F.

34. PC *Report*, vol. IV, p. 715. One element of launch-schedule

pressure for any given launch was the launch date set for the *next* shuttle launch. *Challenger* managers knew that the *Challenger's* next flight, set to put the space probe *Ulysses* in orbit, was set to launch on May 15, leaving a tight time margin to get the *Challenger* ready in time for *Ulysses* to make its space rendezvous (see Chiles, 2001, p. 87).

35. See interviews conducted by the presidential commission (hereafter, PC interview) of: Donald Ketner, March 26, 1986, p. 8; Albert Macbeth, March 14, 1986, p. 4; Brian Russell, March 19, 1986, p. 3; and the author's personal interview of Arnold Thompson, March 23, 1992.

36. See PC *Report*, vol. IV, p. 715, for McDonald's February 25, 1986, testimony.

37. See PC interview of Robert Ebeling, March 19, 1986, pp. 3–4; and PC interview of Allan McDonald, March 19, 1986, pp. 2–3.

38. Personal interview of James D. Smith, January 18, 1991.

39. Jack Kapp, a participant at Thiokol in this early teleconference remembered Lovingood's ending words (though he thought they might be Mulloy's) as "Thiokol, what you need to do now is go back, make an official presentation with viewgraphs, come to an official position, and get back with us as soon as you possibly can" (PC interview of Jack Kapp, March 19, 1986, p. 8).

Lovingood listed participants in that initial teleconference. In his office were himself, J. D. Smith, L. O. Wear, L. F. Adams, K. Coates, B. Brinton (Thiokol), and probably Thiokol's Kyle Speas. In Athens, Georgia, he lists George Hardy; in Florida, Reinartz at his motel and McDonald and Houston at Kennedy Space Center; and at the Wasatch plant in Utah, Kilminster "and others." His listing of McDonald as a participant in this early teleconference is in error, and Brinton attended only at the very end (PC interview of Brinton, March 13, 1986).

40. Judson A. Lovingood, "Notes from January 27, 1986," *PC Report*, vol. V, pp. 932–938.

41. Ibid.

42. See U.S. Congress (1986a, p. 230): "Significant items occurring subsequent to the FRR will also be reported to the AS-SF [Associate Administrator for Space Flight, Jesse Moore]. Actions that can be easily accomplished without safety, mission, or launch impact . . . need not be reported" (NASA Program Directive SFO-PD 710.5A, p. 3).

Excluding Johnson Center managers and engineers at this late point of preparing a launch ignored the fact that official responsibility for launch, mission, and return of shuttle *Challenger* had some weeks earlier been turned over to a group of shuttle element managers making up the Mission Management Team (MMT), a transfer that had taken place immediately after the final Level I flight-readiness review. Lovingood had effectively preempted MMT involvement, giving Marshall sole authority for working through a decision about a new warning of a flight risk, a new assessment of the boosters' actual flight readiness. Marshall's special culture, the origin of Lovingood's sensitivity to protecting Marshall's in-house decision making, is explored below in chapter 3.

NASA's system of reviewing flight readiness of all shuttles, including the special character of the Marshall Center reviews, is described in chapter 3. See also Arnold Aldrich's retrospective comments on flaws in the *Challenger* decision process in PC *Report*, vol. I, 101-103, and more broadly in the Chapter V of volume I.

43. George Hardy, deputy director of Marshall's Science and Engineering Directorate, expressed this view of the primacy of contractor in controlling applications of its products. He testified that during the teleconference, he had said that even though he had agreed with Mulloy's assessment, he also had indicated he "would not recommend launch over

Thiokol's objections" (PC *Report*, vol. V, p. 865). Thiokol's Arnold Thompson reported that it simply never occurred to him or his colleagues that there might be objections to the position that he and his colleagues were presenting, since they were providing data to ensure *safe* flight (personal interview of Arnold Thompson, March 23, 1992).

44. The proof would be the record of 24 previous flights, all safe and flown with O-rings at or above 53 °F.

45. Boisjoly estimated that once individual assignments to obtain engineering data had been made, the engineers each had less than an hour to prepare his chart(s) and presentation before charts had to be sent off to the other centers for the teleconference (Boisjoly, 1987, p. 5; and personal correspondence from R. M. Boisjoly, October 16, 1989, pp. 2–3).

46. PC *Report*, vol. IV, p. 790. Boisjoly describes the sequence, contents, and significance of the charts.

47. The actual launch date of Flight 61C, flown just before the *Challenger*, the most recent launch-delay experience for those waiting for the teleconference to begin, was January 12, 1986. Flight 61C's launch delays were unusual:

1. Launch originally set for December 18, 1985, delayed one day when additional time was needed to close out orbiter aft compartment.

2. Launch attempt December 19 was scrubbed at T–14 seconds because of an indication that the right solid rocket booster hydraulic power unit exceeded RPM redline speed limits. (Later determined to be a false reading.)

3. After an 18-day delay, a launch attempt on January 6, 1986, was halted at T–31 seconds because of accidental draining of approximately 4,000 pounds of liquid oxygen from the external tank.

4. Launch attempt of January 7 was scrubbed at T–9 minutes because of bad weather at both transoceanic abort landing sites (Moron, Spain, and Dakar, Senegal).

5. After a two-day delay, the launch set for January 9 was delayed because of a launch pad liquid-oxygen sensor breaking off and lodging in the number-two main engine prevalve.

6. Launch set for January 10 was delayed two days because of heavy rains.

7. Launch countdown on January 12 proceeded with no delays (search www.Answers.com for "Delays in flight 61C").

48. See the Appendix for Thiokol's charts not presented in the text.

49. Charts whose information can be summarized verbally, like this one, or whose information was unrelated to the engineers' intended argument are presented in the Appendix.

50. Eighty degrees (80°) and 110° arc of blow-by evidence translates to a little more than 8 feet and 11 feet, respectively, around the inside of the two field joints. The Thiokol engineers never converted the degrees arc into feet, but this conversion into foot length, using the Commission's dimensions of the boosters' diameter, may help the reader more clearly to grasp the extent of the blow-by.

51. See Boisjoly's account of the contents and sequence of his teleconference comments, PC *Report*, vol. IV, beginning on page 789, and of his explanation of chart2-2, "Field Joint, Primary Concerns, SRM 25," pp.790–791.

52. "[T]he 15A motor had 80 degrees arc of black grease between the O-rings, and make no mistake about it, when I say black, I mean black just like coal. It was jet black" (testimony of Roger Boisjoly before the Commission, PC *Report*, vol. IV, p. 790).

53. Ibid, p. 791. Boisjoly makes reference here to seeking more refined studies of resiliency that he and Thompson had been trying to arrange. In stating that he lacked data, he revealed his attitude toward the very telling experimental data that he and Thompson had gathered. Boisjoly regarded

that data as merely "preliminary" to a study that would accurately trace the curvilinear course of the ignition transient opening. Really definitive data, he believed, required apparatus that he and Thompson had been trying to get approved and purchased by what Boisjoly regarded as an unresponsive bureaucracy. See Boisjoly (1987, p. 3) where he describes the method and results of Thompson's experiment that clearly demonstrates the effect of temperature on an O-ring's capacity to seal. Described in his account of the experiment, but not easily perceived by an uninstructed reader of it, was the significance of O-ring squeeze as a condition of the O-rings in that experiment. It was the effect of cold temperature on *squeezed* O-rings, the cold keeping their sealing girths squeezed, that degraded the O-rings' capacity to seal, making them unable to recapture their round cross-sectional shape after the squeeze was released, to paraphrase Boisjoly.

54. Boisjoly (1987).
55. PC interview of J. Q. Miller, March 27, 1986, pp, 9–10.
56. Personal interview of Lawrence Mulloy, January 19, 1991, p. 11.
57. Longer compression times should be shown to be associated with greater failure to recover percent of precompression diameter.
58. The notations at the bottom of the chart of erosion depths could be interpreted two ways, depending on whether one was disposed to read safety or danger in the erosion data. The engineers at Thiokol saw the erosion in two joints in the cold flight as a danger signal. Mulloy, Hardy, and others at Marshall regarded impingement erosion as a settled matter: Erosion depths would never reach O-rings' threshold of failure.
59. McDonald & Hanson (2009, p. 103). McDonald indicated (pp. 35–36) that it was his boss, Joe Kilminster, who had

tamped down the blow holes, and that he had done so on every DM and QM motor tested before the DM-7 test. McDonald had confronted Kilminster, indicating that his actions were "stupid."

60. For Hardy's extended explanation of his view of how the joint became sealed, see PC *Report*, vol. V, pp. 868–880.

61. The following sense of "priming" connects the work of Klein (1993, 1997) with the formulations of Abelson (1975, 1976) and Schank (1975), particularly Abelson's concepts of episodic scripts and categorical scripts. From this body of work, Mulloy's responses to Thiokol's presentation can be characterized not only as primed but also as scripted—both episodically and categorically. For example, Mulloy's promise, mirroring Lucas's commitment, "We're going to support these launches on this schedule," is an episodic script, while his and his colleagues' fear of the long pole qualifies as a categorical script. Scripts like these drove much of these deliberations. A script analysis of *Challenger's* entire decision process would illuminate in new ways its linguistic-psychological dimension.

62. This phrase was used by Mulloy in answer to my interview question "If such a justification [for delaying a scheduled launch] were ever required, what kinds of justification would most likely be considered adequate and inadequate?" (personal e-mail from Lawrence Mulloy, September 25, 2000).

63. PC interview of Boisjoly April 2, 1986, p. 40.

64. Personal interview of Allan McDonald, March 20, 1992, pp. 25–27.

65. Tompkins (1993) documents Lucas's aloof and humiliating style of demanding his own conception of high engineering standards and drive for on-time launches. Following are two of 11 similar quotations from managers and technicians taken from Tomkins' post-accident interviews at Marshall: "I feel bad about saying this, but people were afraid to bring

bad news [to Lucas] for fear they would be treated harshly. They didn't want to be chewed out. It was kill the messenger. There was a tendency to push things down, to keep the lid on problems." (p. 163)

"I thought the world of Dr. Lucas, even though he was so rigid and formal. People were afraid to raise problems with him. We started canning and preprogramming what went up to Dr. Lucas. We were afraid of his response. He'd jump all over people if what they said didn't suit him." (p. 164)

66. Personal interview of Lawrence Mulloy, October 19, 2000, tape 2, side1, pp. 2-3.

67. Launching and repairing the Hubble telescope and similar projects brought NASA revenues of the kind promised to Congress when they considered approving funds for the shuttle program.

68. From a personal interview of Lawrence Mulloy conducted by Diane Vaughan, June 8, 1992 (Vaughan 1996, p. 242). See also comments by Keith Coates referring to "umbrella" protection against being the one responsible for holding up a launch in his Commission interview, March 25, 1986 (p. 32), quoted in Vaughan (1996, p. 242).

69. Stanley Reinartz, Mulloy's immediate superior, had only recently been appointed to his position, and his knowledge of booster parts and dynamics was not yet nearly as detailed as Mulloy's, so it fell to Mulloy to investigate and explain the cause of the aborted launch.

70. Personal interview of Lawrence Mulloy, October 19, 2000, tape 2, side 1, p. 2.

71. McDonald remembered the "heat" that the Marshall Center and Mulloy received from the Johnson Center's [Aldrich's] memo: "He [Mulloy] really got chastised. Marshall Space Flight Center got chastised from the Shuttle program about not doing their homework with this unit that was supposed to be qualified and causing this big delay. They were under pressure to get this orbiter, as well as the earlier one, back

because they were both slated to be modified to fly in April. . . . So, there was this pressure now brought on one, the Marshall Space Flight Center, because they had to take the hit first, saying we caused the launch to . . . Mulloy took it on personally, because it was his element, and the first time he'd ever been responsible for that, and there was some question as to whether he'd done enough work to qualify the unit which caused the problem in the first place, . . . and it's expensive to cause one of these launches to be delayed. . . . You've got to look and recognize that pressure there. . . . Lucas is under pressure . . . from both Johnson Space Center, and NASA headquarters, because it was his element that caused the delay. Now, if it had been an orbiter problem, Johnson would have taken the heat. . . . So they got a lot of pressure from that, and there was a lot, a lot of heat, I mean a lot of heat" (personal interview of Allan McDonald, March 20, 1992, pp. 59-62).

72. "The first STS 61C launch attempt in December 1985 resulted in an automatic LPS hold at T–14 seconds and was subsequently scrubbed for a problem later determined to be over-sensitivity in an SRB HPU [hydraulic power unit] electrical control circuit. This was traced to a piece part substitution which introduced a circuit sensitivity characteristic which had been experienced and corrected several years earlier in a similar upgrade of the Orbiter APU [auxiliary power unit] control electronics.

"ACTION: Review Orbiter formal closeout paperwork for this issue and the process for communicating this problem throughout the NSTS system to identify reasons SRB [Solid Rocket Booster] project did not react appropriately." (See "STS 61C Launch," memo received by Reinartz January 21, and by Lucas January 23, 1986, sent to a "distribution" including Mulloy, with copies to Lucas, Kingsbury, and Littles; from MSFC history archives, drawer 25, file "61C 1986," personal document # M3.)

73. In explaining his surprise at Thiokol's argument during the January 27, 1986, teleconference that the *Challenger's* launch should be delayed because of the unusually cold launch temperatures, Mulloy commented to a Commissioner: "This was a surprising conclusion, based on data that didn't seem to hang together, and so I challenged that. And I assure you, sir, that there was no reversal of the tradition of NASA which says prove to me why you can't fly versus prove to me why you can.

"As I say, to me . . . it doesn't make any difference. If somebody is giving me a recommendation and a conclusion that is based upon engineering data, I am going to understand the basis for that recommendation and conclusion to assure that it is logical" (PC *Report*, vol. V, p. 840).

74. NASA's safety system had two parts: the preparation of each space vehicle (the shuttle) as the *hardware* of space flight (including its software), and the actual *use* of the hardware from launch to return in accomplishing missions. Because participants in the *Challenger* deliberations regarded the people and expertise from Thiokol and Marshall as sufficient to settle all the technical issues, and because the issues were in fact settled solely by participants in those two organizations, the second phase of the safety system, with leadership from the Mission Management Team (MMT), headed by Aldrich at the Johnson Space Center, never came into play. On the other hand, there were clear NASA directives dictating that any significant issues arising after the Level I FRR must be handled by the MMT. Because a decision was made at Marshall to include in the deliberations only those at Marshall and Thiokol if the *Challenger* launch went forward, Marshall violated NASA's covering directive.

75. "Flight ready" is in quotes to keep NASA's and the participants' terms but also to reflect the fact that no testing or proof offered during the FRR phase of shuttle preparations could validly or logically imply readiness for actual flight, as

launch and flight conditions could not be known in that phase. Quotes will be used from this point forward to remind the reader of this misleading use of this term.

76. Sagan (1993, p. 258) makes an observation from his studies of accidents that applies to Lucas's impact on decision making in the shuttle program: "Organizations have their stated goals, but they are also strongly influenced by powerful individuals, both inside and outside the organization, who try to shape their goals and manipulate their behavior."

77. Personal interview of Lawrence Mulloy, January 19, 1991, tape 2, side B, pp. 16–17. See also PC interview of Mulloy, April 2, 1986, pp. 61–63.

78. This possibility was never recognized at NASA or even, for some key participants, after the accident.

79. See Klein (1993) for observations on *adaptive* decision priming. Mulloy's decision priming narrowed his focus, a case of *distorted* priming. The most ubiquitous source of priming that militates against accurate perception of a clear shift in normal conditions has come to be known as the confirmation bias (see Kunda, 1999; Nickerson, 1998; Wason, 1960), the tendency to perceive the world in terms of one's already well established schemas, concepts, and principles. It is normally highly adaptive, a matter simply of using one's accumulated experience to understand the ongoing world. The most generalized and analytically useful formulation of this conservative tendency was Piaget's (1952, 1954) work, in which children were seen to "assimilate" new information by using old, familiar schemas when those schemas did not fit the new information, and persisting until they realized that their approach was not working and "accommodated" to the new information by developing more inclusive schemas.

80. Mulloy validates others' phrasing of his wording (PC *Report*, vol. V, p. 843). Mulloy's assessment missed Thiokol's data (Figure 2.7) that contradicted his view, which would have required *Challenger's* O-ring temperature to be close to the

boosters' mean bulk temperature. Figure 2.7, "History of O-ring Temperatures," shows clearly to the contrary, that O-ring temperature follows much more closely the temperature *outside* the booster than the *inside* mean bulk temperature and, further, that the O-rings of the *Challenger's* boosters were both close to its ambient temperature and distant from its mean bulk temperature. The list of those three sites of temperature figures for the seven booster motors represented in Figure 2.7 show that to understand the O-ring dynamics, one had to attend focally to O-ring temperatures alone (personal interview of Lawrence Mulloy, January 19, 1991, tape 2, side B).

81. See Mulloy's narrative of teleconference events, PC *Report*, vol. IV, pp. 612–615.

82. NASA's practice was to designate each flight after flight nine with numbers and letters. The first nine flights were numbered in sequence: Space Transportation System 1 (STS-1), STS-2, etc. For the designations of flights from ten onward, the first number indicated the last digit of the year for which the flight was scheduled to launch; the second digit indicated the location of launch – 1 for Kennedy, 2 for Vandenberg airforce base in California; and the letter indicated the sequence of flight within the year e.g., flight 41B was scheduled for launch in 1984 (4), to be launched from Kennedy (1), and to be the second flight (B) in its year's sequence. The dates of *actual* launch, however, often varied from the indicated year and sometimes the sequence.

83. See PC *Report*, vol. IV, p. 614, for Mulloy's handwritten list of his reasons for rejecting Thiokol's rationale and recommendation. See also PC *Report*, vol. IV, pp. 610–615, for his detailed notes and full-text chronological account of the teleconference discussion. See also Allan McDonald's detailed account of the teleconference in PC *Report*, vol. IV, pp. 740–746.

84. Post-accident sub-scale tests showed that putty even without bubbles showed high variability of pressure resistance. One test showed that putty at 75° F delayed the rise of ignition pressure .530 seconds, while similarly prepared putty at 20° F delayed arrival of that pressure 1.9 seconds, more than three and a half times longer (P.C. *Report*, vol. I, 64-65). That kind of delay in a flight would allow the joint to open before the primary O-ring became actuated, allowing blow-by past both O-rings, causing total joint failure.

85. See volume I of the presidential commission's *Report* (1986, 129-131; 133, Fig. 3, and discussion on p. 156) showing evidence of erosion or blow-by as a function of the air pressure employed in the leak check, where the instance of putty penetration (either erosion or blow-by) rises markedly with pressure greater than 50 psi. This effect of the leak test on the incidence of (impingement) erosion and blow-by was known both at Thiokol and Marshall (P. C. *Report*, vol. I, p. 134). Because the leak test was crucial for safety, its side effects (tolerable impingement erosion and brief blow-by) were acceptable – and proved not to have been a cause in the disaster. The power of the leak check to create bubbles was minor in relation to the pressure created when booster segments were joined ("stacked") in the assembly building at Kennedy. Joining the booster segments forced a comparatively large volume of trapped air into the putty, which could create bubbles or even blow-holes. First discovery of the blow-holes and bubbles had led to thickening of the layer of putty to the point where it oozed out of the joint toward the booster's fuel when segments were joined (email 7.23.14 from Allan McDonald).

86. See McDonald & Hanson (2009), pp. 392–393.

87. This account of McDonald's brief comments just prior to the caucus accords well with other participants' memories of his words. In his testimony before the Commission (PC *Report*, vol. IV, p. 721), McDonald reported having made a more

extended comment, one that expressed more fully the effect on *timing* of the primary O-ring's sealing, it being more distant from the gap it should seal than was true for the secondary O-ring. The several participants who recalled hearing his comment reported the briefer version I have given here, drawn from McDonald & Hanson (2009).

88. Some NASA members at Marshall evidently had understood the Thiokol engineers' warnings about cold O-rings. The idea of heat blankets is not far, in fact, from a post-accident change in the boosters' design: heat tape was provided around each joint to keep the O-rings warm.

89. PC interview of Luther Ben Powers on March 12, 1986, pp. 9–10. Smith's characterization of the trio's conference depicts an engineering approach to the question at hand that was usual for "most engineers":

We were all three standing over in the corner of the room discussing it. . . . John asked Ben what did he think of the situation and Ben did say that he thought we ought to go with the Thiokol engineering recommendation. And we were going to continue discussing that position, well, like most engineers—"Okay, why did you believe that, why did you feel that way? The data is confusing, we got data that says 'okay,' got data that says 'not okay.' Why did you say we should [not] go?" . . . Not agree or disagree, but to understand the position of where he's coming from. (personal interview of James D. Smith, January 18, 1991.)

Smith later elaborated on the context of this conversation. His attempt to elicit the technical views of McCarty, representing the Structures and Propulsion Laboratory, and of Robert Schwinghamer, representing the Materials and Processes Laboratory, was cut short. Just after asking McCarty for the views of his lab, Dr. Wayne Littles, Associate Director for Engineering at Marshall, interrupted their conversation to indicate that Thiokol was now back online to continue the teleconference. Smith never obtained the views of McCarty or Schwinghamer. It was his own view that though the conservative stance would have been to delay, the engineering data were so mixed that no one could stand up and defend a launch delay based on such ambiguous data. As Smith put it, looking at the mixed data that Thiokol had presented that night, he was in a situation where "I can't go right, and I can't go left"; one couldn't prove either danger or safety with the data in front of them. One could only defer to the arguments of Larry Mulloy, who had the responsibility for making a recommendation up the line (personal communication with James D. Smith, August 28, 2009).

Jerry Peoples, a colleague who had been assigned to work with Thiokol engineers on the field joint problems, reported that if he had been asked for his views (he did not participate in the teleconference), he would have agreed: "[I]f I had the data in front of me that Thiokol presented that night, I'd have recommended just like Ben . . . to delay the launch. . . . The reason is for the problem of the O-ring resiliency, which had to do with the performance of the O-ring." (See PC interview of Jerry Peoples, March 12, 1986, pp. 29–32.)

90. Hardy acknowledged his "appalled" comment and explained that what appalled him was the implication that Thompson's experimental data relating O-ring temperature to the time for the secondary O-ring to seal the simulated joint had any relevance to the secondary O-ring's sealing its joint in flight. To his understanding, confident but flawed, if any hot gas got past the primary O-ring, it would occur only in the first 170 milliseconds after ignition but before the joint opened. In that case, the hot gas would immediately cause pressure actuation of the secondary O-ring and bring about sealing of that joint. For the Thiokol engineers not to understand that particular safe dynamic was appalling to

Hardy. See Hardy's full account of his thinking in PC *Report*, vol. V., pp. 887–894.

Hardy's claim that no one in the teleconference was considering how O-rings might fail to seal *after* joint rotation reveals slippage in the Thiokol engineers' communication, hurried under the circumstances. Evidently, Boisjoly's expressions of concern about delaying the timing of sealing in the initial phase of the transient masked his and Thompson's additional concerns about non-resilient O-ring sealing at *any* phase of the ignition transient, given their understanding that the timing of those very phases was itself unpredictable under the expected cold flight conditions.

91. Asked by his Presidential Commission interviewers, Robert Thompson and Emily Trapnell, if there were any formal or informal "structures" for a group getting information up the line to decision makers, Luther Powers referred to polling:

Powers: You say, "Okay, Mr. McCarty, sir, you are the propulsion lab. What's your recommendation?" Put him on the spot. Get him up there and turn the heat up underneath him. He didn't do that. . . . Hardy did not poll.

Thompson: And that's a normal administrative procedure?

Powers: I would have expected him to poll.

Trapnell: At what point?

Powers: During the caucus or before. . . . We've got a lot of technical guys called in here. They're not just sitting around here warming the chairs. Let's see what they think." (PC interview of Luther Ben Powers, March 12, 1986, pp. 24–28)

92. See McDonald's recollections of his remarks and his reasoning (McDonald & Hanson, 2009, p. 105). McDonald also remembered adding that "lower temperatures are in the direction of badness for both O-rings, because they slow down the timing function." While the idea of a delay of sealing was undoubtedly salient in McDonald's mind, the

combined testimony of the participants suggests that his actual words did not convey that idea. Virtually all participants who were not already convinced of the dangers of cold O-rings interpreted McDonald's pointed reference to Hardy's comment as supporting Hardy's point, whose meaning was to reassure that the secondary O-ring would in fact seal the joint if the primary failed in the initial phase of the ignition transient. (See Hardy's extended explanation of his thinking in PC *Report*, vol. V, pp. 864–878.)

93. See Lindstrom's memo to Lucas, "Subject: Discussion with Jerry Mason," February 6, 1985, announcing that Mason had advised "that Garrison will be visiting Beggs, Heflin, Fuqua, and others re second source," with five of Garrison's viewgraphs attached (history archives of Marshall Space Flight Center, Huntsville, Alabama, drawer 27, folder "SRB 1985," personal folder M8).

Garrison's presentation was titled "Is There a Need to Broaden the Industrial Base to Enhance National Security?" and its first point was "Along with other major Shuttle system developers, Morton Thiokol provides high confidence for meeting Shuttle schedule requirements," with a sub-bullet as "All SRM flight set deliveries on schedule."

94. Personal interview of Allan McDonald, March 20, 1992, pp. 107–108.

95. Government interviewers assisted the Presidential Commission in conducting lengthy interviews with all who participated in the prelaunch teleconference. See Thiokol Vice President of Engineering Robert K. Lund's Commission interview, April 1, 1986, pp. 42–43.

96. See Mason's deflection of Commissioner Walker's attempt to get him to confront the fact that "the largest amount of blow-by was at the lowest temperature" (PC *Report*, vol. IV, p, 771).

97. Mason's views of sealing in the boosters' field joints were expressed in detail in his testimony before the Presidential Commission (see volume IV of the PC *Report*, pp. 626–627, 699, 771).

98. See PC *Report*, vol. IV, p. 771, where Mason indicates his relative unconcern for blow-by, being concerned instead about erosion.

99. William Rogers, chairman of the Presidential Commission, had asked Mason about "the nature of the arguments against launch" (PC *Report*, vol. IV, p. 626).

100. PC *Report*, vol. IV, p. 699. In Mason's view, the only way for gas to escape was for an O-ring to be eroded.

101. See Mason's discussion with Commissioner Sally Ride about his thinking about the argon results in PC *Report*, vol. IV, p. 762.

102. Few at Thiokol had anticipated any objection from NASA, as NASA's position had traditionally been, in every FRR up through the most stringent review by the Marshall Center Board, that contractors had to provide convincing evidence that their elements *were* ready to fly. They had never had to prove they were *un*ready to fly. Brian Russell, who worked for McDonald's subordinate, Bob Ebeling, indicated in his Presidential Commission interview that "we felt in our presentation of the data that we had to include all of the data that could possibly be relevant, even though not all of it tended to support our point of view" (PC interview, March 19, 1986, p. 17). Howard McIntosh, who was present in the afternoon discussions at Thiokol but whose management role was case refurbishment and therefore not required in launch processes, was thoroughly convinced as he left early for home that NASA would not proceed with the launch with such cold O-rings.

103. See chart 2-1, Appendix Fig. A. 1.

104. Personal interview of Arnold Thompson, March 23, 1992. See Thompson's final memo, PC *Report*, vol. I, p. 251.

105. Personal interview of Arnold Thompson, March 23, 1992.
106. Gorman, Cooke, and Winner's (2006) well-reasoned argument for a process-oriented conception of "team situation awareness" is relevant to capture the shifts in the teleconference and caucus debate over competing assessments of the shuttle's situation. Thompson's realization here that the trajectory of discussion was about to accelerate in the dangerous direction, and his feeling the need to intervene to change direction, reflects on a small scale the larger turn of events. First, the engineers had believed the initial review of their data and their recommendation would lead more or less straightforwardly to a launch delay. Then Marshall's Mulloy opposed their reasoning with ten reasons of his own and recommended the launch go forward. This led to Mason's intervention, taking leadership back from Mulloy to more direct control at Thiokol. Mason's dominating review now was seen by the two most involved and expert engineers as a move to support not their view but Mulloy's view, reversing their original reasoning and recommendation. Now Thompson, soon followed by Boisjoly, would try to return the course of the group's thought to its original trajectory based on the crucial engineering dynamic of cold temperature effects on O-ring sealing.

The corrective emphasis by Gorman, Cooke, and Winner (2006) on measuring team situation awareness as a process is important. (See also the discussion of Team Holistic Ecology and Dynamic Activity (THEDA) in Cooke et al., 2007). Just as important, however, is the background investigation necessary to reveal *why* the Mulloys are predisposed to oppose interruption of ongoing production, *why* the Masons become so single-minded in controlling the content of discussion to support continued production and to dismiss their technicians' warnings, and *why* the normally laid-back Thompsons are impelled to get out of their seats, walk to the executives' end of the table, and try dissuading them with graphs showing the danger.

107. Testimony of Roger Boisjoly, PC *Report*, vol. IV, pp. 792–793.

108. PC interview with Brian Russell, March 19, 1986, p. 26.

109. Personal interview of Arnold Thompson, March 23, 1992.

110. Thompson and Mason had hunted or fished together on several occasions.

111. Roger Boisjoly, PC Hearings, February 25, 1986, PC *Report*, vol. IV, pp. 792 ff. Corroborated by Thompson in my interview with him on March 23, 1992.

112. PC interview with Joel Maw on March 30, 1986, p. 13.

113. PC interview with Jack Kapp, March 19, 1986, pp. 29–30.

114. Ibid.

115. Ibid., pp. 30–31. Kapp gave this account: Then Mr. Mason made a statement to the effect that, yes, we know that our seal is vulnerable to erosion . . . but we've run extensive tests to show that we can take quite a bit of erosion. . . . He asked engineering . . . "Are you absolutely sure that in your mind you are able to separate out the fact that the seal is less desirable than we would like it to be . . . that your apprehension is not based on the fact that you would like, just generally like, the seal to be better and not on the fact that it was [*sic*: will be] cool?" (Ibid., p. 30).

116. See PC interviews with Brian Russell, March 19, 1986, p. 26, and Jack Kapp, March 19, 1986, pp. 39–40. See also testimony of Roger Boisjoly, PC *Report*, vol. IV, pp. 792–793. One key participant felt strongly that if just one of the other engineering supervisors, especially one who was a close friend of Lund's, had spoken up in support of Boisjoly and Thompson, then Lund, upon whose acquiescence the management decision finally depended, would have held firm to his own group's earlier recommendation, a recommendation he himself had written and presented. Indeed, Mason later named persons who, if they had voiced doubts, would in his view have changed the decision: "If anybody had said,

'Don't fly,' we wouldn't have flown . . . and that included Brinton and McDonald . . . and . . . if Kapp or Sayer had said, 'I think that we're making a mistake,' or that they still had serious concerns" (PC interview of Mason, April 2, 1986, p. 34).

117. See PC interviews of Robert K. Lund, April 1, 1986, p. 44; Brian Russell, March 19, 1986, p. 27; and Jack Kapp, March 19, 1986, p. 34.

118. PC interview with Jack Kapp, March 19, 1986, p. 34.

119. PC interview transcript, Larry H. Sayer, March 20, 1986, pp. 20–23. Alton Keel Jr., executive director of the Presidential Commission, asked Mason directly to explain his comment: "What did you have in mind when you asked him [Lund] to take off his engineering hat and put on his management hat?" Mason replied, "I had in mind the fact that we . . . could not quantify . . . the time for movement of the primary. We didn't have the data to do that, and therefore it was going to take a judgment, rather than a precise engineering calculation, in order to conclude what we needed to conclude" (PC *Report*, vol. IV, p. 773).

120. PC *Report*, vol. IV, p. 725.

121. Boisjoly kept an engineering journal. His entry describing the teleconference and caucus ends with the comment: "I sincerely hope that this launch does not result in a catastrophy [*sic*]. I personally do not agree with some of the statements made in Joe Kilminster's written summary stating that Solid Rocket Motor–25 is okay to fly" (PC *Report*, vol. IV, pp, 684, 686).

122. Note that none of the points of Kilminster's revised rationale address the issue of resiliency or delayed actuation of the primary O-ring and the consequences for passing beyond the brief window of the secondary O-ring's redundancy.

123. PC *Report*, vol. IV, p. 744.

124. Mulloy understood the range of temperatures from 40 °F to 90 °F to apply not to "all components of the solid rocket motor," as McDonald believed, but only to the boosters' propellant MBT, which was expected to be 55° for the *Challenger*. McDonald replied that he thought that interpretation was "ridiculous" (see McDonald's February 25, 1986, notes narrating his discussion with Mulloy, PC *Report*, vol. IV, p. 743).

125. Mulloy's February 14, 1986, notes describe briefly McDonald's additional argument: "Mr. McDonald informed Mr. Reinartz and me that if the MTI engineering concern for the effect of cold was not sufficient cause to recommend not launching, there were two other considerations—launch pad ice and recovery area weather. I stated that launch pad ice had been considered by the mission management team before deciding to proceed and that a periodic monitoring of that condition was planned. I further stated that I had been made aware of the recovery area weather and planned to place a call to Mr. Aldrich and advise him [that] weather in the recovery area exceeded launch commit criteria" (PC *Report*, vol. IV, p. 615).

126. See McDonald's February 25, 1986, notes for the Presidential Commission, PC *Report*, vol. IV, p. 745.

127. The Program Directive (SFO-PD 710.5A) includes the sentence "Significant items occurring subsequent to the FRR [ie., the final FRR at Level I] will also be reported to the AA-SF [Associate Administrator of Space Flight, Jesse Moore, Aldrich's boss]" (see US Congress, 1986a, p. 230.) Thiokol's presentation, recommendation, caucus, and revised recommendation, all on the eve of a launch and in that regard unique, certainly qualify as a "significant item."

128. When William Rogers, chair of the Presidential Commission, asked Mulloy to explain why he had not informed Aldrich, he replied, "At that time, and I still consider today, that was a Level III issue, Level III being an SRB element or

an external tank element or . . . an Orbiter. . . . And we work many problems at the Orbiter and the SRB and the external tank level that never get communicated to Mr. Aldrich or Mr. Moore. It was clearly a Level III issue that had been resolved" (PC *Report*, vol. V, p. 849).

In fact, however, official policy (see previous endnote) called for reporting to Aldrich's level any new condition after the final Level I FRR that might affect flight safety, so the move by Lovingood, setting up the teleconference to exclude Aldrich's level, and by Mulloy in withholding its results from Aldrich, violated the explicit Program Directive referred to in the preceding note.

129. Salmon et al. (2009) find not *overlapping commonality* among team members' situation assessments, as with Endsley and Jones (2001), but rather what Salmon et al. refer to as "*compatible* SA," where team members' situation assessments are defined in terms of their distinct but cooperative roles in performing a given task. Salmon et al. reject Endsley's (1995a, 1999,) conception of an objective situation. From Salmon et al's schema theory: "It is argued that individual team members experience a situation in different ways and therefore that their awareness is compatible rather than shared . . . 'the situation' can indeed be (objectively) defined in all manner of ways but under a schema/system perspective there is a certain futility in this. . . . [The Salmon et al. schema/system account] is in direct contradiction to those that suggest teams possess 'shared' SA (which tacitly assumes 'identical' awareness and an objectively definable situation" (Salmon et al., 2009, p. 204).
Neither Endsley's formulation of a single objective situation assessment nor Salmon and colleagues' view of compatible team members' assessments are sufficient to comprehend the widely distributed, differing, and *conflicting* situations and awarenesses, both objective and subjective, in the *Challenger* decision.

130. The rare opportunity offered by the availability of *Challenger* decision participants' testimony revealed both the detail of their unfolding arguments and the structure of their argumentation, allowing us to see the potent effects on decision outcomes exerted by presumption and burden of proof in the context of high-tech decision making.

131. DeChurch and Zaccaro (2010) argue forcefully from a review of the literature on organizational teams that research and theorizing on team functioning (team mental models, team communication, and the like) that fail to include the effects of wider organizational structures, norms, and competing goals will seriously oversimplify the dynamics actually at work. They argue that a new unit of analysis, the "multiteam system," is required to handle both intra- and inter-team complexities. Their wider, system outlook, with its competing levels and goals, is consistent with the complexities of team and situation evident in the *Challenger* decision making.

132. See Endsley (1995a, 1995b, 1999), and Sarter and Woods (1991).

133. Grosjean and Terrier (1999) show that variations in subjects' "temporal awareness"—concerning sequence of tasks performed and to be performed, and time available to perform future tasks—was related to their performance accuracy and "multiple goal optimization." It is clear that key managers in these deliberations were aware of time pressure but were primed by factors unrelated to the astronauts' or shuttle's safety to complete this countdown to launch, e.g., Mulloy's looking for conclusive proof of danger that would meet Lucas's standards or Mason's attending to an unsigned contract and promises made to meet every launch schedule. The presence of time pressure makes pointedly relevant the idea that speed and accuracy of cognition are conflicting goals. See Fitts (1966) and Wickelgren (1977) for a grounding in the experimental literature and Förster, Higgins, and

Bianco (2003) for an analysis of this tradeoff as a conflict between strategic concerns.

134. My equal emphasis on participants' subjective construals of their situation(s) and on their objective situation(s) contrasts with Endsley's (1995a, 1995b, 1999) widely cited formulation of situation assessment. Even more contrasting with her formulation is the possibility I describe of participants being caught in *two simultaneously objective and conflicting situations.*

135. This kind of causal explanation contrasts sharply with the incremental model of accepting O-ring erosion as harmless employed by Vaughan (1996) in her widely cited analysis of the *Challenger* disaster. I examine her analysis critically in detail elsewhere (Lighthall, 2014c).

136. Those experimental results had been reported months before the teleconference debate to NASA's special-projects office at Marshall, in a memorandum sent by Brian Russell, a member of McDonald's team, with a copy to Larry Wear, Mulloy's immediate subordinate (see PC *Report*, vol. V, 1568–1569). In addition to going to Larry Wear, Mulloy's immediate subordinate, copies of Russell's August 9, 1985, letter went as "blind" copies to Kilminster, McDonald, Ebeling, Boisjoly, Thompson, and others at Thiokol.

137. The abbreviation, FRR, will not be presented in quote marks but the flight readiness review process it abbreviates must still be understood as dangerously misleading, as indicated earlier.

138. The following portrait of Mulloy's ideas, commitments, and reasoning is based on his own accounts in his two lengthy recorded interviews with me, in response to my questions, which, in turn, were based on his own lengthy testimony in the Commission's official interview of him and in public inquiries conducted by Congress and by the Presidential Commission reported in the commission's *Report* (1986).

The references to my interviews are of Larry Mulloy on January 1, 1991, tape 2, side B, particularly at recording numbers 202–210 and 228–250, and on October 19, 2000, the whole of tape 1, side 2, but particularly at recording numbers 141–145, 289–300, 318–355, 450–500, 510–529, and 545–562. The portrait was also drawn from the Commission's official interview, particularly page 64, from PC *Report*, vol. V, pp. 848 and 1537, and from e-mail correspondence with Larry Mulloy from 1991 to 2010. For Larry's continued readiness to add details, to explain, and to correct me, I am deeply grateful.

139. Mulloy acknowledged that the teleconference was not an FRR in the official sense of a review at Level II or I but then explained why his request to Kilminster to sign Thiokol's revised assessment was made: "I might say that another thing that does require a sign-off by the [contractor's] program manager [i.e., Kilminster] is any action that results from anything related to a flight, and this [the teleconference] would certainly fall in that category where concern was raised and an action is assigned to go develop data and then review those data. I view it as part of the flight readiness review process" (PC *Report*, vol. V, p. 863).

140. This is Mulloy's own phrase, expressed to me in an e-mail, describing the kind of evidence required to justify any conclusion about flight readiness.

141. Personal interview of Lawrence Mulloy, January 19, 1991, tape 2, side B. Mulloy succinctly described the two alternative presentations in FRRs that were acceptable and normal: first, a conclusion that one's component was ready to fly (backed, of course, by "credible quantitative engineering analysis or test data"), or, second, a statement that crucial data were lacking to prove readiness.

142. Personal interview of Mulloy, January 19, 1991.

143. Ibid.

144. Mulloy's actual rejection, the night before *Challenger's* launch, of Thiokol's data and reasoning to justify the launch delay is at odds with his retrospective view, in our January 19, 1991 interview, that he would have accepted Thiokol's delay recommendation if it had declared that it was not ready to launch due to insufficient or contradictory data. When he had asked over the telenet for Kilminster's view, Kilminster had replied that he could not recommend launch (See Mulloy's narrative of teleconference events, PC *Report*, vol. IV, 614).

145. See Mulloy's congressional testimony in U.S. Congress (1986b, p. 427).

146. For Hardy's confident view, see PC *Report*, vol. V, pp. 887–894. See also comments on Hardy's reaction and interpretation in K. Speas, "Events leading up to and through the telecon on temperature effect on O-ring performance," 12 February, 1986, microfiche series SSCO37, 0893-0896, National Archives, Washington, DC.

147. Others at Marshall asked for, heard, and then discounted the very different views expressed by the Marshall engineer, Ben Powers, who agreed with Thiokol's position "100 percent," that "it was too cold." His supervisors could not agree because they were ambivalent, perhaps like chief engineer Jim Smith, unable to go right and unable to go left (see PC interview of Luther Ben Powers, March 12, 1986, p. 10).

148. See PC interview of Robert K. Lund, April 1, 1986, pp. 42–43: "Jerry [Mason], as he should have, said, 'Let's discuss this,' and he got up, and he says, 'Let me see if I understand what Mr. Mulloy said.' And he described what Mr. Mulloy said, and everybody said, 'Yeah, that's what he said,' and so we discussed whether that made sense or not, and there were some, particularly Arnie and Roger, that said, no, that doesn't make sense to us because our gut feel still says that resilience is the real issue, and it is not whether the seal is in

one place or the other, and we think that is the overwhelming consideration."

149. Interview of Herb Samuels (pseudonym), Thiokol engineering supervisor, March 23, 1992, p. 20.

150. See PC interview of Jack Kapp, February 19, 1986, p. 30: "Mr. Mason made a statement to the effect that yes, we know that our seal is vulnerable to erosion . . . but we've run extensive tests to show that we can take quite a bit of erosion. . . . He asked engineering . . . 'Are you absolutely sure that in your mind you are able to separate out the fact that the seal is less desirable than we would like it to be . . . that your apprehension is not based on the fact that you would like, just generally like, the seal to be better and not on the fact that it was cool?'"

151. I have in mind here the kind of mental vigilance and discipline that Langer (1989) describes, sharpened in addition by working knowledge of probability and statistics and of the nature, components, process, and practice of formal argument from evidence, e.g., handling presumption, burden of proof, and standards of evidence.

152. Piaget (1952, 1954) and Flavell (1963) found young children "assimilating" new perceptions into previous "schemata" instead of "accommodating" their perceptual systems to the new dimensions of the new information. See also Wason (1960; Lord, Ross, and Lepper (1979); Koehler (1993); Nickerson (1998); and Kunda (1999) for research on adults showing the same tendency to hold on to established modes of thinking in face of new, invalidating information.

153. See, for example, Fitts (1966), Wickelgren (1977), and Hollnagel (2009).

154. See Tversky and Kahneman (1973), Schwarz et al. (1991), and Colin and Campbell (1992).

155. See Fischhoff and Johnson's (1997) discussion of creative tensions within distributed decision-making systems where they warn that when a dynamic balance—e.g., between production

and safety—"is lacking, the organization is in a state of crisis, vulnerable to natural events or to hostile actions that exploit its imbalances. The crisis is particularly great when the need for balance is not recognized or cannot be admitted or when an *experiential gulf separates management and operators*" (p. 233, emphasis added).

156. For example, launching a shuttle before the heat effects and sealing dynamics in the previous shuttle's booster joints could be analyzed.

157. See "Effect of flight rate on spare parts," PC *Report*, vol. I, pp, 173–175, 176–177. Recall also the shortage of parts that led to substitution of a faulty part whose malfunction caused a long delay in a launch, a delay embarrassing to Lucas and to Mulloy (see Chapter 3).

158. Mulloy told me how United States Boosters, the manufacturers of the boosters' forward and aft skirt assemblies, had "re-competed" that contract, resulting in a lower price for NASA (interview of L. B. Mulloy, October 19, 2000, tape 1, side 1).

159. See "STS 61C Launch," memo received by Reinartz on January 21 and by Lucas on January 23, 1986, sent to a "distribution" including Mulloy, with copies to Lucas, Kingsbury, and Littles (MSFC history archives, drawer 25, file "61C 1986," personal document M3).

The term "operational" was early used by President Reagan as he announced the end of the testing phase of shuttle flight (the first four shuttle flights), indicating that the shuttle program would now be in a position to carry out space missions routinely. The term carried the clear implication that the shuttle no longer required testing, that its properties were fully known, that it was a workhorse vehicle—all contradicted repeatedly by, among other things, the many launch delays of many flights, most especially that of 61C just preceding the *Challenger*.

160. Everyone understood the obvious fact that as each shuttle was being assembled and tested to meet its design and updated specifications, the shuttle was not ready for flight (under normal conditions) until proven so on the basis of engineering data. That is, it was presumed unready until certified "flight ready."

161. Although participants were no doubt aware of time pressure, their training and experience did not equip them to grasp the cognitive, communicative, and decision-making effects of restricted time, much less to voice the fact of these deficits or their clear implication that the usual FRR standards of data completeness never could be met under that kind of time restriction. Yet the whole matter would be different if the focus had been not on proving danger but rather on proving the shuttle safe, a view elaborated in Chapter 7.

The effect of time pressure to degrade perceptual and cognitive performance is a finding with a long history (see Fitts, 1966; Wickelgren, 1977). It has received various labels, most usually "speed-accuracy trade-off."

162. Dekker and Woods (2010, p. 138) comment on one aspect of this distance: "One marker of [organizational] resilience is the distance between operations as management imagines they go on and how they actually go on."

163. Readers familiar with the work of Jean Piaget (1952, 1954; Flavell, 1963) will recognize how his concepts apply aptly to the situation of the engineers trying to expand the managers' grasp of the new situation. The key managers were "assimilating" the engineers' warning and data to their previous schemas instead of accommodating their schemas to the new information.

164. See Chapter VII of Volume I of the Presidential Commission *Report*, "The silent safety program," for the Commission's critical assessment of deficiencies in reporting

problems and in-flight anomalies, the failure to collect "trend data," communication failures, and the effect that the concept of "operational" had on assumptions that shuttle flights were routine. See especially the report by Wiley C. Bunn, head of Marshall's Quality Assurance program, that his office actually had on hand the unassembled trend data before the launch but did not examine it: "Had we done that the data just jumps off the page at you" (PC *Report*, vol. I, p. 155).

165. Ibid, p. 152. See Lighthall (2014b) for an analysis of those decisions.

166. Of course, *Situations* may well arise more than once in such organizations.

167. See The Hon. Lord Cullen (1990) and Paté-Cornell (1993). Learning from the Piper Alpha accident: A Postmortem analysis of technical and organizational factors. *Risk Analysis, 13*(2), 215-232.

168. Lipsitch , et al (2012).

169. See also the penetrating account of the decision making preceding the *Columbia* shuttle disaster by Cabbage and Harwood (2004, especially pp. 59–72).

170. The possibility of such a situation being assessed and decided immediately or through unexpressed internal debate by a single person in authority exists and is perhaps most likely in an emergency military or corporate setting (see McCuistion, 2012, and Jaffe, 2012, for punitive responses to experts' informing managers of dangerous situations), but even there, a senior officer will depend on the subordinate technicians who first discover the new condition and who are most expert in the technical context and equipment performance of that discovery. That dependency of managers on technicians stems directly from the differentiation among segments of expertise and authority distributed across roles, locations, and levels of command in highly organized enterprises.

Personal observations and interviews at the Cook nuclear power plant in Bridgman, Michigan suggest that regular cycles of operator training, the structured practice of delegating emergency decision-making power to control room operators, and routinized operator responses to a wide array of danger scenarios in a program of danger simulations can, together, mitigate the kind of decision-making weaknesses revealed in the *Challenger* and *Columbia* disasters. However, while the word culture is prominent in the Cook managerial discourse, that discourse is still to be informed by the discipline and methods of cultural anthropology, especially ethnography – a potentially serious organizational blindness, a condition not confined to this otherwise resilient (Woods, 2006) high-tech safety-critical enterprise.

171. Scholars familiar with Piagetian writings (Piaget, 1952, 1954; Flavell, 1963) will recognize the tendency—exhibited here in these managers' holding on to the inaccurate mental models that "worked" for them—to "assimilate" new information to familiar schemas, thus failing to "accommodate" their schemas to the new dimensions of reality, where reality can be correctly perceived only after experiencing cognitive "disequilibrium" in which they realize their familiar schemas no longer work.

172. The reader may wonder why participants would *presume* danger just before the *Challenger* launch when it had been preceded by the complete string of 24 successful flights. Participants, especially managers, who (1) recognize that the space shuttle venture enters a still relatively uncharted domain with entirely new technology and (2) have been taught to understand the stark difference between subjective probability and objective probability (see, for example, Slovik, 2000) and to understand that the basis for figuring probabilities of either success or failure in space exploration is still very unstable—and therefore that this shuttle effort and any future space exploration must be framed as

experimental, not as "operational"—would understand the wisdom of presuming danger and the danger of presuming safety in settling any safety-danger issue.

173. The general rule is that he who brings a claim must prove it. In criminal cases, the government is always the party bringing the case. For a penetrating analysis of how presumption and burden of proof can determine the outcome of arguments, arguments in any context over any issue, see Gaskins (1995). See also Cooper (2003) for the distinction between "legal" burden of proof and "evidential" burden of proof.

174. See Fischhoff and Johnson (1997). Discussing distributed decision-making systems, they comment that "the fundamental management problem remains the simple one of determining what is relevant" (p. 231).

175. Too complete, that is, given the time available for clarifying the significance of each piece of evidence.

176. Remember, inclusion of *all* evidence in FRRs was a norm that Lucas reinforced by publicly humiliating anyone omitting some relevant piece of data.

177. The issue of which conditions should require or trigger presumption of one competing value over the other can be complicated. See Greenberg, Gould-Saltman, and Schneider (2006) for complications in child custody cases. See also Yablon (2003) for complications of presumption and burden of persuasion more generally.

Applying the presumption of danger in high-tech explorations in unforgiving environments, however, given the high stakes of human life, is simpler. Presuming danger is required by the magnitude and multidimensionality of *inevitable and unforgiving unknowns* in such enterprises, usually in the form not of straightforward causal effects but rather of highly *interacting* conditions.

178. See McCuistion (2012) and Jaffe (2012) for descriptions of technical experts' frontline observations of deviations from

operating norms, deviations communicated to managers who then both ignored the warnings and acted on their own to ensure continuation of the aberrant and, in the end, disastrous practices.

179. For the frequency of offshore hydrocarbon drilling disasters, see www.offshorttechnology.com and www.foxfirm.com (workplace accidents/severe injuries — oil rig/oil platform injuries).

180. A strong professional norm in engineering limits the role of engineers and technical specialists to technical advising only. Decisions about any organizational decision implied by that technical advice are the province of managers. In high-tech settings, and many other organizations, this division of functions brings the danger of managers acquiring mental models of technical dynamics that suffer from incompleteness or inaccuracies. For an engineer to ask a manager to give an account of the manager's technical understanding, however, crosses the advice-giving line into holding managers accountable. Managers hold subordinates, including engineers, accountable. Upward accountability by subordinates who evaluate their managers, a valuable tool in a safety-promoting organization, is rare (but see Flin, 2006, p. 231 for an example).

181. NASA's impressive, multidimensional "knowledge management" system (Rogers, 2005, 2006; Day & Rogers, 2006; Rogers & Ryschkewitsch, 2008), created in response to the *Columbia* accident, was adapted specifically for NASA's project structure. Knowledge management focuses primarily on developing, sharing, and "reapplying" ground-level operating knowledge within and across NASA, but makes no specific provision for knowledge transfer to NASA from the disciplines of the human sciences.

182. I analyze elsewhere deficiencies similar to these, but even more shocking, in the *Columbia* shuttle disaster (Lighthall, 2014a).

183. In response to the *Challenger* and *Columbia* accidents NASA instituted a multidimensional program of knowledge acquisition and sharing to transform itself into a learning organization. Its centralized and local practices can be found in Rogers (2005, 2006) and in Rogers & Ryschkewitsch (2008).

184. On conceptual complexities of "culture": Abu-Lughod (1986, 1991), Boddy (1989), Deflem (1991), Duranti (1994), Geertz (1973,1983), Goffman (1963, 1967), Ortlieb (2010), Shweder (1991), and Turner (1969); on the intricacies of applied anthropology: Baba (1989, 2006), Cerfkin (2010), Gamst (1977), Moore (1997), Schwartzman (1989, 1993), and Van Maanen (2001).

The listings of this endnote and of the next five endnotes sample only minimally a much larger corpus of scholarly works dealing with each of these domains, but they do indicate the range of expertise that must be recruited to bring into these high-tech enterprises the new dimensions of skill and insight required to achieve an effective balance of production and safety.

185. The varied perspectives needed are reflected in the following sample: Cook and Nemeth (2006); Flin (1996, 2003, 2006); Hale and Heijer (2006); Hollnagel, Woods, and Leveson (2006); Piaget (1952, 1954); Schraagen, Militello, Ormerod, and Lipshitz (2008); Weick and Sutcliffe (2001); Wickens (2002); Woods (2006); and Zohar and Luria (2003). The intellectual disposition that Langer (1989, 1997) refers to as mindfulness would seem particularly relevant to detecting important but unexpected shifts in conditions.

186. At least two prominent meanings have been given in the organizational literature to "resilience." One is the capacity to recover production capacity from mishap and adversity. Such resilience is in the service of production. The recovered processes and capacities referred to in that resilience

do not support safety. They crowd it out. The other meaning of resilience in the literature is explicitly in the service of safety. It is this meaning that must be enacted.

187. See Peterson (2008, p. 2): "[H]ierarchical organization has some features that can create serious problems. Most importantly, hierarchy permits separation [of] possession of technical knowledge relevant to ensuring safe and efficient organization [from] possession of authority to commit organizational resources to a particular course of conduct."

188. See Hutchins's (1995) examination of the cognitive complexities of navigating a large ship, Emerson's (1962, 1972) explorations of power-dependence relations, Roberts's (1993) organizational analysis, Maier's (2013) conception of servant leadership, and especially the studies of the bases of power and influence by French and Raven (1959); Koslowsky, Schwarzwald, and Ashuri (2001); Raven (1992); and Raven, Schwarzwald, and Koslowsky (1998).

189. On the effects of stress on deliberations: Hammond (2000); DeCaro et al. (2011); Bhagat, Allie, and Ford (1991); Bourne and Yaroush (2003), Hockey (1983, 1997); Lazarus (1966); Schooler, Dougall, and Baum (1999); and Shanteau and Dino (1993). For research on how time pressure (need for speed) affects perceptual-cognitive effectiveness (accuracy), see Fitts (1966), Hollnagel (2009), and Wickelgren (1977).

For conceptual and empirical research on situation assessment and awareness, see Endsley (1995a, 1995b, 1997); Endsley and Jones (2001); and Gorman, Cooke, and Winner (2006); and also Grosjean and Terrier (1999) and Salmon et al. (2009).

190. See Ashworth and Blake (1996); Billig (1996); Cooper (2003); Gaskins (1995); Greenberg, Gould-Saltman, and Schneider (2006); Lu and Lajoie (2008); and Osborne (2010).

191. An organization capable of studying and improving its own structures, norms, and processes requires a kind of leadership geared to safety, production, *and* organizational self-study. Empirical and conceptual studies of leadership are legion and are reviewed in Zaccaro and Klimoski (2001) and Zaccaro and DeChurch (2011). Bass and Riggio (2006) describe and show evidence for a "transformational leadership," complemented by Bolman and Deal's (1997) perspective on "reframing organizations." Zaccaro (2002) assesses the social intelligence required of the transformational leader; Langer (1989, 1997) explores "mindlessness" and "mindfulness," qualities of attention and openness required; Hogarth (2001) explores the intuitive dimension of mindfulness; Patterson et al. (2013) explore intuitive decision making in a simulated environment, and Klein (2003) and colleagues (Phillips, Klein, & Sieck (2007) explore intuition and expertise in natural settings; Einhorn and Hogarth (1978) consider the persistence of invalid confidence in one's judgment—a barrier to mindfulness; Tindale (1993) reviews error tendencies in the decision making of individuals and groups; and Hackman (2002) considered how team leaders can lay the groundwork for "great performances." Eagly and Johnson (1990) and Herrera, Duncan, Green, and Skaggs (2012) assess sex and gender differences in leadership, and Goodwin (2009) explores professional vision.

Theory and insights relevant for effective organizational improvement are treated in Argyris (2004); Argyris and Schön (1994, 1996); Jarvis (2006); Langer (1989, 1997); Lighthall (2004); Mattingly (1991), Rochlin, La Porte, and Roberts (1987); Schein (1993); and Schön (1995).

Skills and experience supporting a self-studying organization are exhibited in Carroll, Perin, and Marcus (1991), Carroll, Rudolph, and Hatakenaka (2002); Fiore, Rosen, Smith-Jentsch, and Salas (2010); Haldane (2013); Lighthall (1989, 2000); Lighthall and Allan (1989); Loughran et al.

(2004) for teachers' studies of their own teaching practices; Lundy, Laspina, Kaplan, Fastman, and Lawlor (2007); PwC (PricewaterhouseCooper, 2013); Rogers (2006); Schön (1991); Schneider (1985); and U.S. Army Combined Command (1993).

Complexities of group and intergroup processes are explored in Cannon-Bowers, Salas, and Converse (1993); Cannon-Bowers, Salas, Blickensderfer, and Bowers (1998); Cicourel (1990); Cooke, Salas, Cannon-Bowers, and Stout (2000); Cronin and Weingart (2007a, 2007b); DeChurch and Zaccaro (2010); Duffy (1993); Edmondson, Bohmer, and Pisano (2001); Espinosa and Clark (2014); Fiore et al. (2010); Gorman, Cooke, and Amazeen (2010); Salas, Cannon-Bowers, and Koslowski (1997); and Salas, Cooke, and Rosen (2008). Dimensions of decision-making processes are explored in Bearman et al. (2010); Janis (1972); Janis and Mann (1977); Klein (1993); Klein et al. (1993); Marks, Zaccaro, and Mathieu (2000); McGrath (1990); Orasanu and Connelly (1993); and Hammond et al. (1986).

Dynamics of individual cognition relevant to functioning well (or poorly) in organizational improvement are exhibited in Abelson (1975, 1976), Kahneman and Tversky (1986), Kirschner and Whitson (1997), Saks and Kidd (1986), and Schank (1975).

192. See also my analysis of the knowledge voids in the *Columbia* disaster (Lighthall, 2014a).

193. See Rogers (2006) for an adaptation of the U.S. Army's after-action reviews (U.S. Army Combined Command, 1993); see also Wabb (2009).

194. The participants in the *Challenger* deliberations exemplify the kinds of position, role, and specialization that high-stakes technical deliberations and decisions involve in the *Situation* I have described. Effective simulations of *Situations* require that range of participants.

195. The Donald C. Cook nuclear facility in Bridgman, Michigan, for example, contains two exact replicas of its online control rooms for its two power units. The replicas are used regularly to conduct simulated emergencies demanding operators' responses. Simulations are now video taped so that participants are able to review and discuss areas of strength and weakness. This is the kind of reflexive study and learning needed more widely in these high-tech safety-critical organizations for them to become learning organizations.

196. Theory and insights relevant for effective organizational improvement are treated in Argyris (2004); Argyris and Schön (1994, 1996); Jarvis (2006); Langer (1989, 1997); Lighthall (2004); Mattingly (1991), Rochlin, La Porte, and Roberts (1987); Rogers (2005, 2006); Rogers & Ryschkewitsch (2008); Schein (1993); and Schön (1995).

References

Abelson, R. P. (1975). Concepts for representing mundane reality in plans. In D. G. Bobrow & A. M. Collins (Eds.), *Representation and understanding: Studies in cognitive science* (pp. 273–309). New York, NY: Academic Press.

Abelson, R. P. (1976). Script processing in attitude formation and decision making. In J. W. Payne & J. S. Carroll (Eds.), *Cognition and social behavior* (pp. 33–45). Hillsdale, NJ: Lawrence Erlbaum.

Abu-Lughod, L. (1986). *Veiled sentiments: Honor and poetry in a Bedouin society*. Berkeley: University of California Press.

Abu-Lughod, L. (1991). Writing against culture. In R. G. Fox (Ed.), *Recapturing anthropology: Working in the present* (pp. 137–162). Santa Fe, NM: School of American Research Press.

Abu-Lughod, L., & Lutz, C. A. (1990). Introduction: Emotion, discourse, and the politics of everyday life. In C. A. Lutz and L. Abu-Lughod (Eds.), *Language and the politics of emotion* (pp. 1–23). Cambridge, UK: Cambridge University Press.

Argyris, C. (2004). *Reasons and rationalizations: The limits to organizational knowledge*. New York, NY: Oxford University Press.

Argyris, C., & Schön, D. (1994). *Theory in practice: Increasing professional effectiveness*. San Francisco, CA: Jossey-Bass.

Argyris, C., & Schön, D. A. (1996). *Organizational learning II: Theory, method and practice*. Reading, MA: Addison-Wesley.

Ashworth, A., & Blake, M. (1996). The presumption of innocence in English criminal law. *Criminal law review, 306*, 314.

Baba, M. (1989). Organizational culture: Revisiting the small-society metaphor. In P. Sachs (Ed.), *The anthropology of work review, 10*, 7-10. Special Issue: Anthropological approaches to organizational culture. Washington, DC: Society for the Anthropology of Work.

Baba, M. 2006. Anthropology and business. In H. James Birk (Ed.), *Encyclopedia of anthropology* (pp. 83–117). Thousand Oaks, CA: Sage.

Bass, B. M. (1998). *Transformational leadership: Industrial, military, and educational impact.* Mahwah, NJ: Erlbaum.

Bass, B. M., & Riggio, R. (2006). *Transformational leadership* (2nd Ed.). Mahwah, NJ: Prentice Hall.

Bearman, C., Paletz, S. B. F., Orasanu, J., & Thomas, M. J. W. (2010). The breakdown of coordinated decision making in distributed systems. *Human factors, 52*(2), 173–188.

Bhagat, R. S., Allie, S. M., & Ford, D. L., Jr. (1991). Organizational stress and symptoms of life strain: An inquiry into the moderating role of styles of coping. *Journal of social behavior and personality, 6,* 163-184.

Billig, M. (1996). *Arguing and thinking: A rhetorical approach to social psychology* (2nd Ed.). Cambridge, UK: Cambridge University Press.

Boddy, J. (1989). *Wombs and alien spirits: Women, men, and the Zar cult in Northern Sudan.* Madison: University of Wisconsin Press.

Boisjoly, R. M. (1987). Ethical decisions—Morton Thiokol and the space shuttle *Challenger* disaster. Paper presented at the annual meetings of the American Society of Mechanical Engineers, Boston, MA, Fall, 1967.

Bolman, L. G. & Deal, T. E. (2013). *Reframing organizations: Artistry, choice, and Leadership.* (5th Ed.). San Francisco, CA: Jossey-Bass.

Bourne, L. E., Jr., & Yaroush, R. A. (2003). Stress and cognition: A cognitive psychological perspective. *National Aeronautics and Space Administration Grant Number NAG2-1561 Final Report.* Available at: www.humansystems.arc.nasa.gov/eas/download/non_EAS/Stress_and_Cognition.pdf

Bruno, L. C. (1994). Challenger explosion. In N. Schlager (Ed.), *When technology fails: Significant technological disasters, accidents, and failures of the twentieth century* (pp. 609–616). Detroit, MI: Gale Research.

Buljan, A., & Shapira, Z. (2005). Attention to production schedule and safety as determinants of risk taking in NASA's decision to launch the Columbia Shuttle. In W. H. Starbuck & M. Farjoun (Eds), *Organization at the limit: Lessons from the Columbia disaster* (pp. 140-156). Malden, MA: Blackwell.

Cabbage, M., & Harwood, W. (2004). *Comm check... The final flight of shuttle* Columbia. New York: Free Press.

Cannon-Bowers, J. A., Salas, E., Blickensderfer, E., & Bowers, C. A. (1998). The impact of cross-training and workload on team functioning: A replication and extension of initial findings. *Human Factors, 40*, 92–101.

Cannon-Bowers, J. A., Salas, E., & Converse, S. (1993). Shared mental models in expert team decision making. In J. Castellan Jr. (Ed.), *Current issues in individual and group decision making* (pp. 221–246). Hillsdale, NJ: Erlbaum.

Carroll, J. S., Perin, C., & Marcus, A. A. (1991, December). Organizational learning at nuclear power plants. *Report of the panel meeting, nuclear power plant advisory panel, on organizational learning,* MIT Sloan School of Management, Cambridge, MA, October 17–18.

Carroll, J. S., Rudolph, J. W., & Hatakenaka, S. (2002). *Organizational learning from experience in high-hazard industries: Problem investigation as off-line reflective practice* (Working Paper 4359-02). Cambridge: MIT Sloan School of Management. Available at: http://ssrn.com/abstract_id=305718

Cerfkin, M. (2010). *Ethnography and the corporate encounter.* New York, NY: Berghahn Books.

Chiles, J. R. (2001). *Inviting disaster: Lessons from the edge of technology.* New York, NY: Harper Collins.

Cicourel, A. V. (1990). The integration of distributed knowledge in collaborative medical diagnoses. In J. Gallagher, R. Kraut, & C. Egido (Eds.), *Intellectual teamwork: Social and technological foundations of cooperative work* (pp. 221–241). Hillsdale, NJ: Lawrence Erlbaum.

Colin, M., & Campbell, L. (1992). Memory accessibility and probability of judgments: An experimental evaluation of the availability heuristic. *Journal of personality and social psychology, 63*(6), 890–902.

Cook, R. I., & Nemeth, C. (2006). Taking things in one's stride: Cognitive features of two resilient performances. In E. Hollnagel, D. D. Woods, & N. Leveson (Eds.), *Resilience engineering: Concepts and precepts* (pp. 205–221). Burlington, VT: Ashgate.

Cook, R. I., & Woods, D. D. (2006). Distancing through differencing: An obstacle to organizational learning following accidents. In E. Hollnagel, D. D. Woods, & N. Leveson (Eds.), *Resilience engineering: Concepts and precepts* (pp. 329–338). Burlington, VT: Ashgate.

Cook, R. I., Woods, D. D., & Miller, C. (1998). *A tale of two stories: Contrasting views on patient safety.* Chicago, IL: National Patient Safety Foundation.

Cooke, N. J., Salas, E., Cannon-Bowers, J. A., & Stout, R. (2000). Measuring team knowledge. *Human factors, 42,* 151–173.

Cooke, N. J., Gorman, J. C., Duran, J. L., & Taylor, A. R. (2007). Team cognition in experienced command and control teams. *Journal of experimental psychology: Applied, 13*(3), 146-157.

Cooper, S. (2003). Human rights and legal burdens of proof. Retrieved from http://webjcli.ncl.ac.uk/2003/issue3/coope 3.html

Cronin, M. A., & Weingart, L. R. (2007a). Representational gaps, information processing, and conflict in functionally diverse teams. *Academy of management review, 32,* 761–774.

Cronin, M. A., & Weingart, L. R. (2007b). The differential effects of trust and respect on team conflict. In K. J. Behfar and L. L. Thompson (Eds.), *Conflict in organizational groups:*

New directions in theory and practice (pp. 205–228). Evanston, IL: Northwestern University Press.

Cullen, The Hon. Lord W. Douglas (1990). *The public inquiry into the Piper Alpha disaster.* London: H.M. Stationery Office, 2 volumes.

Day, R., & Rogers, E. (2006, January). Enhancing NASA's performance as a learning organization. *ASK Magazine, 22,* 1-5. Retrieved from http://appel.nasa.gov/2006/01/01/enhancing-nasas-performance-as-a-learning-organization/

DeCaro, M. S., Thomas, R. D., Albert, N. B., & Beilock, S. L. (2011). Choking under pressure: Multiple routes to skill failure. *Journal of experimental psychology: General, 140,* 390–406.

DeChurch, L. A., & Zaccaro, S. J. (2010). Perspective: Teams won't solve this problem. *Human factors, 52*(Special Issue), 329–334.

Deflem, M. (1991). Ritual, anti-structure, and religion: A discussion of Victor Turner's Processual Symbolic Analysis. *Journal for the scientific study of religion, 30,* 1–25.

Dekker, S. W. A., & Woods, D. D. (2010). The high reliability organization perspective. In E. Salas, F. Jentsch, & D. Maurino (Eds.), *Human factors in aviation* (2nd ed., pp. 123–146), New York, NY: Elsevier. Retrieved from http://sidney-dekker.com/wp-content/uploads/2013/01/CH005.pdf

Duffy, L. T. (1993). Team decision making and technology. In N. J. Castellan, Jr. (Ed.), *Individual and group decision making—current issues* (pp. 247–266). Hillsdale, NJ: Lawrence Erlbaum.

Duranti, A. (1994). *From grammar to politics: Linguistic anthropology in a western Samoan village.* Berkeley: University of California Press.

Eagly, A. H., & Johnson, B. T. (1990). Gender and leadership style: A meta-analysis. *Psychological bulletin, 108,* 233–256.

Edmondson, A. C., Bohmer, R. M. J., & Pisano, G. P. (2001).

Disrupted routines: Team learning and new technology implementation in hospitals. *Administrative science quarterly, 46*, 685–716.

Einhorn, H. J., & Hogarth, R. M. (1978). Confidence in judgment: Persistence in the illusion of validity. *Psychological review, 85*, 395–416.

Emerson, R. M. (1962) Power-dependence relations. *American sociological review, 27*:31-40.

Emerson, R. M. (1972) Exchange theory, Part I: A psychological basis for social exchange. In J. Berger, M. Zelditch, and B. Anderson, (Eds.), *Sociological theories in progress*, vol. 2 (pp. 38-57). Boston, MA: Houghton Mifflin.

Endsley, M. R. (1995a). Toward a theory of situation awareness. *Human factors, 37*(1), 32–64.

Endsley, M. R. (1995b). Measurement of situation awareness in dynamic systems. *Human factors, 37*(1), 65–84.

Endsley, M. R. (1997). The role of situation awareness in naturalistic decision making. In C. E. Zsambok & G. Klein (Eds.), *Naturalistic decision making* (pp. 269–283). Mahwah, NJ: Lawrence Erlbaum.

Endsley, M. R. (1999). Situation awareness in aviation systems. In D. J. Garland, J. A. Wise, & V. D. Hopkins (Eds.), *Handbook of aviation human factors* (pp. 257–276). Mahwah, NJ: Lawrence Erlbaum.

Endsley, M. R. (2000). Theoretical underpinnings of situation awareness: A critical review. In M. R. Endsley & D. J. Garland (Eds.) *Situation awareness analysis and measurement* (pp. 1-24). Mahwah, NJ: Lawrence Erlbaum.

Endsley, M. R., & Jones, W. M. (2001). A model of inter- and intra-team situation awareness: Implications for design, training and measurement. In M. McNeese, E. Salas, & M. Endsley (Eds.), *New trends in cooperative activities: Understanding system dynamics in complex environments* (pp.46-67). Santa Monica, CA: Human Factors and Ergonomics Society.

Espinosa, J. A., & Clark, M. A. (2014). Team knowledge representation: A network perspective. *Human factors, 56,* 333–348.

Fiore, S. M., Rosen, M. A., Smith-Jentsch, K. A., & Salas, E. (2010). Toward an understanding of macrocognition in teams: Predicting processes in complex collaborative contexts. *Human factors, 52,* 203–224.

Fischhoff, B., Slovik, P., Lichtenstein, S., Read, S., & Combs, B. (1978). How safe is safe enough? A psychometric study of attitudes toward technological risks and benefits. *Policy sciences, 9,* 127–152.

Fischhoff, B., & Johnson, S. (1997). The possibility of distributed decision making. In Z. Shapira (Ed.), *Organizational decision making.* (pp. 216–237). Cambridge, UK: Cambridge University Press.

Fitts, P. M. (1966). Cognitive aspects of information processing: III. Set for speed versus accuracy. *Journal of experimental psychology, 71*(6), 849–857.

Flavell, J. H. (1963). *The developmental psychology of Jean Piaget.* Princeton, NJ: D. Van Nostrand.

Flin, R. (1996). *Sitting in the hot seat: Leaders and teams for critical incident management.* Chichester, England: Wiley.

Flin, R. (2003). Men behaving badly? Senior managers and safety. *Human factors and ergonomics in manufacturing, 13*(4), 1–8.

Flin, R. (2006). Erosion of managerial resilience: From VASA to NASA. In E. Hollnagel, D. D. Woods, & N. Leveson (Eds.), *Resilience engineering* (pp. 223–234). Burlington, VT: Ashgate.

Förster, J., Higgins, E. T., & Bianco, A. (2003). Speed/accuracy decisions in task performance: Built-in trade-off or separate strategic concerns? *Organizational behavior and human decision processes, 90,* 148-164.

French, J. R. P., Jr., & Raven, B. H. (1959). The bases of social power. In D. Cartwright (Ed.), *Studies in social power* (pp. 150–167). Ann Arbor, MI: Institute for Social Research.

Gamst, F. C. (1977). An integrating view of the underlying premises of an industrial ethnology in the United States and Canada. *Anthropological quarterly, 50,* 1–8.

Gaskins, R. H. (1995). *Burdens of proof in modern discourse.* New Haven, CT: Yale University Press.

Geertz, C. (1973). *The interpretation of cultures.* New York, NY: Basic Books.

Geertz, C. (1983). The way we think now: Toward an ethnography of modern thought. In C. Geertz, *Local knowledge: Further essays in interpretive anthropology.* (pp. 147–166). New York, NY: Basic Books.

Goffman, E. (1963). *Stigma: Notes on the management of spoiled identity.* Englewood Cliffs, NJ: Prentice-Hall.

Goffman, E. (1967). *Interaction ritual: Essays on face-to-face behavior.* New York, NY: Pantheon Books.

Goodwin, C. (2009). Professional vision. In A. Duranti (Ed.), *Linguistic anthropology* (2nd ed., pp. 452–478). West Sussex, England: John Wiley.

Gorman, J. C., Cooke, N. J., & Amazeen, P. G. (2010). Training adaptive teams. *Human factors, 52*(2), 295–307.

Gorman, J. C., Cooke, N. J., & Winner, J. L. (2006). Measuring team situation awareness in decentralized command and control systems. *Ergonomics, 49,* 1312–1325.

Greenberg, L. R., Gould-Saltman, D. J., & Schneider, R. (2006). The problem with presumptions–A review and commentary. *Journal of child custody, 3*(3/4), 141–174, and available at: http://jcc.haworthpress.com

Grosjean, V., & Terrier, P. (1999). Temporal awareness: Pivotal in performance? *Ergonomics, 42*(11), 1443–1456.

Guttentag, J. M. & Herring, R. J. (1986). *Disaster myopia in international banking.* Essays on international finance, No. 164,

Princeton, NJ: International finance section, department of economics, Princeton University.

Hackman, J. R. (2002). *Leading teams. Setting the stage for great performances.* Cambridge, MA: Harvard Business School Press. See also www.leadingteams.org

Haldane, A. G. (2009). Why banks failed the stress test. Draft paper for the Marcus-Evans Conference on Stress Testing, 9-10 February, 2009. Available at: http://www.bis.org/review/r090219d.pdf

Hale, A., & Heijer, T. (2006). Defining resilience. In E. Hollnagel, D. D. Woods, & N. Leveson (Eds.), *Resilience engineering: Concepts and precepts* (pp. 35–40). Burlington, VT: Ashgate.

Hamburg, J. (1987). *An account of the final hours of the space shuttle* Challenger *January 28, 1986—etched forever.* Special section, Orlando Sentinal, FL.

Hammond, K. R. (2000). *Judgment under stress.* New York, NY: Oxford University Press.

Hammond, K. R., Stewart, T. R., Brehmer, B., & Steinmann, D. O. (1986). Social judgment theory. In H. R. Arkes & K. R. Hammond (Eds.), *Judgment and decision making: An interdisciplinary reader* (pp. 56–76). New York, NY: Cambridge University Press.

Herrera, R., Duncan, P. A., Green, M. T., & Skaggs, S. L. (2012). The effect of gender on leadership and culture. *Global business and organizational excellence, 31,* 37–48.

Hockey, G. R. J. (Ed.). (1983). *Stress and human performance.* Chichester, England: Wiley.

Hockey, G. R. J. (1997). Compensatory control in the regulation of human performance under stress and high workload: A cognitive-energetical framework. *Biological psychology, 45,* 73–93.

Hogarth, R. M. (2001). *Educating intuition.* Chicago, IL: University of Chicago Press.

Hollnagel, E. (2013a). A tale of two safeties. *Nuclear safety and simulation, 4*, 1-9.

Hollnagel, E. (2013b). From safety-I to safety-II: A white paper. *Eurocontrol.* Available at: www.skybrary.aero/bookshelf/books/2437.pdf

Hollnagel, E. (2009). *The ETTO Principle: Efficiency-thoroughness trade-off—Why things that go right sometimes go wrong.* Burlington, VT: Ashgate.

Hollnagel, E., Woods, D. D., & Leveson, N. (Eds.). 2006. *Resilience engineering.* Burlington, VT: Ashgate.

Howard, M. W. & Kahana, M. J. (1999). Contextual variability and serial position effects in free recall. *Journal of experimental psychology: Learning, memory, and cognition, 25*, 923-941.

Hutchins, E. (1995). *Cognition in the wild.* Cambridge, MA: MIT Press.

Jaffe, S. (2012). Countrywide whistleblower reveals rampant mortgage fraud part of "everyday business." Retrieved from www.rawstory.com/rs/2012/07/21/countryside-whistle-blower-reveals-rampant-mortgage-fraud-part-of-everyday-business/

Janis, I. L. (1972). *Victims of groupthink.* Boston, MA: Houghton Mifflin.

Janis, I. L., & Mann, L. (1977). *Decision making: A psychological analysis of conflict, choice, and commitment.* New York, NY: Free Press.

Jarvis, P. (1987). *Adult learning in the social context.* Beckenham, England: Croom Helm.

Jarvis, P. (2006). *Towards a comprehensive theory of human learning.* New York, NY: Routledge.

Kahneman, D., & Tversky, A. (1986). Choices, values, and frames. In H. R. Arkes & K. R. Hammond (Eds.), *Judgment and decision making: An interdisciplinary reader* (pp. 194–210). New York, NY: Cambridge University Press.

Kahneman, D. & Tversky, A. (1974). Judgment under uncertainty: Heuristics and biases, *Science 185*, 1124-1131.

Kirshner, D. & Whitson, J. A. (1997). *Situated cognition: Social, semiotic, and psychological perspectives.* Mahwah, NJ: Lawrence Erlbaum.

Klein, G. A. (2003). *Intuition at work.* New York: Doubleday.

Klein, G. A. (1993). A recognition-primed decision (RPD) model for rapid decision making. In G. Klein, J. Orasanu, R. Calderwood, & C. E. Zsambok (Eds.), *Decision making in action: Models and methods* (pp. 138–147). Norwood, NJ: Ablex.

Klein, G. A. (1997). An overview of naturalistic decision making applications. In C. E. Zsambok & G. Klein (Eds.), *Naturalistic decision making* (pp. 49–69). Mahwah, NJ: Lawrence Erlbaum.

Klein, G., Orasanu, J., Calderwood, R., & Zsambok, C. E. (Eds.). (1993). *Decision making in action: Models and methods.* Norwood, NJ: Ablex.

Koehler, J. J. (1993). The influence of prior beliefs on scientific judgments of evidence quality. *Organizational behavior and human decision processes, 56*, 28–55.

Koslowsky, M., Schwarzwald, J., & Ashuri, S. (2001). On the relationship between subordinates' compliance to power sources and organizational attitudes. *Applied psychology: An international review, 50*, 455–476.

Kunda, Z. (1999). *Social cognition: Making sense of people.* Cambridge, MA: MIT Press.

Langer, E. J. (1989). *Mindfulness.* Reading, MA: Addison-Wesley.

Langer, E. J. (1997). *The power of mindful learning.* Reading, MA: Addison-Wesley.

La Porte, T. R. (1996). High reliability organizations: Unlikely, demanding, and at risk. *Journal of contingencies and crisis management. 4*(2), 60-71.

Lazarus, R. S. (1966). *Psychological stress and coping processes.* New York, NY: McGraw-Hill.

Leveson, N., Dulac, N., Marais, K., & Carroll, J. (nd, circa 2010). Moving beyond normal accidents and high-reliability organizations: A systems approach to safety in complex systems. Available by Google search: Sunnyday.mit. edu/papers/hro-final.doc

Lewis, R. S. (1988). Challenger: *The final voyage*. New York, NY: Columbia University Press.

Lighthall, F. F. (1989). Making and transcending local adaptations: A pragmatic constructivist perspective on "participation." In R. J. Magjuka & S. B. Bacharach (Eds.), Structuring participation in organizations (pp. 1-26). *Research in the sociology of organizations, 7.*

Lighthall, F. F. (2000). How can our practice of self study of our professional practices contribute a new (and needed) form of accountability?: A regular collaboration with students. In J. Loughran & T. Russell (Eds.), *Exploring myths and legends of teacher education* (pp. 154–158). Proceedings of the 3rd international conference on self-study of teacher education practices, Herstmonceux Castle, East Sussex, England.

Lighthall, F. F. (2004). Fundamental features and approaches of the *s-step* enterprise. In J Loughran, M. L. Hamilton, V. K. LaBoskey, & T. Russell (Eds.), *International handbook of self-study of teaching and teacher education practices, Part One* (pp. 193–246). Dordrecht, The Netherlands: Kluwer Academic Publishers.

Lighthall, F. F. (2014a). *The* Columbia *disaster: Choice points, gaps, dangerous thinking.* Available at: www.high-techdangers.com

Lighthall, F. F. (2014b). *Case study: A pre-empted near miss.* Available at: www.high-techdangers.com

Lighthall, F. F. (2014c). *Basic flaws in Vaughan's analysis of the* Challenger *accident.* Available at: www.high-techdangers. com

Lighthall, F. F., & Allan, S. D. (1989). *Local realities, local adaptations—Problem, process, and person in a school's governance.* London, England: Falmer Press.

Lipshitz, R., & Shaul, O. B. (1997). Schemata and mental models in recognition-primed decision making. In C. E. Zsambok & G. Klein (Eds.), *Naturalistic decision making* (pp. 293–340). Mahwah, NJ: Lawrence Erlbaum.

Lipsitch, M., Plotkin, J. B., Simonsen, L., & Bloom, B. (2012). Evolution, safety, and highly pathogenic influenza viruses. *Science 336*(6088) Special Issue, 1529–1531.

Lord, C. G., Ross, L., & Lepper, M. R. (1979). Biased assimilation and attitude polarization: The effects of prior theories on subsequently considered evidence. *Journal of personality and social psychology, 37*(11), 2098–2109.

Loughran, J., Hamilton, M. L., LaBoskey, V. K. & Russell, T. (Eds.), (2004). *International handbook of self-study of teaching and teacher education practices*. Dordrecht, The Netherlands: Kluwer Academic Publishers.

Lu, J., & Lajoie, S. P. (2008). Supporting medical decision making with argumentation tools. *Contemporary educational psychology, 33*, 425–442.

Lundy, D., Laspina, S., Kaplan, H., Fastman, B. R., & Lawlor, E. (2007). Seven hundred and fifty-nine (759) chances to learn: A 3-year pilot project to analyse transfusion-related near-miss events in the Republic of Ireland. *Vox sanguinis*, 1–9.

Mahler, J. G., & Casamayou, M. H. (2009). *Organizational learning at NASA: The* Challenger *and* Columbia *Accidents*. Washington, DC: Georgetown University Press.

Maier, M. (2013). The imperative for servant-leadership: Reflections on the (enduring) dysfunctions of corporate masculinity. In R. Burke & C. D'Agostino (Eds.), *Gender in organizations: Men as allies or adversaries to women's career advancement*, (pp. 93–117). Cheltenham, UK: Edward Elgar.

Marais, K., Dulac, N., & Leveson, N. (2004). Beyond normal accidents and high reliability organizations: The need for an alternative approach to safety in complex systems. Paper presented at the Engineering Systems Division Symposium, MIT, Cambridge, MA, March 29-31, 2004.

Marks, M. A., Zaccaro, S. J., & Mathieu, J. E. (2000). Performance implications of leader briefings and team-interaction training for team adaptation to novel environments. *Journal of applied psychology, 85,* 971–986.

Marcus, G. E. & Fischer, M. M. J. (1999). *Anthropology as cultural critique: An experimental moment in the human sciences.* Second edition. Chicago: University of Chicago Press.

Mattingly, C. F. (1991). Narrative reflections on practical action: Two learning experiences in reflective story telling. In D. Schön (Ed.), *The reflective turn: Case studies in and on practice* (pp. 235-257). New York, NY: Teachers College Press.

McClelland, D. C. (1953). *The achievement motive.* New York: Appleton-Century-Crofts.

McClelland, D. C. (1961). *The achieving society.* New York: D. Van Nostrand Co.

McConnell, M. (1987). Challenger: *A major malfunction.* Garden City, NY: Doubleday.

McCuistion, N. N. (2012). Whistleblowers: Inside the mortgage meltdown. Retrieved from www.frtv.org/2012/10/21/whistleblowers-inside-the-mortgage-meltdown/

McDonald, A. J. (1989). *Return to flight with the redesigned solid rocket motor* (AIAA Paper No. 89-2404). 25th Joint Propulsion Conference, Monterey, CA.

McDonald, A. J. & Hanson, J. R. (2009). *Truth, lies, and O-Rings: Inside the space shuttle* Challenger *disaster.* Gainsville: University Press of Florida.

McGrath, J. (1990). Time matters in groups. In J. Gallagher, R. Kraut, & C. Egido (Eds.), *Intellectual teamwork: Social and technological foundations of cooperative work* (pp. 23–62). Hillsdale, NJ: Lawrence Erlbaum.

Moore, S. (1997). The ethnography of the present and analysis of process. In R. Borofsky (Ed.), *Assessing cultural anthropology* (pp. 362–374). New York, NY: McGraw-Hill.

National Commission on the BP *Deepwater Horizon* Oil Spill and Offshore Drilling. (2011). *Deep water: The gulf oil disaster and the future of offshore drilling*. Washington, DC: United States Government Printing Office.

National Commission on the Causes of the Financial and Economic Crisis in the United States (2011). *The financial crisis inquiry report*, Official Government Edition, Washington, DC: United States Government Printing Office.

Nickerson, R. S. (1998). Confirmation bias: A ubiquitous phenomenon in many guises. *Review of general psychology, 2* (2): 175–220.

Orasanu, J. M., & Backer, P. (1996). Stress and military performance. In J. E. Driskell & E. Salas (Eds.), *Stress and human performance*, (pp. 89–125). Mahwah, NJ: Lawrence Erlbaum.

Orasanu, J., & Connelly, T. (1993). The reinvention of decision making. In G. Klein, J. Orasanu, R. Calderwood, & C. E. Zsambok (Eds.), *Decision making in action: Models and methods*, (pp. 3–20). Norwood, NJ: Ablex.

Ortlieb, M. (2010). Emerging culture, slippery culture: Conflicting conceptualizations of culture in commercial ethnography. In M. Cerfkin (Ed.), *Ethnography and the corporate encounter: Reflections on research in and of corporations*, (pp. 185–210). New York, NY: Berghahn Books.

Osborne, J. (2010). Arguing to learn in science: The role of collaborative, critical discourse. *Science, 328,* 463–466.

Paté-Cornell, M. E. (1990). Organizational aspects of engineering system safety: The case of offshore platforms. *Science, 250,* 1210–1217.

Paté-Cornell, M. E. (1993). Learning from the Piper Alpha accident: A Postmortem analysis of technical and organizational factors. *Risk analysis, 13*(2), 215-232.

Patterson, R. E., Pierce, B. J., Boydstun, A. S., Ramsey, L. M., Shannon, J., Tripp, L., & Bell, H. (2013).Training intuitive decision making in a simulated real-world environment. *Human factors, 55*, 333–345.

Perrow, C. (1984). *Normal accidents: Living with high-risk technologies*. New York: Basic Books, Inc.

Peterson, M. J. (2008). Appendix H: Assessing responsibility. In M. J. Peterson, *International dimensions of ethics education in science and engineering case study series: Bhopal Plant disaster*. Retrieved from www.umass.edu/sts/ethics

Phillips, J. K., Klein, G., & Sieck, W. R. (2007). Expertise in judgment and decision making: A case for training intuitive decision skills. In D. J. Koehler & N. Harvey (Eds.), *Blackwell handbook of judgment and decision making*, (297-315). Malden, MA: Blackwell Publishing.

Piaget, J. (1952). *The origins of intelligence in children*. New York, NY: International Universities Press.

Piaget, J. (1954). *The construction of reality in the child*. New York, NY: Basic Books.

Presidential Commission on the Space Shuttle *Challenger* Accident. (1986). *Report* (Vols. I-V). Washington, DC, United States Printing Office.

PwC (PricewaterhouseCooper) (2013). Stress testing: Failures on the horizon? *Regulatory brief*, November, 2013. Albany, NY: PwC Financial Services Regulatory Practice.

Raven, B. H. (1992). A power/interaction model of interpersonal influence: French and Raven 30 years later. *Journal of social behavior and personality*, 7, 217–244.

Raven, B. H., Schwarzwald, J., & Koslowsky, M. (1998). Conceptualizing and measuring a power/interaction model of interpersonal influence. *Journal of applied social psychology*, 28, 307–332.

Reason, J. (1990). *Human error*. Cambridge, England: Cambridge University Press.

Reinartz, S. R. (1986). *Notes: Jan. 27, '86 8:35–11:00PM @ KSC.* [Memo to NASA headquarters from SA01/Stanley R. Reinartz]. Subject: Personal Documentation, Marshall

Space Flight Center Archives (stamped received February 20, 1986; no MSFC archive drawer number).

Roberts, K. H. (Ed.). (1993). *New challenges to understanding organizations*. New York, NY: Macmillan.

Roberts, R. C., Flin, R., & Cleland, J. (2015). Staying in the zone: Offshore drillers' situation awareness. *Human factors*, 57(4), 573-590.

Robison, W., Boisjoly, R., Hoeker, D., & Young, S. (2002). Representation and misrepresentation: Tufte and the Morton Thiokol engineers on the *Challenger. Science and engineering ethics*, *8*, 59–81.

Rochlin, G. I., La Porte, T. R., & Roberts, K. H. (1987). The self-designing high-reliability organization: Aircraft carrier flight operations at sea. *Naval war college review*, Autumn, 76–90.

Rogers, E. W. (2005). Building a healthy learning organization at the NASA Goddard Space Flight Center. Prepared for presentation at the First International Forum on Integrated System Health Engineering and Management in Aerospace, November 7-10, 2005, Napa, CA. Available at: www.nasa.gov/centers/goddard/pdf/289024main_Rogers_Knowledge_Mgmt.pdf

Rogers, E. W. (2006). Introducing the pause and learn (PaL) process: Adapting the army after-action review process to the NASA Project World at the Goddard Space Flight Center. (White paper circulated at Goddard Space Flight Center, revised June 8, 2006). Available at: www.nasa.gov/centers/goddard/pdf/287922main_PaLwhitepaperV3.pdf

Rogers, E. W. & Ryschkewitsch, M. (2008). Knowledge reapplication: Enhancing organizational learning at NASA. Discussion paper, Office of the Chief Engineer, NASA HQ, Washington, DC, December, 2008. Available at: www.nasa.gov/sites/default/files/files/NASALearningAs-Posted-09032013.pdf

Rogers, E. W. (2009). The NASA learning organization: How NASA reapplies its knowledge for mission success. (Principles and components of NASA's process, presented in slides.) Available at: www.nasa.gov/centers/goddard/pdf/467921main_NASA_Learning_Organization.pdf

Sachs, P. (1995). Transforming work: Collaboration, learning and design. *Communications of the ACM, 38*, 36–44.

Sagan, S. D. (1993). *The limits of safety: Organizations, accidents, and nuclear weapons.* NJ: Princeton University Press.

Saks, M. J., & Kidd, R. F. (1986). Human information processing and adjudication: Trial by heuristics. In H. R. Arkes & K. R. Hammond (Eds.), *Judgment and decision making: An interdisciplinary reader* (pp. 213–242). New York, NY: Cambridge University Press. (Originally published in the *Law and society review*, 1980, *15*, 123–160.)

Salas, E., Cannon-Bowers, J. A., & Koslowski, S. W. J. (1997). The science and practice of training: Current trends and emerging themes. In J. K. Ford, S. W. J. Koslowski, K. Kraiger, E. Salas, & M. Teachout (Eds.), *Improving training effectiveness in work organizations* (pp. 357-368). Mahwah, NJ: Lawrence Erlbaum.

Salas, E., Cooke, N. J., & Rosen, M. A. (2008). On teams, teamwork, and team performance: Discoveries and developments. *Human factors, 50*, 540–547.

Salas, E., Goodwin, G. F., & Shawn, C. B. (Eds.). (2008). *Team effectiveness in complex organizations: Cross-disciplinary perspectives and approaches.* New York, NY: CRC Press.

Salmon, P. M., Stanton, N. A., Walker, G. H., & Jenkins, D. P. (2009). *Distributed situation awareness: Theory, measurement and application to teamwork.* Surrey, England: Ashgate.

Sarter, N. B. & Woods, D. D. (1991). Situation awareness: A critical but ill-defined phenomenon. *The international journal of aviation psychology, 1*(1), 45-57.

Schank, R. C. (1975). The structure of episodes in memory. In D. Bobrow & A. Collins (Eds.), *Representation and understanding:*

Studies in cognitive science (pp. 237–272). New York, NY: Academic Press.

Schein, E. (1993). On dialogue, culture, and organizational learning. *Organizational dynamics, 1993* (Autumn), 40–51.

Schneider, W. (1985). Training high-performance skills: Fallacies and guidelines. *Human factors, 27*(3), 285–301.

Schön, D. A. (Ed.). (1991). *The reflective turn: Case studies in and on educational practice.* New York, NY: Teachers College.

Schön, D. A. (1995). Causality and causal inference in the study of organizations. In R. F. Goodman & W. R. Fisher (Eds.), *Rethinking knowledge: Reflections across the disciplines* (pp. 69–101). Albany: State University of New York Press.

Schooler, T., Dougall, A., & Baum, A. (1999). Cues, frequency, and the disturbing nature of intrusive thoughts: Patterns seen in rescue workers after the crash of flight 427. *Journal of traumatic stress, 12*, 571–585.

Schraagen, J. M., Militello, L. G., Ormerod, T., & Lipshitz, R. (Eds.). (2008). *Naturalistic decision making and macrocognition.* Aldershot, England: Ashgate.

Schwartzman, H. B. (1989). *The meeting: Gatherings in organizations and communities.* New York, NY: Plenum.

Schwartzman, H. B. (1993). *Ethnography in organizations.* Newbury Park, CA: Sage.

Schwarz, N, Strack, F., Bless, H., Klumpp, G., Rittenauer-Schatka, H., & Simons, A. (1991). Ease of retrieval as information: Another look at the availability heuristic. *Journal of personality and social psychology, 61*(2), 195–202.

Seife, C. (2003). *Columbia* disaster underscores the risky nature of risk analysis. *Science, 299*, 1001.

Shanteau, J., & Dino, G. A. (1993). Environmental stressor effects on creativity and decision making. In O. Svenson & A. J. Maule (Eds.), *Time pressure and stress in human judgment and decision making* (pp. 293–308). New York, NY: Plenum.

Shweder, R. A. (1991). *Thinking through cultures.* Cambridge, MA: Harvard University Press.

Shweder, R. A. (2003). *Why do men barbecue? Recipes for cultural psychology*. Cambridge, MA: Harvard University Press.

Simons, D. J., & Ambinder, M. S. (2005). Change blindness: Theory and consequences. *Current directions in psychological science, 14,* 44–48.

Slovik, P. (2000). *The perception of risk*. London, England: Earthscan.

Spinner, J.. (2004, Fall). Simulator brings realistic training to sailors. *Undersea warfare—The official magazine of the us submarine force*. Retrieved from http://www.navy.mil/navy data/cno/n87/usw/issue_24/sim.htm

Starbuck, W. H., & Stephenson, J. (2005). Making NASA more effective. In W. H. Starbuck & M. Farjoun (Eds.), *Organization at the limit: Lessons from the* Columbia *disaster,* (pp. 309–335). Oxford, England: Blackwell.

Strauch, B. (2004). *Investigating human error: Incidents, accidents, and complex systems*. Burlington, VT: Ashgate.

Suchman, L. A. (1987). *Plans and situated actions: The problem of human-machine communication*. Cambridge, UK: Cambridge University Press.

Swets, J. A. (Ed.). (1964). *Signal detection and recognition by human observers*. New York, NY: Wiley.

Swets, J. A., Dawes, R. M., & Monahan, J. (2000). Psychological science can improve diagnostic decisions. *Psychological science in the public interest, 1*(1), 1-26.

Tindale, R. S. (1993). Decision errors made by individuals and groups. In J. Castellan Jr. (Ed.), *Current issues in individual and group decision making* (pp. 109-124). Hillsdale, NJ: Erlbaum.

Tompkins, P. K. (1993). *Organizational communication imperatives: Lessons of the space program*. Los Angeles, CA: Roxbury.

Tompkins, P. K. (2005). Apollo, Challenger, Columbia: *The decline of the space program*. Los Angeles, CA: Roxbury.

Tufte, E. R. (1983). *The visual display of quantitative information*. Cheshire, CT: Graphics Press.

Tufte, E. R. (1997). *Visual explanations*. Cheshire, CT: Graphics Press.

Turner, V. (1969). *Ritual process: Structure and anti-structure*. Chicago, IL: Aldine.

Tversky, A., & Kahneman, D. (1973). Availability: A heuristic for judging frequency and probability. *Cognitive psychology, 5*(2), 207–232.

US Army Combined Command. (1993). *A leader's guide to after-action reviews*. Training Circular (TC) 25-20.

US Congress. (1986a). *Investigation of the* Challenger *accident*. Report of the House Committee on Science and Technology, 99th Congress, Second Session, Report 99-1016. Washington, D.C: US Government Printing Office.

US Congress. (1986b). *Investigation of the* Challenger *accident*. Hearings before the House Committee on Science and Technology, 99th Congress, Second Session, No. 137, vol. 1. Washington, DC: US Government Printing Office.

US Congress. (1986c). *Investigation of the* Challenger *accident*. Hearings before the House Committee on Science and Technology, 99th Congress, Second Session, No. 139, vol. 2. Washington, DC: US Government Printing Office.

US Congress. (1986d). *Space shuttle accident*. Hearings before the Senate Subcommittee on Science, Technology, and Space of the Committee on Commerce, Science, and Transportation, 99th Congress, Second Session, No. 99-986. Washington, DC: US Government Printing Office.

US District Court for the Eastern District of Louisiana. (2014). in re: Oil spill by the oil Rig "Deepwater Horizon" in the Gulf of Mexico, *Findings of fact and conclusions of law: phase one trial*. Case 2;10-MD-02179-CJB-SS, Document 13355, 9.4.2014.

Van Maanen, J. (2001). Afterwords: Natives R us: Some notes on the ethnography of organizations. In D. Gellner & E. Hirsch (Eds.), *Inside organizations: Anthropologists at work* (pp. 233–261). Oxford, England: Berg.

Vaughan, D. (1996). *The* Challenger *launch decision: Risky technology, culture, and deviance at NASA.* Chicago, IL: University of Chicago Press.

Vaughan, D. (2005). System effects: On slippery slopes, repeating negative patterns, and learning from mistakes? In W. H. Starbuck & M. Farjoun (Eds.), *Organization at the limit: Lessons from the* Columbia *accident* (pp. 41–59). Malden, MA: Blackwell.

Wabb.[Blog author] (2009). *A lightweight post mortem process.* Retrieved from http://akfpartners.com/techblog/2009/09/03/a-lightweight-post-mortem-process/

Wason, P. C. (1960). On the failure to eliminate hypotheses in a conceptual task. *Quarterly Journal of experimental psychology, 12*(3), 129–140

Weick, K. E., & Sutcliffe, K. M. (2001). *Managing the unexpected: Assuring high performance in an age of complexity.* San Francisco, CA: Jossey-Bass.

Wickelgren, W. A. (1977). Speed-accuracy tradeoff and information processing dynamics. *Acta psychologica, 41,* 67–85.

Wickens, T. D. (2002). *Elementary signal detection theory.* New York, NY: Oxford University Press.

Woods, D. D. (2006). Essential characteristics of resilience. In E. Hollnagel, D. D. Woods, & N. Leveson (Eds.), *Resilience engineering: Concepts and precepts* (pp. 21-34). Burlington, VT: Ashgate

Yablon, C. M. (2003). A theory of presumption. *Law, probability and risk, 2,* 227–236. Retrieved from http://lpr.oxfordjournals.org/content/2/3/227.full.pdf

Zaccaro, S. J. (2002). Organizational leadership and social intelligence. In R. Riggio (Ed.), *Multiple intelligences and leadership,* (pp. 29–54). Mahwah, NJ: Erlbaum.

Zaccaro, S. J., & DeChurch, L. A. (2011). Leadership forms and function in multiteam systems. In S. J. Zaccaro, M. A. Marks, & L. A. Zaccaro (Eds.), *Multiteam systems: An orga-*

nization form for dynamic and complex environments (pp. 253–288). New York, NY: Routledge/Taylor Francis.

Zaccaro, S. J., & Klimoski, R. (2001). The nature of organizational leadership. In S. J. Zaccaro & R. Klimoski (Eds.), *The nature of organizational leadership: Understanding the performance imperatives confronting today's leaders* (pp. 3–41). San Francisco, CA: Jossey-Bass.

Zohar, D., & Luria, G. (2003). Organizational meta-scripts as a source of high-reliability: The case of an army armored brigade. *Journal of organizational behavior, 24*, 837–859.

Zohar, D., & Luria, G. (2004). Climate as a social-cognitive construction of supervisory safety practices: Scripts as proxy of behavior patterns. *Journal of applied psychology, 89*, 322–333.

Zsambok, C. E. (1997). Naturalistic decision making: Where do we go from here? In C. E. Zsambok & G. Klein (Eds.), *Naturalistic decision making* (pp. 3–16). Mahwah, NJ: Lawrence Erlbaum.

Author Index

Notes: This index lists authors of cited works. Topics and personnel are listed in separate Subject Index. Page numbers followed by n and a number refer to a numbered note on that page.

DeCaro, M. S., 227n189
DeChurch, L. A., 215n131,
    228n191, 229n191
Deflem, M., 226n184
Dekker, S. W. A., 221n162
Dino, G. A., 227n189
Dougall, A., 227n189
Duffy, L. T., 229n191
Dulac, N., 187n13
Duncan, P. A., 228n191
Duran, J. L., 210n106
Duranti, A., 226n184

E
Eagly, A. H., 228n191
Edmondson, A. C., 179,
    229n191
Einhorn, H. J., 228n191
Emerson, R. M., 168, 227n188
Endsley, M. R., 107, 187n10,
    187n12, 214n129, 215n132,
    216n134, 227n189
Espinosa, J. A., 229n191

F
Fastman, B. R, 229n191
Fiore, S. M., 228n191, 229n191
Fischer, M. M. J., 187n12
Fischhoff, B., 219n155, 224n174
Fitts, P. M., 159, 168, 215n133,
    219n153, 221n161, 227n189
Flavell, J. H., 219n152, 221n163,
    223n171
Flin, R., 225n180, 226n185
Ford, D. L. Jr., 227n189
Förster, J., 215n133
French, J. R. P. Jr., 168, 227n188

G
Gamst, F. C., 226n184
Garland, D. J., 187n10, 187n12
Gaskins, R. H., 224n173,
    227n190
Geertz, C., 226n184
Goffman, E., 226n184
Goodwin, C., 228n191
Gorman, J. C., 210n106,
    227n189, 229n191
Gould-Saltman, D. J., 224n177,
    227n190
Green, M. T., 228n191
Greenberg, L. R., 224n177,
    227n190
Grosjean, V., 215n133, 227n189
Guttentag, J. M., 169

H
Hackman, J. R., 228n191
Haldane, A. G., 169, 228n191
Hale, A., 226n185
Hamilton, M. L., 228n191
Hammond, K. R., 227n189,
    229n191
Hanson, J. R., 191n31
Harwood, W., 2, 222n169
Hatakenaka, S., 228n191
Heijer, T., 226n185
Herrera, R., 228n191
Herring, R. J., 169
Higgins, E. T., 215n133
Hockey, G. R. J., 227n189
Hogarth, R. M., 228n191
Hollnagel, E., 159, 176,
    219n153, 226n185, 227n189
Howard, M. W., 169
Hutchins, E., 227n188

J
Jaffe, S., 3, 185n6, 222n170, 224n178
Janis, I. L., 229n191
Jarvis, P., 228n191, 230n196
Jenkins, D. P., 214n129, 227n189
Johnson, B. T., 228n191
Johnson, S., 219n155, 224n174
Jones, W. M., 214n129, 227n189

K
Kahana, M. J., 169
Kahneman, D., 169, 219n154, 229n191
Kaplan, H., 229n191
Kidd, R. F., 229n191
Kirschner, D., 229n191
Klein, G. A., 187n12, 198n61, 202n79, 228n191, 229n191
Klimoski, R., 228n191
Klumpp, G., 219n154
Koehler, J. J., 219n152
Koslowski, S. W. J., 229n191
Koslowsky, M., 168, 227n188
Kunda, Z., 202n79, 219n152

L
LaBoskey, V. K., 228n191
Lajoie, S. P., 227n190
Langer, E. J., 158, 219n151, 226n185, 228n191, 230n196
La Porte, T. R., 187n13, 228n191, 230n196
Laspina, S., 229n191
Lawlor, E., 229n191
Lazarus, R. S., 227n189
Lepper, M. R., 219n152
Leveson, N., 187n13, 226n185

Lighthall, F. F., viii, 2, 144, 147, 150, 168, 216n135, 222n165, 225n182, 228n191, 229n192, 230n196
Lipshitz, R., 187n12, 226n185
Lord, C. G., 219n152
Loughran, J., 228n191
Lu, J., 227n190
Lundy, D., 229n191
Luria, G., 226n185

M
Maier, M., 227n188
Mann, L., 229n191
Marais, K., 187n13
Marcus, A. A., 228n191
Marcus, G. E., 187n12
Marks, M. A., 229n191
Mathieu, J. E., 229n191
Mattingly, C. F., 228n191, 230n196
McClelland, D. C., ix
McConnell, M., 66
McCuistion, N. N., 3, 185n6, 222n170, 224n178
McDonald, A. J., 191n31
McGrath, J., 229n191
Militello, L. G., 226n185
Moore, S., 226n184

N
Nemeth, C., 226n185
Nickerson, R. S., 159, 168, 169, 202n79, 219n152

O
Orasanu, J., 187n12, 229n191
Ormerod, T., 226n185

T
Taylor, A. R., 210n106
Terrier, P., 215n133, 227n189
Thomas, M. J. W., 229n191
Thomas, R. D., 227n189
Tindale, R. S., 228n191
Tompkins, P. K., 198n65
Tripp, L., 228n191
Turner, V., 226n184
Tversky, A., 169, 219n154, 229n191

U
U.S. Army Combined Command, 229n191

V
Van Maanen, J., 226n184
Vaughan, D., viii, 63, 181, 186n9, 189n24, 199n68, 216n135

W
Wabb, 229n193
Walker, G. H., 214n129, 227n189
Wason, P. C., 169, 202n79, 219n152
Weick,K. E., 226n185
Weingart, L. R., 229n191
Whitson, J. A., 229n191
Wickelgren, W. A., 159, 168, 215n133, 219n153, 221n161, 227n189
Wickens, T. D., 226n185
Winner, J. L., 210n106, 227n189
Woods, D. D., 176, 215n132, 221n162, 226n185

Y
Yablon, C. M., 224n177
Yaroush, R. A., 227n189

Z
Zaccaro, S. J., 215n131, 228n191, 229n191
Zohar, D., 226n185
Zsambok, C. E., 229n191

Subject Index

Notes: Authors of works cited are listed in separate Author Index. Page numbers followed by t refer to a table on that page. Page numbers followed by f refer to a figure on that page. Page numbers followed by n and a number refer to a numbered note.

A

Achilles' heel, 179

Adams, L., 14t

Aldrich, Arnold, 67, 96–97, 111, 129, 134, 135, 170

Ambient Temperature (AMB), 54

Argon gas, 51, 86–87, 112

Argument
    characteristics of, 145–146
    reframed *Challenger* deliberations, 159–162
    See also Evidence-based argument; Presumption, case, and burden of proof

Atlantis shuttle, 185n1

B

Beggs, James M., 83

Blow-by of hot gas
    in cold temperatures, 39
    discounted threat to O-rings, 76–77, 85–86, 170
    in engineers' argument to delay launch, 42–58 (*See also* Charts presented in teleconference)
    and erosion of O-rings, 25
    on warm flight, 28–30

Blow hole, 20–21

Boisjoly, Roger, 182
    discounting of chart 4-3, 86, 112
    engineers' argument to delay launch, 40–41, 44–48, 58
    experiments on sealing capacity, 27
    on Lucas' standards of analysis, 60–61, 62
    Mason's concept of sealing problem, 85–86
    off-line caucus, attempt to delay launch, 87, 89–91, 110, 116
    as participant in decision to launch, 11, 14t, 15
    reframed argument for *Challenger* deliberations, 160–161

Boosters
    contract for manufacture of (*See* Contract considerations between NASA and Thiokol)
    field joints, dynamics in, 16–22
    manufacture and design of, 17–20, 18f

solid evidence criteria not met, 158

Clevis, 19, 20f, 21–22

Coates, Keith, 14t, 37

Cold temperatures
  basic events in decision to launch, 9–12
  discounted threat to O-rings, vi, 75–76, 85
  and O-ring sealing capacity, 11, 12, 25–28, 29, 30, 87–88
  plus squeeze of O-rings, 25–28, 52–53
  rationale for launch delay, 36, 38, 39–40, 44–46

Columbia shuttle disaster, viii, 2, 144, 147, 150, 151

Communication situations
  safety undermined by time restriction and degraded thought, 135–136
  between Thiokol and NASA, 108–110

Complexity. *See* High-technology complexity

Confirmation bias, 122–123, 168, 169, 202n79

Conflict management, 121

Consequential thought processes, 167–168

Contract considerations between NASA and Thiokol, 33–36, 82–84, 116, 129, 130–131, 171

Control cards, electronic, 64–65, 66–68
  See also Parts substitution, leading to launch delay

Cook nuclear power plant, Michigan, 223n170, 230n195

Credible quantitative engineering analysis or test data, 60, 62, 111, 132, 153, 217

Cultural anthropology, 176

Culture. *See* Organizational culture

Culture at Marshall, developed by Lucas, 38, 59, 71, 130
  Lucas' FRR: six dimensions, 72–74

D

Danger(s)
  awareness of three kinds, 165
  in decision making, vii–viii, 2–5
  in development of *Situation*, 145–146, 149–151
  formal argument, case and sides, 156–157
  in generic *Situation*, 125–126
  vs. production, 123–124
  and protective form of argument for safety, 145–146
  threats to safety, 165–172
  See also High-tech disasters; Safety

Data. *See* Evidence

Decision making
  complexities in *Situations*, 151
  conditions of distributed, 101–103
  dangers in, vii–viii, 2–5

emergency power to,
222–223n170

training and practice for
emergency decision,
178–179

Decision to launch
basic events in, 9–13
final rationale to launch by
Thiokol management,
93–94, 95f
participants in decision to
launch, 13–16, 14t
See also Teleconference

Deeper, farther, and faster,
165–166

Deepwater Horizon oil spill, 3,
185n6

Default side, as component of
formal argument, 156

Delta thinking/practice, 74, 112,
134–135, 170

Demanding standards, as
dimension of FRR culture, 73

Demonstration motors (DM),
53–54

Disaster myopia, 169

Disasters. *See* High-tech disasters

Disastrous decision making,
vii–viii, 2–3

Discovery shuttle, 185n1

Distributed decision making,
conditions of, 101–103

E

Ebeling, Bob, 10, 14t, 32, 36, 57

Education in decision making in
high-tech enterprises,
167–169

Electronic control cards, 64–65,
66–68
See also Parts substitution,
leading to launch delay

Endeavour shuttle, 185n1

"Engineering decision," 32, 36, 37

Engineering standards set by
Lucas, 60–62, 68, 120, 153

Engineers
vs. managers, a danger of
decision-making, 3, 4–5,
122–123
safety undermined by
managerial distance from
technical discoveries,
137–138
upward accountability of
technical understanding,
225n180
See also Managers *vs.* engineers;
Thiokol engineers

Enterprise shuttle, 185n1

Ergonomics, vii

Erosion in O-rings, 24–25,
85–86

Evidence
as component of formal
argument, 157–158, 160
knowledge gap as dangerous
condition, 167–172
mixed, and competing values,
153–155
protection against threats to
safety, 177

Evidence-based argument, vii, 2,
5, 146, 153–162
formal argument: eight basic
components, 155–159

FRR. *See* Flight readiness review (FRR)

G
Garrison, U. Edwin, 35, 36, 83, 84
Gaskins, Richard H., 181
Goethe, Johann Wolfgang von, x
Green ball theory, 84

H
Hardy, George
  deficiency in accepting engineers' warning, 115–116
  mental model of O-rings sealing, 147–148
  as participant in decision to launch, 14t, 15, 37
  reactions to engineers' argument to delay launch, 58–59, 81
Health and wellness monitoring metaphor, 173–175
High-tech disasters
  dangers in decision making, vii–viii, 2–5
  development of *Situation*, 144
  safety-protecting organizational culture needed, 173
  training and practice for emergency decision, 178–179
High-technology complexity, 2, 30, 101–102
  example of context of, 142–144

Horseshoe game with engineers, 66, 71, 130, 141
Houston, C., 14t
Hubble telescope, 199n67
Human causes of disaster, vii, 3, 146
Human failure
  of investigation as dangerous condition, 172
  in organizational levels, 169–172
  to understand deeper, farther, and faster, 165–166
Human sciences, current knowledge void in high-tech enterprises, 168
Humiliation from Lucas, 61–62, 71, 130, 140, 170, 198n65

I
Ice on launch pad, 96
Ignition transient, 21, 22, 39, 44–45, 78
Impingement erosion of O-rings, 24–25, 30, 42, 43f, 86, 94
In-house control at Marshall, 65–67, 135, 170
Integrated electronic assembly (IEA), 64
Internal market between NASA and Congress, 127–131, 171

J
Jacques, Bob, 181
Johnson Space Center, Houston
  FRR Level II reviews, 69
  memo on Flight 61C delay in launch, 65, 66–67, 68, 170

as participant in decision to
launch, 16
Lund, Robert
in engineers' argument to
delay launch, 55–57, 59
off-line caucus, decision to
launch, 89, 90, 92–93, 117,
118
as participant in decision to
launch, 10, 12, 14t, 15
in preparation of rationale
for launch delay, 36, 37, 39
reframed argument for
Challenger deliberations,
161

M

Macbeth, W., 14t
Macroergonomics, vii, viii, 6, 97
Managerial decision, 32–33
Managers *vs.* engineers
accountability of technical
understanding, 225n180
a danger of decision-making,
3, 4–5, 122
mental models of, 147–149,
166
safety undermined by
managerial distance from
technical discoveries,
137–138
technical disputes, as
dangerous condition,
166–167
technical disputes, protection
against threats to safety, 177
Market pressures, in production
against safety, 127–131

Marshall Center Boards, 70–72,
73
Marshall's Office of Reliability
and Quality Assurance
(MRQA), 138
Marshall Space Flight Center,
Alabama
culture of, developed by
Lucas, 38, 59, 71, 130
engineering standards set by
Lucas, 60–62, 68, 120, 153
in-house control, 65–67, 135,
170
Lucas' FRR culture, 72–74
off-line caucus deliberations,
80–81
participants in decision to
launch, 13–16, 14t
teleconference, 10, 37, 41
See also NASA
Marshall's Science and Engineering
Directorate, 15, 37, 38, 81,
138
Mason, Jerald
biasing conditions, 123–124
call for off-line caucus, 78
conception of O-ring sealing
problem, 85–87, 89,
147–148
contract considerations,
33–36, 82–84, 87, 116
deficiency in accepting
engineers' warning,
116–119
off-line caucus, decision to
launch, 89–93
as participant in decision to
launch, 11–12, 14t, 15

objection on O-rings and
temperature in Flights 51C
and 51E, 27, 30
as participant in decision to
launch, 11–12, 13, 14t
parts substitution problem
(*See* Parts substitution,
leading to launch delay)
preparatory FRR, 70
reactions to engineers'
argument to delay launch,
51, 58–59, 74–75
reframed argument for
Challenger deliberations,
160–161
view of teleconference as
Marshall Center FRR,
110–113, 135
Multiple layers of disaster, 1
Multiple simultaneous objective
situations, 119, 120

N
NASA
communication situation
with Thiokol engineers,
108–110
contract considerations with
Thiokol, 33–36, 82–84,
116, 129, 130–131, 171
failure of investigating
human processes, 172
flight designations, 203n82
launch schedule, 62–63,
102–103, 128, 130
reporting policy violation,
38, 96–97, 118, 135, 170,
201n74

safety review system, Flight
Readiness Reviews, 69
See also Johnson Space
Center, Houston; Kennedy
Space Center, Florida;
Marshall Space Flight
Center, Alabama
Near miss situation, 144, 150, 151
Nozzle joints, 43, 47f, 48, 75, 76

O
Objective situations
Congress's budget for space
program, 131
engineers' correct situation
assessment, 105–107
Mason's, 116
multiple simultaneous, 119,
120
understanding, 103–105
Organizational culture
a danger of decision-making,
3, 5
for safety, five protections
required, 174–178
of safety protection, 172–173
Organizational levels, human
failure in, 169–172
Organizational separation, a danger of decision-making, 3, 4–5
O-rings
basic events in decision to
launch, 10–12
blow-by on warm flight,
28–30
cold temperatures and
rationale for launch delay,
36, 39–40

in engineers' argument to
delay launch, 42–58 (*See
also* Charts presented in
teleconference)
engineers' correct situation
assessment, 105–107
experiments on sealing
capacity, 15, 27–28, 29, 46,
48, 49–50, 56, 58–59, 148
final rationale to launch, 94,
95f, 96
function, and hot exhaust
gas, 16–17, 20–22
Mason's faulty conception of
sealing problem, 85–87, 89,
147–148
Mulloy's discounted threat of
cold temperature, 75–78,
85, 114–115
rates of changes, as example
of high-technology
context, 143–144
reframed argument for
Challenger deliberations,
160–161
sealing capacity, 11, 12, 26,
39–40
temperature plus squeeze,
25–28, 52–53
timing and spacing of field
joints, 22–24, 23f, 43–44

P
Participants in decision to
launch, 13–16, 14t, 193n39
Parts cannibalized, 172
Parts substitution, leading to
launch delay, 64–65, 66–67,
68, 128–129, 170, 200n72,
220n157
Peoples, Jerry, 206n89
Piper Alpha oil and gas disaster, 3
Powers, Luther Ben, 14t, 80–81,
160, 182
Presidential Commission on
Space Shuttle *Challenger*
Accident, 83–84, 181
on Marshall's silent safety
program, 139, 221n164
Report, technological
dynamics, vi
Presumption, case, and burden
of proof, 124, 125, 132, 146,
149, 154, 159–160, 167
Primary O-rings
erosion of, 24–25, 42–43
timing and spacing of field
joints, 22–24, 23f
See also O-rings
Privileged side, as component of
formal argument, 156
Probing, as dimension of FRR
culture, 73, 132, 135, 140,
146
Production against safety,
127–141
biasing conditions, 123–124
as dangerous condition,
165–166
market pressures, 127–131,
139
on-time ethos, 133–134
organizational conditions
undermining safety,
134–139, 141

Temperature. *See* Cold
temperatures
Thiokol, Inc., contract with
NASA, 33–36, 82–84, 116,
129, 130–131, 171
Thiokol engineers
basic events in decision to
launch, 9–13
charts presented in evidence
to delay launch, 42–58 (*See
also* Charts presented in
teleconference)
communication situation
with NASA, 108–110
correct situation assessment,
105–107
embedded argument to delay
launch, 39–42
lack of formal argumentation
and debate, 155–159
mental models, shifting of,
148
in off-line caucus, final
attempt to delay launch,
87–91
reactions to cold weather
reports, 31
See also Engineers
Thiokol group, Utah
conditions preventing
agreement about situation,
108–110
off-line caucus deliberations,
78–79, 82–93
off-line caucus final rationale
to launch, 93–94
participants in decision to
launch, 13–16, 14t

teleconference, 10, 37 (*See
also* Teleconference)
Thompson, Arnold, 182
communication situation
with NASA, 108–110
engineers' argument to delay
launch, 40, 49, 50–51, 87
experiment and engineers'
correct situation
assessment, 106
experiments on O-ring
sealing capacity, 15, 27, 29,
46, 48, 49, 56, 58–59, 148
Mason's concept of sealing
problem, 85, 116
memo on O-ring seal
problem, 88–89
off-line caucus, attempt to
delay launch, 87–89, 91
as participant in decision to
launch, 11, 14t, 15
reframed argument for
Challenger deliberations,
160–161
Thompson, Robert, 207n91
Threats. *See* Danger(s)
Time, limited, in decision-
making, 4, 122–123
knowledge void of human
sciences, 168, 177
regulation of resources, 159
safety undermined by
degraded thought,
135–136, 221n161
See also Speed-accuracy trade
off
Timing, in O-rings in field
joints, 22–24, 23f, 43–44

Training and practice for
emergency decision,
178–179
Trapnell, Emily, 207n91

U
United States Boosters, 220n158
U.S. Congress, internal market
with NASA, 127–131, 171
U.S. Department of Defense,
192n33

V
Validation, as component of
formal argument, 157
Values, 154–155, 158–159, 160
Vandenberg Air Force, 82,
192n33
Vaughan, Diane, 181
    See also entry in Author Index
Vehicle Assembly Building, 17

W
Wear, Larry, 14t, 28, 73–74
Wellness monitoring metaphor,
173–175
Wiggins, C., 14t, 92, 117
Wright, Mike, 181